AF530662

History of Modern India

The Origin of Asian Democracy

History of Modern India

The Origin of Asian Democracy

P.S. Choudhary

KUNAL BOOKS
New Delhi-110 002

KUNAL BOOKS
4648/21, First Floor,
Ansari Road, Daryaganj,
New Delhi-110002
Phones: 011-23275069, 9811043697
E-mail: kunalbooks@gmail.com
Website: www.kunalbooks.in

History of Modern India: The Origin of Asian Democracy

© Publisher

First Published 2010

Reprint 2018

ISBN: 978-81-910085-6-2

{All rights reserved, No part of this publication may be reproduced stored in a retrieval system or transmitted, in any form or by any means, mechanical, photocopying, recording or otherwise, without prior written permission of the publisher}.

Published in India by Prem Singh Bisht for Kunal Books, and Printed at Milan Enterprises, Delhi.

Preface

Democracy is a political government carried out either directly by the people (direct democracy) or by means of elected representatives of the people (Representative democracy). The term is derived from the Greek: *dnmokratva* "rule of the people", which was coined from *dkmos* "people" and *kratos* "power", in the middle of the fifth-fourth century BC to denote the political systems then existing in some Greek city-states, notably Athens following a popular uprising in 508 BC.

Democracy is a political system in which all the members of the society have an equal share of formal political power. In modern representative democracy, this formal equality is embodied primarily in the right to vote. The history of democracy - the history of empowering people by giving them a say in their political entities - duces back from its origins in the ancient world to its re-emergence and rise from the 17th century to the present day. Although it is generally believed that the concepts of democracy and constitution were created in one particular place and time - identified as Ancient Athens about the year 508 BC - there is evidence to suggest that democratic forms of government, in a broad sense, may have existed in several areas of the world well before the turn of the 5th century.

Asia has the promise of democracy with democratically elected Governments in all of South Asia and in many other parts of the region. Countries in Asia have adopted different systems and models id democracy that have been influenced by their historical past. Countries like Bhutan and Maldives, two of the world's youngest democracies, have forget new paths, one responding to the vision of its King and the other to the yearning of its people. Democracies in Asia need to grow organically in line with local traditions, cultures and environment. Inclusive civic participation to expand the base of democracy and empower those without a voice is vital for deepening and sustaining democracy in Asia.

India's political experiment as a sustainable and successful democracy should logically provide a workable model for all the other South Asian nations. The global community has hailed and held up India as a democratic model that could be emulated by the rest of South Asia. In the destabilized South Asian security environment that exists today this truism could not be more realistic and true. Most South Asian nations with the exception of Pakistan recognize this reality. South Asian nations, again with the exception of Pakistan have witnessed as to how the Indian political democracy and democratic governance have facilitated India's remarkable economic resurgence with sustained high rates of economic growth. This besides other national attributes of power has facilitated the world to take notice of India as an emerging global power. The moot question that arises is as to why other South Asian nations which became independent about the same time should be floundering around searching for stability and peace.

The basic guiding principles of democracy - such as freedom of expression, inclusive participation and equal access to justice - are common to all. Each country must develop its own tools and mechanisms to put these principles into action. Because the democracy a nation chooses to develop depends on its history and circumstances, countries will necessarily be differently democratic. But in all countries democracy is about much more than a single decision.

P.S. Choudhary

Contents

1

The Indian Subcontinent

The Indian subcontinent, also Indian Subcontinent and other terms, is as region of the Asian (and, in turn, the Eurasian) continent on the Indian tectonic plate south of the Himalayas, forming a peninsula which extends southward into the Indian Ocean. Historically forming the whole of greater India or the territories of the British Raj, the region now comprises the countries of India, Pakistan, and Bangladesh; it often also includes Nepal, Bhutan, and offshore Sri Lanka. It may also include the island country of Maldives.

The region may also include the disputed territory of Aksai Chin, which was part of the British Indian princely state of Jammu and Kashmir, but is now administered as a part of the Chinese autonomous region of Xinjiang.

A booklet published by the United States Department of State in 1959 includes Afghanistan, Ceylon (Sri Lanka), India, Nepal, and Pakistan as part of the" Subcontinent of South Asia".

When the term Indian Subcontinent is used to mean South Asia, the islands countries of Sri Lanka and the Maldives are sometimes not included, while Tibet and Nepal are included and excluded intermittently, depending on the context. Due to similar scope, the terms" Indian subcontinent" and" South Asia" are used by some academics interchangeably.

Due to political sensitivities, some prefer to use the terms "South Asian Subcontinent", the "Indo-Pak Subcontinent", or simply "South Asia" or "the Subcontinent" over the term "Indian subcontinent". According to some academics, the term "South Asia" is in more common use in Europe and North America, rather than the terms "Subcontinent" or the "Indian Subcontinent". Indologist Ronald B. Inden argues that the usage of the term "South Asia" is getting more widespread since it clearly distinguishes the region from East Asia; however, opinion on this is divided.

Geographically, the Indian subcontinent is a peninsular region in south-central Asia, rather resembling a diamond which is delineated by the Himalayas on the north, the Hindu Kush in the west, and the Arakanese in the east, and which extends southward into the Indian Ocean with the Arabian Sea to the southwest and the Bay of Bengal to the southeast. With all seven countries included, the area covers about 4.4 million km^2 (1.7 million mi^2), which is 10% of the Asian continent or 2.4% of the world's land surface area.

Most of this region rests on a distinct tectonic plate, the Indian Plate (the northerly portion of the Indo-Australian Plate), and is isolated from the rest of Asia by mountain barriers. It was once a small continent before colliding with the Eurasian Plate about 50-55 million years ago and giving birth to the Himalayan range and the Tibetan plateau. In addition, it is also home to a variety of geographical features, such as glaciers, rainforests, valleys, deserts, and grasslands.

The Indian subcontinent generally comprises the countries of India, Pakistan, and Bangladesh; it often also includes Nepal, Bhutan, and offshore Sri Lanka and may include the Maldives. Overall, it accounts for about 34% of Asia's population (or over 16.5% of the world's population) and is home to a vast array of peoples.

LAND AND PEOPLE

India has always been a mystery to the West. The glitter of her gold kindled the imagination of Herodotus and lured Alexander the Great in his drive eastward. Marco Polo, after having seen the splendor of the court of Great Khan of China, described southern India as the noblest and richest country in the world. And countless monuments, ravaged by time but even now resplendent with magnificence and beauty, make one believe that there was no exaggeration in the stories of India told by the enthusiastic traveling merchant of Venice. Centuries later these and similar stories inspired the great Portuguese and Spanish captains in their travels along the African coast and brought Columbus to the shores of America. They all sought the riches of India. Were those riches real or imaginary?

There are majesty and melancholy in Indian scenery. Endless plains, parched soil, meager vegetation dying under the cruel sun, here and there cluster of huts hardly distinguishable from the stony fields around them. The monotonous panorama is brightened by lines of crenelated walls on the horizon, gates flanked by towers, ruins of temples and mausoleums, and skeletons of castles overlooking the valley from hills encircled by battlements. Everywhere traces of history, teeming with battles and violence. Such is the typical scenery of India, cradle and tomb of so many civilizations.

One sees the traces of devastation left in these borderless plains by centuries of invasion and internal struggles for power. But one also feels the peaceful achievements of the vanished peoples, and the tremendous wealth sacrificed to the Moloch of war by the onetime rulers of these plains. Great religions were born on Indian soil, human creative genius has left indelible traces, and a great concentration of economic power was achieved here before the era of prosperity dawned in the West.

There are few monuments in the world comparable to the temples carved in the living rock at Ajanta and Ellora. The cathedral of Chartres is probably the only religious monument in the western world comparable to the architectural jewel of Belur. It depicts the descent of the Ganges to the earth - crowds of people and flocks of animals converging from all sides to the new source of life, and jubilant divinities and celestial guardians in heaven. In the center of the commotion one sees the tiny figure of the pious King Arjuna, whose constant prayer moved the immortals to award the river to the thirsty people. Arjuna prayed for a thousand years while standing on one leg with hands stretched out to the gods. Thus an unknown artist saw him, and thus he stands after another thousand years in the granite block at the crossing of two dusty country roads.

LAND OF CONTRASTS

The standard of living of most people in India is pathetially low. There are, however, few places in the world where poverty of the masses is combined with so ostentatious a display of wealth. Barefooted crowds, men and women in rags who have never earned more than their daily bread; beggars everywhere, around the temples, in front of railroad stations and hotels, in bazaars, on highways, cripples and robust fellows, old and young, even babies in the arms of their mothers or their six-year-old sisters, taught to stretch out their tiny palms before they learn to walk.... And along with all this, magnificent palaces, private mansions with fabulous gardens, huge hotels, and modern office buildings. The British-built government quarters in New Delhi, second to none among western capitals, epitomize the contrast.

At first sight, this striking contrast between luxury and extreme poverty seems to be the heritage of the colonial era. Such an inference, however, is only partly true. The gulf between the rich potentates and the starving masses was already characteristic of the social system in India when the British set foot on her soil. The traders and adventurers who brought the British colors to the land of the Great Moghuls and maharajahs were neither surprised nor shocked by the social conditions did they find. Rather they tried to make the best of them by maneuvering for a solid foot-hold. They succeeded in cultivating the friendship of the local rulers.

The British colonial administration that superseded the East India Company was not responsible for the caste system and the exploitation of the peasants by the landlords and moneylenders. It is to be blamed only for not having changed these conditions. British colonial administration brought order and peace to the country, built highways, railroads, harbors, established banks, opened universities. The foundations of modern industries were laid. But the colonial administration followed the policy of changing local customs as little as possible. The westernized economic sector remained isolated from the bulk of the Indian economy, and the latter, together with the archaic social system, were left stagnating while the economy in western nations was advancing rapidly.

Symbolic of the Indian economy is the use of cow manure as fuel, not only in villages but also in town slums. "We are talking about the atomic age while living in the cow-dung era," Prime Minister Nehru once remarked. On Indian highways we met strings of loaded donkeys and crowds of women with large dung-filled baskets on their heads - tragic caravans that carry the precious nutrient of exhausted soil to the town where poor people burn it to prepare their scanty food.

Along the highways we observed women moving in files, bending over each piece of dung, throwing it in the air and catching it in the baskets. And strangely, many of these women were wearing silver bracelets, silver ringlets on their ankles, gold earrings. The gold and silver hoarded in villages is estimated at many billions of dollars. Gold markets operate in almost every city and are patronized not only by the rich but also by people who live in misery and yet have preserved some crumbs of their inheritance.

Another striking contrast in the Indian scene is between the illiteracy of the masses and a brilliant intelligentsia. In the universities and government bureaus - not only in New Delhi but also in provincial governments - one meets men who have absorbed all that Oxford or Cambridge could offer and at the same time have preserved their old ways of life. They are proud of their education but equally proud of their country. Conceding that India is backward, they try to minimize the importance of the appalling illiteracy of the people, stressing, unconvincingly, that the masses in India though illiterate are not uneducated.

The intelligentsia is the ruling class in modern India. The proportion of scholars and thinkers in the upper layer of her bureaucracy is probably higher than among professional politicians in more developed nations. When they told us about their task and their plans, we felt that they were men of courage and vision. Yet there is something unreal about them: The contrast between their dreams and the cruel facts of life around them is too deep -atomic age versus cow dung, in Nehru's bitter words.

THE YOUNG REPUBLIC

India is full of anachronisms - one of the world's oldest civilizations and an infant nation emerging from political chaos. In all her long, stormy, and colorful history, she has known only a few brief periods of existence as a united independent nation. She was united for a short time under the rule of the great and wise king Asoka in the third century B.C., and again under the Moghuls in the seventeenth century, but the British took over a country that was a hodgepodge of more or less independent princedoms. Under British domination an effective centralized administration was established in the peninsula, but politically India remained divided among several dozen provinces and hundreds of formally semi-independent states.

The first task of the government of the independent Indian Republic was to bring these states together. And the government has mastered this Herculean task. "I believe in our capacity in India...in winning over the people rather than fighting them," said Nehru. "If we settled the Indian States problem, it was not only by goodwill but also by the pressures that were exercised, whether by the new government of India or the people of the States.

Also there was the friendly approach to settle it in a friendly way, not to crush them....We paid heavy sums of money as privy purses to the princes....We thus brought about a very major political change without...the tremendous expenses of a conflict."

This was indeed a considerable achievement. Nearly a decade after maharajahs were removed from the political scene, they still maintain a grip over the people's imagination. We saw their full-length portraits in university halls and public places, figures from an oriental tale, in fantastic uniforms or robes studded with diamonds and other precious stones, leaning on glittering curved swords. We listened while a university professor explained to us in an awesome half whisper: "Our Highness in 1915...The father of Our Highness in 1865.... The grandmother of Our Highness...." Not a single time did he call the former rulers by name, or use the pronouns he, his, their. Even "His Highness" did not seem to him respectful enough.

The question of rulers was solved, but a more difficult problem remained - the language. The 1951 census reported 845 languages and dialects in India, including 63 non-Indian tongues. More than nine-tenths of the population reported that one or another of the 15 main languages was their mother tongue (Hindu, Urdu, Hindustani, Telega, Marathi, Tamil, and so on). About 12 million persons spoke one or another of the 23 tribal languages, 18 million used one of the other 24 languages, and some 3 million named one of 720 various dialects.

The overwhelming difficulties the young republic faces in organizing civilian administration, the judiciary, and the schools for this multilingual humanity are illustrated by current troubles connected with administrative reform. Not all politically mature intellectuals in India believe that the reform was well conceived and skillfully timed, but it is difficult for a foreign observer to weigh the arguments pro and con. The general idea is to consolidate small administrative units - some of them corresponding to the old feudal princedoms - into larger provinces, the borders of which will conform as closely as possible to the distribution of the major languages, so that the language prevailing in each province will become its official local language, together with Hindi, the official language of the Union.

Not infrequently, however, a region delineated as a province includes areas where people speak different languages. It may happen that the linguistic minority consists of politically inarticulate people with only a handful of intellectuals who pretend to represent their aspirations. Such self-styled leaders are naturally interested in converting their land into a separate province and taking over its administration. They oppose the reform and insistently demand rearrangement of the proposed administrative borders.

The issue of linguistic minorities has proved an excellent pretext for agitation by Communist groups. Under their guidance local super nationalist movements have developed into a nationwide wave of strikes, street demonstrations, riots, clashes with police. The government has met the acts of violence with firmness but has demonstrated great patience in negotiations with the opposition, occasionally making concessions that would guarantee the rights of the minority. Nehru has used all his eloquence and personal prestige to quell the movement, appealing to the patriotism of the people, calling on them to preserve national unity. Almost everywhere he has succeeded in settling the disputes in a democratic way, by persuasion.

GENTLENESS AND VIOLENCE

The outbreaks of violence kindled by administrative reforms puzzle western observers. Throngs of tribesmen from remote mountains, armed with clubs and knives, have descended into valleys to contest the allocation of a city that most of them had never seen before. The Indians are a peaceful and friendly people with a ready smile for a foreigner. If one stops in the street to take a picture, he will find himself instantaneously surrounded by curious people, joking and laughing, fighting in a friendly way for a better place in the picture. But there is a subdued spirit of violence in this gentle crowd, and our Indian friends told us that a trifle can set off an explosion.

We did not witness any scene of violence and saw only one minor demonstration in Bombay. This was a peaceful demonstration but there was something uncanny about it. A group of young men, not more than a hundred in all, appeared in front of our hotel to protest against the hotel's serving beef in its dining room. They carried posters and shouted in chorus. Bystanders translated their slogans for us: "The cow is our mother!"" Do not kill our mother!" " Do not eat cow meat!"

The shouting was accompanied by fanatical gestures and gave an impression of conviction, sincerity, and passion. The hotel people told us that this was an organized demonstration and the boys were professional noisemakers paid for their services. Whether or not this was true, I felt that the indignation of these men against the hotel's practice was genuine and that they might eventually give way to their feelings in violence.

This insignificant scene evoked other tragic events. Gentle people with suppressed emotions may eventually lose control of them and act with a brutality and ruthlessness contrary to their nature. Was this not the origin of the terrible explosion that accompanied the partition of India? India and Pakistan are full of memories of these days. Half a million Hindus and Muslims were slaughtered. Nobody knows which side was responsible for the first bloodshed, but rumors spread like wildfire: "The Hindus are butchering the Muslims" and "The Muslims are killing the Hindus." Both sides called for retaliation. In mixed communities along the new frontiers between India and Pakistan, Hindus and Muslims fled from the long knives of their neighbors.

A professor of Karachi University told us about his personal experience:

"There was no bad feeling between us. The Muslims and the Hindus lived peacefully together. Then suddenly hell broke out. People ran for their lives. I served as commissioner for refugees. Train after train arrived in Karachi, packed with men and women insane from fear. I met each train at the railroad station. One train arrived with only two men alive, the engineer and the fireman. All the cars were packed with dead bodies - men, women, and children, all with their throats cut. Blood everywhere, not a single child left alive.... My people did the same thing, ambushed caravans, stopped trains, murdered any Hindu who fell into their hands...."

The Hindus told us similar stories about those days, perhaps the darkest days in all Indian history, but nobody had a plausible explanation of how and why those horrors happened. Is gentleness only a superficial varnish and cruelty the true nature of these people? Or are they kind and friendly in their normal environment while the violent explosions come as fits of collective insanity? Do not similar questions arise when one thinks of sudden outbursts of hatred and barbarism in other countries?

Strangely enough the sad story of Hindu-Muslim massacres did not change our general impression of India as a land of peaceful, warmhearted people. Indeed were they not this kind of people, they would not have recognized such a man as Gandhi as their spiritual leader and national hero.

BETWEEN THE WEST AND THE EAST

What is India's position in the ideological clash between the West and East? India has answered this question in her

Constitution. She is a parliamentary democracy. The Constitution of India proclaims freedom of speech and expression, assembly, association, movement, residence, acquisition and disposal of property, practice of any profession, and the carrying on of any occupation, trade, and business (Article 19). It guarantees religious freedom, protects cultural interests of minorities, and provides for adequate compensation to citizens in the event of compulsory acquisition of their property by the state (Article 22).

India's Parliament consists of two chambers: the Council of State *(Rajya Sabha)*, in many respects similar to the British House of Lords, and a democratically elected House of the People *(Lok Sabha)*, a replica of the British House of Commons. She has a President elected by an electoral college consisting of elected members of the Central Legislature and Legislative Assemblies of the various states. The Council of Ministers headed by the Prime Minister is appointed by the President of India but responsible collectively to the House of the People (Article 74).

The Supreme Court consists of judges appointed by the President (not subject to confirmation by the Parliament). The state governors, chief executives of provinces, are appointed by the President and, in turn, appoint the local councils of ministers. Legislative power in the state is exercised by democratically elected assemblies subordinated to the jurisdiction of the Union Parliament. There is nothing in this Constitution remotely reminiscent of the Soviet system or totalitarianism in general. From the beginning to the end it is democratic and British in spirit.

Indeed India's political system is similar to the one many among her intellectuals learned to know and respect in British universities, in the years of their apprenticeship in political thinking. They may criticize some British institutions and especially British foreign policy; but do not British intellectuals likewise criticize their own country? The fact remains: Great

Britain is the political frame of reference for Indians almost as much as for the British themselves.

When they speak of democracy they think of Great Britain, and when they talk of socialism they use this term in the Fabian rather than the Marxian sense, as a series of social reforms carried out by an enlightened and benevolent élite, for the general welfare, without class struggle. In this sense the Indians are far from being neutral in the historical clash of ideas of our time. They have rejected the Communist idea of progress through brute force and dictatorship and have chosen the road of evolution followed by the free western nations.

DEMOCRACY AND CAPITALISM

What makes the attitude of India somewhat confusing to American observers is that Indian political leaders and intellectuals at large make a clear distinction between democracy and capitalism. The West - and primarily the United States - represents for them both ideas: democracy as the principle of political organization, capitalism as the pattern of economic system. They accept the first idea and reject the second again quoting Nehru:

"Some people mix up democracy with capitalism," he advised the Standing Committee of the National Development Council. "I really do not understand it. Simply because democracy has grown in some capitalist countries, it does not mean that democracy is an essential part of capitalism or vice versa. They imagine that any kind of socialism necessarily means authoritarianism. It does not, at least in the theory; in practice, I do not know how the country will develop. Democracy must mean removal of disparities. That is quite simple."

This is quite simple indeed. But what is the capitalism that Nehru rejects in favor of socialism? Does he not have in mind the economic system that prevailed in England and elsewhere in the nineteenth century? The economic system has greatly changed since that time in modern democratic countries, perhaps more radically in the United States than anywhere else. The modern economic system includes developments which Nehru expects from democracy and calls socialism.

Capitalism, he explains in another part of his speech, "has had its day in the broad sense of the word. And, indeed, capitalism even in England and elsewhere is different from what it was in the nineteenth century. It is changing in England; maybe it is not changing fast enough, but it is changing. Now, should we go through the same old process and then ultimately try to reverse it and come back and try to change it? We have got the choice before us and we have the experience of others...."

Nehru is right. Since India has chosen to follow the road of democracy, she must mold her economy by taking the best she finds in modern institutions in other democratic countries. She may, for example, emulate the American credit policy, collective bargaining, and unemployment compensation system, British health insurance and selective nationalization, Swedish consumer cooperatives, Danish farm cooperatives, and so on. She may call the combination of all these measures socialism, but that label will not change the fact that this is precisely what we, in the West, describe as our modern economic system.

INDIAN NATIONALISM

Like other young nations India is in a state of nationalist ferment. Indian nationalism, however, is free from blind hatred of foreigners. Indian patriots feel no grudge against their former colonial masters. Did not the sweetness of victory offset the bitterness of the long fight for independence? Did not the British leave India graciously? Is not Lord Mountbatten a friend of the Indians?

After all that we have read and heard about India's hatred of the British rule, we were surprised to find evidence of pro-British feelings at almost every step: Gorgeous monuments to

British monarchs, viceroys of India, and other statesmen of the British Crown; Queen's and King's streets and places in all the cities; pictures of illustrious lords in university halls. There is no doubt that of all the westerners the British are the most popular in India.

They come here as if returning home. They have friends in government, academic circles, the business community, and the press. They meet people with whom they established friendships in Oxford and Cambridge. India's independence has not broken the cultural and personal ties between Indian and British intellectuals. Perhaps these ties are even stronger than before because both parties now meet on the basis of equality.

The outbursts of Indian nationalists against colonialism are not directed against Great Britain. By definition, colonialists and imperialists are rich and carefree. These adjectives do not apply to the British. Is not that country having a hard time? And a strange thing happens: When an Indian intellectual thunders against modern colonialism, he is aiming his diatribe at the United States.

The nationalism of Indian intellectuals is apparent in their exaggerated appraisal of the role of their country in world affairs. Her clash with Pakistan is, of course, closer to them than unification of Germany or the conquest of eight East European countries by the USSR after World War II. Kashmir is the central issue of their country's foreign policy and perhaps their attitude toward regional military alliances, SEATO, the United States, and the USSR would have been different if the peninsula had not been split into two independent nations after the end of the British rule.

Another manifestation of nationalism in India is the sensitivity of its intellectuals to lack of respect for their country on the part of foreigners. When they suspect a western guest - a diplomat, newsman, or simple tourist - of feelings of superiority or condescension toward their country, they respond with arrogance. On the other hand, when they discover in their guest a sincere interest in their problems they treat him with Oriental friendliness. In domestic affairs Indian nationalism appears to be a positive, constructive elation rather than a state of xenophobia, resentment, and suspicion against foreigners.

India bristles with enthusiasm. Not only the intellectuals but people with little or no education talk politics, discuss the Five-Year Plan and the outlook for industrialization. A man on the street cannot understand, of course, the intricacies of capital formation, public and private investments, methods of defraying the proposed public outlays, and so on. But the people have heard of the Plan and believe that it will change their lives. People trust their government, its wisdom, and its integrity. Complaints of abuses and corruption are rare and limited to local administration. Although the general standard of living in India has not improved appreciably in recent years, people are confident that improvement will come and are willing to wait. Have they not waited for centuries without any hope of improvement?

We found two schools of thought among the Americans we met in India. Some were embittered, complained about the difficulties of the American businessmen in dealing with local authorities, portrayed Nehru as a fellow-traveler, and saw India's future in dark colors. They had little sympathy with our plans for lectures on socio-economic questions and warned us that we would face hostile and suspicious audiences. Other Americans gave a totally different picture. They had friends among Indian intellectuals and sympathized with the country's aspirations.

Indian newspapers are not always fair to the United States. Some have specialized in America-baiting. To them the United States is the incarnation of monopolistic capitalism, neo-imperialism, and colonialism. Some editorials consist of motheaten clichés from start to finish. Some impressed me as dull, as if their authors themselves were tired of the litany they were rewriting for the hundredth time. But the critical and caustic remarks of Indian newspapers about Mr. Dulles, NATO, and SEATO can hardly be described as vicious propaganda of hate. Indeed they are no more antiAmerican than some essays of our domestic columnists. Certainly it would be erroneous to conclude from their language that the people of India are anti-American.

In our travels we met no sign of hostility or suspicion of us as Americans. Everywhere, in lectures, seminars, and public conferences, we faced friendly and responsive audiences, full of interest in and good will toward the United States. It is true that this attitude was often combined with resentment against United States policy toward India. The resentment was based on a regrettable accumulation of misunderstandings.

In the debates that followed each lecture, listeners occasionally came out with loaded questions: "Why does the United States arm Pakistan against us?" "Do you believe that regional military alliances serve the cause of peace?" "Do you not think that billions of dollars spent for armaments could be diverted toward more constructive aims?" It was easy to explain and defend the intentions of the United States government against the reproaches hidden behind such questions. Often our explanations were met with applause. But even when the audience remained unsatisfied, we felt that we were facing friends whom we had failed to persuade rather than enemies.

Apart from his absorbing duties as the strong man and head of an active government, he is a tireless, ubiquitous public speaker. He gives sometimes twenty speeches a week, often in the open under a blazing sun. From all parts of India people call on him to address them on the occasion of breaking ground for a dam, a bridge, a school house, or the celebration of commencement at a university, unveiling a monument, opening a public park, the anniversary of some local historical event.

People travel hundreds of miles to see and hear him. They feel unhappy and are not interested in any substitute when he declines their invitation.

And since Nehru likes crowds, enjoys the adoration of the common people, and, most of all, hates to disappoint people who show so much affection for him, he goes on speaking day after day. Moreover by his nature he is a fighter, and he misses no occasion to address an unsympathetic or hostile crowd wherever troubles arise and his government faces opposition from Communists or reactionary elements. No superman can find new and important ideas for so many speeches, and it is natural that Nehru occasionally either repeats himself or contradicts his previous statements. Such contradictions are not infrequent.

He is not afraid to change his mind when new facts come to his attention or changed conditions cast a new light on a problem. His skill on the platform is unbelievable. In almost every appearance he finds words that kindle enthusiasm in the crowd and catch headlines in newspapers all over the nation. What is his message to the people? Whatever the occasion, Nehru tells the people that India is a wonderful country facing her destiny, depending on the common people to make her prosperous and happy. They have only to preserve their faith and courage, work hard, put the interest of the nation above their egoism, and keep together.

Perhaps this is oversimplifying the political philosophy of Nehru. But simple statements are not hollow generalities. The fate of a nation depends on its faith in itself and its feeling of unity. To maintain this feeling in the people is the task of a national leader. On the plane of morale Nehru follows the footsteps of his great teacher, Mohandas Gandhi, but he took the helm under changed political and economic conditions, to face new problems and carry out new responsibilities. Despite the deep difference between the two men, Nehru is the direct successor of Gandhi as the spiritual leader of the nation.

To western observers his nationalism may appear excessive, but a man whom his countrymen identify with the nation must be nationalist. Nehru is a product of two civilizations - the Indian and the western. All his political philosophy reflects his British education. But his policy is Indian, and when he talks about world affairs he thinks of his country rather than of the world as a whole. It is futile and pointless to criticize single statements by Nehru. A leader of a great nation in a state of revolution cannot weigh every word; polish every sentence in his speeches. Often in technical questions he has to rely on his advisers.

Those who try to influence public opinion in India by undermining Nehru's prestige only strengthen his position as the focal point of Indian nationalism. They would do better to criticize the political and economic philosophy that prevails in India today without blaming Nehru personally for ideas he shares with the men in his environment. What counts in a popular leader is the direction in which he leads the people. And this is certain: Nehru is leading India in our direction and is among the outstanding champions of the free world.

And what about his flirting with the Soviets? The red carpet rolled out before Kruschev and Bulganin? The delay in reprimanding Russia for the Hungarian debacle? In speeches of Nehru one finds critical remarks about the United States as well as about the USSR (rarely about Great Britain). His attitude toward foreign countries is largely determined by the vicissitudes of his own foreign policy, which is as selfish as the foreign policy of other nations. Indeed "neutralism" as professed by him is not indifference toward the ideological contest between the free world and the Soviet block, but partly isolationism similar to the United States isolationism in the nineteenth century and partly an attempt to play each side against the other in pursuit of his nationalist policy.

For some reason India was brought to believe that the United States was barring her way in her dispute with Pakistan.

Closer ties with the USSR promised to strengthen her position in the United Nations, and the government was delighted to shake the hand Moscow was extending. We may deplore this step as contrary to our own policy, but we are hardly qualified to condemn it.

INDIAN SPIRITUALITY

The Indians delight in debates and logical fencing. For a western guest it is sometimes difficult to follow their reasoning because of the difference in language. They speak English, often beautiful English, but use certain words and concepts in their own way. One such concept that appears frequently in their talk is spiritual values, or spiritualism, or as we would say, spirituality. Nehru himself does not like these terms. "Talking of India's spiritualism does not help us," he says; "it just confuses the issues."

He prefers to speak of Indian aspirations and goals in more realistic terms: Increasing production, developing a society based on justice and equality, and so on. But we heard Indian westernized journalists, well dressed, well housed, and well fed, talking about spiritual values as a characteristically Indian message to the world. And interviewing rich Americans and Europeans arriving at India's shores, they often let frustrated society ladies and clubwomen repeat that they came to India to find peace of soul in this land of spiritual values, away from the materialism of the western world.

Actually if the term 'spiritual values' mean anything, it means about the same thing that we call 'human values' in politics and economics: Justice, equality, respect for human dignity, compassion. It is difficult to understand how the British-educated intellectuals of India, familiar with western civilization and the modern economic system, have overlooked the fact that in the past century and especially in the recent fifty years progress in western society has consisted precisely in the rise of human values.

Indeed few among them realize that the difference between the modern economic system and the classical capitalism of the middle of the nineteenth century is in the predominance of human values over property values. It seems that the Indians who have visited the United States have been so impressed by our material standard of living that they have had no time to notice the other, more important, features of our society: Respect for labour, internal freedom of the individual, opportunity for all, glorification of individual abilities and initiative as compared with inherited wealth!

Strangely enough, precisely these human values are insufficiently emphasized in the discussion of economic planning in modern India. Its aim is essentially a democratic and prosperous economy, but in discussing the different aspects of development its intellectuals occasionally deviate from this aim toward ideas borrowed from Moscow, which practically mean that human progress is less important than technical progress in a mechanistic, vulgarly materialistic sense. One of India's mysteries is the fact that so many among her intellectuals who are humanitarians in the depth of their hearts seem to be more interested in building new factories than in water supply, sanitation, elementary schools, social security.

However, what is to some extent neglected in public discussion is provided by private initiative. Charity is more important in India than in many modern western communities. Whether the difference is in the stage of development of social conscience or in the type of the western and eastern societies, the term human values rarely appears in the discussion of India's economic plans. A substitute for this term is the idea of the socialist society that India is building.

2

The Government of British India

The government of British India is a government of a dependency of the British Crown. As such its powers are derived from and defined by Parliament, and it may therefore be called a derivative government. A government of this type is not national in origin, nor is it autonomous. But India is a continent without nationalities, and for seven hundred years it has either been under foreign rulers or plunged in anarchy. Its vast territory has been incessantly split up and parcelled out among foreign conquerors and contending dynasties; its population is internally divided to a degree unparalleled elsewhere even in Asia. British rule in India can find a good title, as the lawyers say, in the conditions preceding it.

It succeeded to the Mughal Empire in the last throes of dissolution. It was welcomed by the Indian peoples, who co-operated willingly in promoting its dominion, and whom it saved from the anarchy which was grievously wasting them. It is to this day accepted by the peoples and princes of India as the best government of which they have knowledge, and as freely admitting them to its councils and to responsible office. All the subordinate and much of the superior work of the administration are performed by Indians. In that sense the government of British India is a national government.

The evolution of this government is one of the most remarkable chapters of political history. We have seen that in 1858 an Act was passed by Parliament transferring the government of India from the East India Company to the Crown, and that Queen Victoria's memorable Proclamation of November 1, 1858, which has been justly called the Magna Charta of India, announced to the peoples of India the principles on which British rule would be conducted. And if we are content to start from this point, we can point to a series of Acts of Parliament building up the present fabric of the Indian government. But unless we go further back, half the contrivances which this fabric exhibits are not intelligible to us. We should not know how they came into being or for what purpose.

Again, we should be ignorant of the process by which the Crown of England acquired this great dominion beyond the seas. What says the Queen's Proclamation on this point? It says that the Crown with the advice and consent of Parliament had resolved to take upon itself the government of the territories in India," heretofore administered in trust for us by the Honorable East India Company." What does this mean? How came a trading company to be the trustee for the Crown of a great dependency?

A comprehensive legal phrase like "trust" is sometimes used to cover a doubtful position. In the third quarter of the eighteenth century the British people and Parliament awoke to the fact that the East India Company had become possessed of an immense territory in India, where it was exercising sovereign rights, raising armies, making peace and war, and generally incurring responsibilities too vast for a trading association. The Company claimed to hold its territorial acquisitions as its private property, and at first Parliament was not disposed to challenge seriously the claim, but contented itself with exacting for the British treasury an annual tribute of £400,000.

But the Company's debts and the confusion of its affairs in India re-opened the question, and convinced the nation that a radical reform was necessary. The remedy devised by Parliament was Lord North's famous Regulating Act of 1778, which remodelled the governing body of the Company, established a Governor-General and council for Bengal, and set up a supreme court of justice in Calcutta. It was under this Act that Warren Hastings was appointed Governor-General. The Act was a sign that Parliament recognised a national responsibility for the empire created by the Company, but it left the question of ownership unsettled. It left the Company in possession of its territories and revenues for the term of its charter.

The Regulating Act proved to be seriously defective. Warren Hastings had unexpected difficulties with his council and with the Supreme Court, and was plunged through no fault of his own into a series of exhausting wars with the Mahrattas and other native states. The affairs of the Company were constantly before Parliament, and formed the occasion for much party warfare, culminating in the impeachment and trial of Warren Hastings. Whig and Tory statesmen alike recognised that the Company's exercise of sovereign powers was a danger to England, and that a complete change of system was imperatively required.

They differed as to how the change should be effected. Was the Company to be put on one side, and the government and patronage of India vested in the ministry of the day? Or was the Company still to administer and appoint to offices, while being brought under the supervision and control of the ministry? The second alternative was followed by Pitt in his famous Act of 1784. The constitution created by Pitt is known as the" double government" system. It endured with some minor changes till 1858, when the Crown assumed the direct government of India; and many of its features have been retained in the present constitution of the Indian government. Its importance therefore can hardly be over-rated.

The essence of the "double government" system was that the substance of authority passed from the Company to the

Crown. The Company reigned but in important matters did not govern. It retained the patronage in respect of Indian appointments, though the approval of the Crown was required to the appointment of the Governor-General, the Governors of Madras and Bombay, and the Commander-in-Chief. The real authority in important matters was vested in a Board of Control. This Board consisted of six privy councilors (nominees, of course, of the ministry), but its powers were virtually exercised by its President, who was a cabinet minister. The Board saw all the correspondence from India and no order could be sent to India by the Court of Directors without its approval.

The Board could also draw up orders and require the Court to send them to India. Further, there was a special arrangement by which the Board could send to India and receive from India correspondence marked" secret" without the contents being made known to the Court of Directors. Under this system the home ministry was virtually responsible for the policy pursued in India, and became accountable for the same to Parliament. It left the detailed administration to the Company, but as it had a final voice in the selection of the Governor-General; it could make sure that the person appointed to that high office was at one with it on large questions of policy. In that sense he was a "parliamentary" Governor-General, because he was the choice of the ministry, and the ministry was responsible to Parliament for his acts.

From the passing of Pitt's Act of 1784 the East India Company may be said to have administered India as" trustees for the Crown," though the phrase was not used until a much later date. It is so used in the Act of 1833 renewing the Company's charter on the condition, among others, that it ceased to be a trading association in India. Pitt's system retained the Governor-General and his council as the supreme executive authority, but gave the former the right to over-rule his council if occasion required. The Governor-General in Council was also given the power to make laws, at first in an informal way under the name of "regulations," but subsequently in the form of Acts and with the formalities of a legislature.

It is obvious that the double government system could be altered at any time into direct single government by the Crown with little difficulty. When the change was determined on after the mutiny, a Secretary of State for India took the place of the President of the Board of Control, and was given the assistance of a council, the members of which, as regards Indian experience, took the place of the Court of Directors. In India the system of government was not affected. The Governor-General in Council remained, and the Governor-General continued to be a "parliamentary" Governor-General, responsible to Parliament through the medium of the ministry. In its immediate effect the change in fact was one rather of spirit than in the actual structure of the government.

In the words of King Edward's Proclamation, "it sealed the unity of Indian government and opened a new era." It was the visible sign of the incorporation of India into the British Empire. It brought the Indian peoples and princes into immediate relations with the Crown and gave a direct objective to their loyalty. It was a pledge that the government would be administered with a sole eye to their benefit. It was also a pledge that their rights and privileges would be scrupulously maintained, their religions and customs respected, and that they would be freely and impartially admitted to offices in the public service.

Since 1858 many changes have been made in the system of Indian administration, but the main structure is unaltered. These changes may generally be ascribed to three causes-the ever-growing mass of business and increasing duties of the administration, the necessity for decentralising the government, and the policy of giving the Indian people a larger voice and a larger share in the management of public affairs. The central or supreme government in India is that of the Governor-General in Council. It is commonly spoken of as "the Government of India," to distinguish it from the local governments. In 1858 the council consisted of four "ordinary" or full-time members, the Commander-in-Chief being usually added as a fifth or "extraordinary" member.

Owing to the growth of business the ordinary members have now been increased to six. But this is not the full extent of the change. In 1858 the council worked as a collective body. Now each member has his own department, and disposes of the great bulk of the work as a departmental minister, only the most important questions being reserved for consideration by the Governor-General in Council. In other words the departmental and cabinet system of our government and of other modern governments has been established in India with the happiest results as regards economy of labour and dispatch of business.

A much more important change or constitutional development is found in the rise of the legislative council of the Governor-General. The supreme law-making power for India is Parliament. But Parliament has wisely contented itself with settling the framework or, as a continental statesman would say, the "organic laws" of government in India, and with delegating to a legislative body in India the power of making detailed laws subject to the approval of the Crown. The problem has always been as to how this legislative body should be constituted.

There are cogent reasons why an autocratic government with powers derived from an external source, such as the Indian government is, should have a prevailing voice in the making of the laws which it administers. But clearly it should not have the sole voice; the voice of the people should also be heard. Parliament therefore began in 1861 in a tentative way to lay the foundations in India of a deliberative assembly to which the function of making laws should be entrusted. It enacted that the Governor-General and his executive council might, under certain conditions, sit as a legislative council, one of these conditions being the addition of twelve purely "legislative" members, of whom six at least were to be persons not in the public service. The tiny plant of those days has since grown into a large and vigorous assembly.

The legislative council of the Governor-General now contains in all sixty-six members, of whom thirty are non-officials. The latter are either returned by specified electorates or are otherwise the representatives of specified classes. The legislative council is no longer confined to the work of making laws. It debates the detailed provisions of the annual budget estimates, and divides on resolutions concerning these. Its members may put questions to the executive government. They may move resolutions on matters of public interest, and debate and take divisions upon them. In these ways the legislative council is now associated with the government in the general work of the administration. Its attitude is necessarily that of a critic, though by no means always an unfriendly critic.

If its presence keeps the executive authorities on their mettle, they are given an opportunity which they greatly value of putting the government case in debate before the council. A clean-handed and efficient government has generally a good defence for its policy, and need not fear its critics if it can meet them fairly in debate. The experience of the last two years (Lord Morley's *Indian Councils Act* was enacted by Parliament in 1909) is distinctly satisfactory in this and other respects. The enlarged council has brought the executive government nearer to the people, and has made its motives more intelligible to them. But the legislative council is not a Parliament. Its powers have been strictly limited by the British Parliament, from whom they are derived. It cannot turn out the executive government, it cannot stop supplies, it cannot enforce the resolutions that it passes.

For all that it exercises a great and salutary influence on the general administration as an organ of public opinion. It shapes the laws of the country, and it can propose new laws to meet the needs of a progressive society. An interesting case in point is the bill for establishing a partial system of compulsory elementary education which Mr. Gokhale, the leader of the Indian national party in the council, has recently introduced. During the recent recess its distinguished author has toured through the country and has addressed many public meetings, with the very proper object of explaining the provisions of the measure and conciliating opinion in its favour, just as we are accustomed to see public men in this country do in a similar case. This is an instance of the quickening effect which the recent constitutional reforms are exercising over public life in India.

The Government of India, as the supreme executive authority in India, exercises its powers in two ways. Certain departments of the state it keeps in its own hands and directly administers: others it has made over to the local governments: and in respect of these it contents itself with supervision and general control. In the former class are included the army and defence of the country, political relations with foreign states, the management of the finances, the currency and the debt, the railways, the post and telegraphs. The second class virtually includes the general internal administration of the country. In 1833 British India consisted of the three provinces or presidencies as they were called, of Bengal, Madras, and Bombay.

The Governor-General in Council administered Bengal and had a controlling power over the governments of the other presidencies. Now there are eight important governments, including Madras and Bombay, besides the two frontier chief commissionerships. Madras and Bombay are under what is called council government, namely, a Governor appointed by the Crown, and an executive council of three members. In Bengal the Lieutenant-Governor has recently been given an executive council of two members.

Four other provinces-the Punjab, the United Provinces of Agra and Oudh, Eastern Bengal and Assam, Burma-are governed by a Lieutenant-Governor without an executive council. In each of these seven provinces there is a provincial legislative council, modelled on the lines of the legislative council of the Governor-General, and empowered to discuss the provincial finances and other administrative matters relating to the province. These provincial councils are of considerable size; they consist largely of unofficial members representing constituencies or classes; within certain limits they make the laws of their respective provinces; and they are the mouthpiece of the educated community, such as at present it is, of the province.

This system of a number of subordinate governments and of a central government for supervision and control recognises the fact that India is a continent and not a single country. No other arrangement would be practicable. At first sight it seems to resemble the plan adopted in uniting the provinces of Canada in the Dominion Government and the Australian Colonies in the Commonwealth of Australia. But there is an important difference. In the Canadian and Australian cases the separate colonies existed before union was thought of. Their rights had to be carefully defined and safeguarded by the Act of Parliament incorporating them into a union. The federal government thus created is based on a constitutional law which cannot be changed except on certain strictly defined conditions.

The case of India is different. There is no constitutional instrument determining the relation of the Government of India and the local governments. The Government of India has supreme and undivided authority, subject, of course, to the home government. It is a unitary and not a federal government. The local governments are its agents, and they derive their various powers from it. This does not mean that the local governments lead a precarious existence, enjoying independence one day and losing it the next. The Government of India and the home government believe too firmly in decentralisation for that to be possible. The process is steadily in the direction of enlarging the powers of the local governments, and the very fact that there is no written constitution and that a mistake in one direction or the other can be repaired without political strife, makes advance the easier.

Let us see how the system actually works, taking first the case of finance. All the revenues of British India, whether collected by the local governments or by the central government, are paid into one exchequer. Of the total roughly one-third is made over to the local governments as their share. They have the spending of some twenty-six millions sterling out of seventy-eight millions. The share of the local governments is settled in the following manner. Certain heads of revenue have been made over entirely to them; of others they receive not less than one-half; others again belong entirely to the Government of India. Thus the Government of India retains all receipts from customs, railways, opium, posts, and telegraphs, and half the receipts from land revenue, excise, income-tax, stamps.

The local governments manage the latter sources of revenue, and have a direct financial interest in developing them. As to expenditure, similar arrangements are observed. The Government of India defrays the cost of the railways and other departments directly managed by it; and share with the local governments the cost of the land revenue and other departments, the revenue of which is divided. The system may seem intricate, and in its details it is. But the broad principle is that the local governments meet the needs of the internal administration of the country from certain sources of revenue made over to them. It is their interest to develop these revenues and to expend them to the best advantage.

The local government touches the citizen at many points: the central government is far away. The local government dispenses patronage: creates and appoints to offices. It provides law courts and judges; medical men, hospitals and dispensaries; makes roads and bridges; helps struggling municipalities with grants for drainage and water-supply; regulates the collection of the revenue and sits in judgment on the conduct of the officials. To the ordinary citizen it is *the* government so far as he is concerned. Public feeling in India is therefore beginning to take shape in provincial moulds. The enlarged legislative councils which have been set up in the several provinces encourage this tendency.

The local council discusses the provincial budget, and realises that more money could be locally spent with advantage. It sees that of the revenues collected in the province a large part goes to the central government and is spent on objects, such as national defence, that do not directly concern the province. It does not question the necessity for such expenditure, but it is inclined to think that it might be met in some other way than from revenues collected in the province, or that other provinces have been more favorably treated. The growth of a public spirit provincial in its aims is an interesting fact in modern India. It has to be reckoned with in other matters than finance, as was seen in the case of the partition of Bengal.

The most distinctive feature in Indian administration is the "district." It is the administrative unit. Every province is divided into districts, each of which is of the size of one of the larger English counties. "In India," Sir John Strachey has said, in his book to which reference has been already made, "where an absolute government is administered by a small body of foreigners far more advanced in civilisation than the people of the country itself, the most essential condition of safety to the rulers, and of good government to the people, is that authority should be strong, and authority cannot be strong unless it is concentrated. In every district of British India the government has its representative, in whom all executive civil authority centres."

This officer is usually called the" district magistrate and collector," and as a rule he is a member of the Indian civil service. He is the chief magistrate of the district, but he is a great deal more than a magistrate. He is ultimately responsible for the maintenance of the public peace, and for ensuring obedience to the laws. In most provinces he has authority over the police, and all the magisterial courts and jails are under his supervision. His title of collector is misleading. In England a" collector" is a petty officer who collects rates and taxes. In India the" collector" is the head of the general administration of the district. The term is full of history. It takes us back to the time of Clive and of Warren Hastings, when the right of collecting the revenues of Bengal was ceded to the Company, while the government of the province remained in native hands.

The Company's officers were then collectors of the land revenue and nothing more. Later on, when the Company took over the administration of the province, the collector became responsible both for collecting the revenue and for the general administration of the district. The collection of the revenue is only one of his duties. He is concerned with every aspect of the land system, with the condition of agriculture, the health and well-being of the population, and the working of the district and borough councils. The local government turns to him for information and advice on all questions." Upon his energy and personal character," it has been said," depends ultimately the efficiency of our Indian government."

The duties of government in India are in many respects much wider than in the United Kingdom. The British took over India in a state of economic nakedness. There were no roads, docks, harbours, canals, hospitals, schools, colleges, printing presses, or other requirements of eivilised life, and neither the disposition nor the means on the part of the population to provide them. British rule had to play the part of a universal provider and special providence: and having started in that line it has continually extended its functions.

"It manages a vast forest property, and is a large manufacturer of salt and opium. It owns the bulk of the railways in the country and directly manages a considerable portion of them; and it has constructed and maintains most of the important irrigation works. It owns and manages the postal and telegraph systems. It has the monopoly of note issue, and it alone can set the mints in motion. It acts for the most part as its own banker, and it occasionally makes temporary loans to presidency banks in times of financial stringency. With the co-operation of the Secretary of State it regulates the discharge of the balance of trade as between India and the outside world, through the action of the India council's drawings. It lends money to municipalities, rural boards and agriculturists, and occasionally to the owners of historic estates."

To these hybrid duties may be added those that spring from the prescriptive right of the ruling power to a share in the produce of the land. Save where (as in Bengal) the government has commuted the claim, it re-assesses from time to time the cash value of its share. This is called "making a settlement of the land revenue." It keeps up land surveys and registers in which every field, the name of the occupier, the crop, the rent are shown. It intervenes between landlords and tenants for the protection of the latter. It manages the estates of indebted or otherwise disqualified proprietors. In the Punjab and in some other tracts it prevents the transfer of land from the agricultural to the non-agricultural classes.

Further, the state in India is directly responsible in a degree unknown in England for police, education, sanitation, medical relief, and ordinary public works. Lastly, in times of drought it undertakes" famine relief" measures on the scale of a great campaign. Government so extensive as this means large establishments. Some three million persons are returned in the census as employed in the public service. The majority of this army is merely petty local offices, such as village headmen, watchmen, or accountants. But the number of well paid responsible posts is very large, according to English ideas. Indians hold all but the highest posts, and their share in the latter is continually increasing.

In 1903 of twenty-eight thousand posts carrying salaries of £60 a year and upwards, only six thousand five hundred were held by Europeans. This may be taken to represent the entire European element in the whole civil administration. The Indian civil service, which is recruited by open competition in England, consists of about twelve hundred and fifty members, of whom sixty-five are Indians. In every high court one or more of the judges are Indians. The executive council of the Governor General, and those of Bombay, Madras, Bengal, each contain an Indian member. These facts and figures give some idea of the extent to which the government of British India is carried on by the people of the country.

In considering whether the European leaven is excessive, sufficient, or insufficient, it should be borne in mind that the administration is European in methods and in guiding principles and that for many posts technical and professional qualifications are required which Indians do not at present possess. A word may be here said about the laws which are in force in India and the courts by which they are administered. How far do they observe the principles of European justice and morality? The question opens an interesting chapter of history. At first the British courts in Bengal administered native law.

They found the Muhammadan criminal law universally in force, and applied it to Muhammadans and Hindus alike. In civil cases they applied the personal law of the parties. They also were guided by the principle that no act committed in consequence of a rule of caste in native families should be deemed a crime. This principle saved practices such as human sacrifice, exposure of children, the burning of widows, the burying alive of lepers. The Muhammadan criminal law also abounded in matter which was equally objectionable according to European ideas. By degrees the British courts shook themselves free from the worst features of native law. Suttee or widow burning in 1829 was definitely made a penal offence.

But it was not until 1862, when the penal code was brought into force that the procedure of the courts and a good deal of the substantive law began to conform generally to European ideas of morality. The penal code prohibits a good many acts which were not offences in Muhammadan or Hindu eyes. It has taught a new morality. The law in this respect has been a schoolmaster. In civil matters, where family caste or religion is affected, the personal or law of the parties still applies. The Muhammadan retains his law of divorce, the Hindu his law about plurality of wives. There is opposition here between our ideas and those of the East, but it is too firmly rooted in radical differences of civilisation, religion and race to be removed by the law-giver.

Of the Indian courts of law hard things are often said. It is said that they are expensive to the litigant and dilatory: that they are over-run by petty lawyers and very technical: that they administer a procedure and legal system which are far in advance of the need of poor and humble folk. These complaints are often made about courts of civil justice in other countries. They are no doubt true in part as regards the Indian courts. But the bitterest critic of the Indian courts is obliged to admit that the great majority of the Indian judges are now clean handed.

This is a notable and most encouraging fact. It denotes a notable rise in the average level of public morality. It is due to education, to the moral teaching of the penal code, and to the example set by European public servants. It is also due to adequate salaries and pensions, permanency of employment, and good prospects of advancement. The government in British India is a good master, and on the whole is well served.

3

War and the Search for a New Order

It is not necessary, for the purpose of understanding modern India, to study in detail the stages by which India moved towards independence, but there are four aspects Of that progress which require our attention, since they govern conditions in India to-day. First, the fact that, notwithstanding the struggle between the British Government and the Congress over three decades, the final transfer of power was a voluntary act, in no way extorted by force has had a profound effect on relations between Britain and independent India. Secondly, the gradualness of the progress towards self-government gave time for parliamentary institutions to take root, and for Indians to be trained in higher administration. Thirdly, the parliamentary character of the self-governing institutions introduced by Britain made partition unavoidable; while, finally, the long-drawn-out transition led to the consolidation of the Congress into the powerful party, firmly committed to a planned semi-socialist economy, which rules India to-day.

It is a significant fact that the first, short step towards fardistant self-government was taken when Britain was in a position of absolute and unquestioned authority. The Mutiny had been completely crushed and not even an incipient nationalist movement had yet come into being. Wise administrators nevertheless recognised that the British rulers were dangerously out of contact with their Indian subjects, and Bartle Frere wrote of 'the perilous experiment of continuing to legislate for millions of people, with few means of knowing, except by rebellion, whether the laws suit them or not'. To remedy this lack of contact, in 1861 the Legislative Council was for the first time expanded to include a small number of non-officials nominated by the Governor-General and similar Councils were established in the Provinces.

Although the Governor-General's choice was not limited by statute, in practice the majority of non-officials nominated by him were, right from the start, Indians. Their number was, however, small and the educative effect of the 1861 Act was less than that of the steps taken in the eighth and ninth decades of the century to establish local self-governing bodies. Committees, composed of both Indians and Europeans, were set up in some Provinces to deal with health, education and similar matters, and with the purpose of affording opportunities for participation in self-government, as well as of associating Europeans and Indians in joint action.

A little later, regular municipalities and local boards were created on an elective basis, and Lord Ripon frankly thought of them 'not primarily with the view to improvement of administration ... but as a measure of political and popular education'. In some respects the early results of this development were disappointing: Indians of standing tended to hold aloof from these bodies and District Magistrates so dominated them that they were regarded almost as departments of government. When this phase passed some decades later, and non-officials replaced the District Magistrates as Chairmen, there was a marked deterioration in the standard of administration and many observers regarded the system as a failure.

A sounder view of these later years would perhaps be that local self-government provided the educated classes with a valuable experience of the working of the representative principle, as well as of the technique of committee work and law-making. When the next constitutional change took place in 1892, the Indian National Congress had existed for seven years. Its moderate attitude, and the experience of politics gained through it by a limited class of Indians, justified an advance. The scope of the Provincial Councils was expanded and, although it was still considered premature to apply the elective principle to them, certain commercial associations, municipalities, universities and other bodies were given the right to put forward names which the Government would accept if it thought fit. In practice, the suggested names were almost always accepted.

The new Councils on the whole worked well, and although the new Hindu militancy associated with Tilak in Bombay, and with the anti-partition agitation in Bengal, had created a good deal of unrest and some violence, it was considered possible to embark on a further advance in 1909. The Morley-Minto reforms of that year abolished the official majorities in some of the Provincial Legislatures and introduced a system of election, though the constituencies were not general, but consisted of municipalities, district boards, Chambers of Commerce, landholders and other special interests. John Morley denied that these reforms were intended to lead to the establishment of the Parliamentary system in India, and declared that, if that had been the aim; he would have had nothing to do with them.

It is difficult to know what he meant and it is abundantly clear that the reforms did, in fact, amount to a decisive choice of the Parliamentary system as the foundation of future self-government. By the time of the next constitutional advance in 1919, the political atmosphere had become charged with electricity. Resentment at the overwhelmingly British character of the superior services was keen, and Britain was charged with having been consistently false to the declaration, first enunciated in the 1833 Charter, and frequently repeated, that 'no subject of Her Majesty should by reason only of his religion, place of birth, descent, colour or any of them be disabled from holding any place, office or employment under the company'.

The demand for still more liberal institutions had gathered strength rapidly under the educative influence of the Morley-Minto reforms and was further stimulated by the consciousness of the magnificent part which India had played in the First World War. Additional weight was given to this demand by the pact-destined, unfortunately, to prove very temporary-entered into between the Hindus and Muslims at Lucknow in 1916. Edwin Montagu, Secretary of State for India, was in tune with the spirit of the times in India and truly represented the most progressive thought of war-time England, when, on August 20, 1917, he made the most momentous announcement in Indian history: 'The policy of His Majesty's Government, with which the Government of India is in complete accord, is that of the increasing association of Indians in every branch of the administration and the gradual development of self-governing institutions with a view to the progressive realisation of responsible government in India as an integral part of the British Empire.'

The announcement in effect repudiated Morley's attitude and made it clear that the goal for India was parliamentary self-government, and the resulting Government of India Act of 1919 set India firmly on the path to that goal. The Act distinguished between Central and Provincial subjects and so laid the foundations of future federation. Within the Provincial sphere it established the system of dyarchy, under which elected Ministers had charge of certain departments, while officials remained in control of others. A few years earlier, such an advance would have been hailed with delight, but the atmosphere had been poisoned, first by the agitation against the Rowlatt Acts which it had been necessary to enact in order to deal with terrorism, and, secondly, by the Punjab Rebellion, the events of the Jallianwala Bagh, and General Dyer's infamous 'crawling order'.

The Reforms were accordingly denounced by important sections of the Congress as hopelessly inadequate. After a good deal of vacillation, Gandhi threw in his lot with the extremists and the Non-Co-operation Movement was launched. We are not concerned with the history of that sterile movement, or with the terrorist activity which naturally grew out of it. It is doubtful if non-co-operation or its successor, civil disobedience, advanced self-government by a single day. On the other hand, it engendered a racial bitterness, which has fortunately disappeared since the transfer of power, and a disregard of law and order which has left an enduring mark on the youth of India.

It also prevented the growth of that sense of joint responsibility between elected Ministers and official members of the Provincial Councils which it had been hoped would lead insensibly to true Cabinet government. Nevertheless, dyarchy gave Indian public men valuable administrative and parliamentary experience and taught the public the use of the ballot box. In the writer's judgement it was an essential preliminary to full parliamentary self-government.

The Government of India Act of 1935, which followed the Simon Commission, the Round Table Conferences, and the Joint Select Committee of 1933, carried the progress towards self-government a long stage further. The Provinces were made autonomous in many important respects, while elected Ministers obtained full control over Provincial affairs, subject only to certain reserve powers vested in the Governor. Officials disappeared altogether from the Provincial Legislatures. At the outset the Congress treated the new Constitution with great suspicion and contended that the Governor's special powers would render Ministers unable to discharge their responsibilities.

These fears were soon overcome and, on taking office, Ministers discovered not only that they possessed the substance of power, but also that British officials were their strongest defenders. The 1935 Act set the final seal on parliamentary government as the pattern which would in due course be adopted by a self-governing India. It is useless to discuss the suitability or otherwise of that form of government for the conditions and background of India. Educated Hindus, brought up on the English classics of the nineteenth century, had become deeply impregnated with the belief in parliamentary institutions and regarded all other systems of government as vastly inferior.

The establishment of parliamentary government in India was indeed the logical consequence of British work and influencethe end-product which gave meaning to all that had gone before. The 1935 Act also contemplated the establishment of an all-India Federation, with something very near responsible government at the centre, but this was to be conditional on the accession of half of the Indian States. It will be remembered that it was largely an historical accident whether any particular area was brought under direct British rule and incorporated in a province of British India, or was left under the rule of a hereditary *rajah* or *nawab*.

During some phases British policy had avoided extensions of direct rule wherever possible, while in other periods, notably during the time of Dalhousie, every opportunity had been taken to pension off Indian princes and absorb their territories in British India. By 1935, the resulting map of India was like a patchwork quilt, with 562 Indian States scattered amongst the eleven Provinces and five Chief Commissionerships of British India. These States varied greatly in importance and degree of independence. Some were little more than the domains of feudal landlords, while others were great semi-independent kingdoms, whose rulers were very jealous of any encroachment on their prerogatives.

Many of the States had treaties governing the relations between them and the British Government, whilst all were controlled in those relations by the doctrine of paramountcy.

That doctrine was never defined, save perhaps, in the cryptic phrase 'paramountcy must remain paramount. The combined effect of treaties and paramountcy was that defence and external affiairs were in the hands of the Crown, while for other purposes most of the States were virtually independent, except for the possibility of intervention by the Viceroy in the event of gross misrule.

The political department, whose officers represented the Viceroy in the States, tended as a rule to resist interference with the rights of the rulers, and it could fairly be said that the Viceroy left the Indian States to govern them well or badly, unless intervention became quite unavoidable. There is room for difference of opinion as to the wisdom or otherwise of this policy. Its defenders argue that it made for stability and was merely an honest fulfilment of Britain's original engagments with the princes, while critics maintain that many of the smaller States were run solely for the benefit of their rulers and that they had become an anachronism which would have been swept away but for British protection.

The link between British India and the Indian States was provided by the Viceroy, who, as Governor-General, was the head of the administration of British India, while as Viceroy he represented the Crown in relation to the States. As India approached self-government, it was clear that this link would be severed when the Governor-General became the purely constitutional head of the State in British India.

There would thus be a complete gulf between the two parts of India and there might even be radical divergence of policy in important matters. Federation was conceived as a method of bridging this gulf and the intention of the Government of India Act, 1935, was to weld the Provinces of British India and the States into a great Federation. There were many practical difficulties in the way of such a process. Although at least some of the States were very well administered and in advance of

British India in education and other matters, the democratic ideas with which the politicians of British India were then obsessed had made little headway in the States.

The difficulty of establishing a federal legislature, two-thirds of the members of which would be elected by democratic processes from British India, while the remaining third would be nominated by autocratic rulers, was obvious. The real difficulty, however, arose not so much from the nature of the problem itself, as from the lack of wisdom on the part of the princes and the Indian National Congress alike. The accession of a State to the Federation was to be governed by an instrument of accession, which would specify the subjects in respect of which power was to be transferred from the State to the Federal Centre.

Lord Linlithgow, a great Viceroy, who realised that federation, was the best hope of India, strove valiantly between 1937 and 1939 to persuade the princes to accede, and there is little doubt that at that time they could have made a satisfactory bargain as to the limitations on the authority of the Federal Centre. They failed to understand that they could never hope for a recurrence of such favourable terms and threw away their last chance of effective survival. In this attitude they were to a considerable extent encouraged by the political unwisdom of the Congress Party in 1937 in embarking on a policy which Coupland has described as 'undisguised hostility to the States Governments and of open encouragement of agitation within and without the States against them'.

Just as the Congress mass campaign against the Muslims at this time was one of the ultimate causes of the demand for partition, in the same way the militant Congress campaign in the States resulted in a definite hardening of the attitude of the Princes, who not unnaturally feared inclusion in a federation in which the Congress, in its new militant mood, would be the predominant factor. It is no exaggeration to say that, by its unhappy timing of these campaigns, the Congress helped to kill the federal scheme and perhaps destroyed the last chance of preserving a united India. Nevertheless, this unwisdom on the part of the Congress cannot excuse the obstinacy and blindness of the princes in 1937.

It is by no means certain that they could in a case have survived as islands of autocracy in a sea of popular government, but by their refusal to join the Federation then, they made their own destruction inevitable. In order to understand the final steps leading to the transfer of power, we must go back a little and consider briefly the position of the Muslims during the formative years of modern Indian political thought. The Muslims felt that it was they, rather than the Hindus, who had lost as a result of the replacement of the Mughal Empire by British rule.

Under the Mughals, although Hindus were often employed in high office, the ultimate power was generally in Muslim hands, and as *Qazis, zemindars* or courtiers, Muslims occupied a privileged position. The substitution of English for Islamic law, and the abolition of Persian as the official language, was greatly resented by the Muslims, who failed to imitate the more flexible-minded Hindus in taking to the new system. The Hindus rapidly filled all important posts open to Indians and the Muslims were left sullen and helpless.

Hinduism and Islam both underwent militant revivals in the latter half of the nineteenth century and the sullenness of the Muslims was fanned into open hostility, fully reciprocated by the Hindus, which led to numerous, serious, communal riots before the century was over. When Western-educated Hindus began to talk of democratic forms of government, the Muslims became profoundly apprehensive.

They were conscious that the Hindus outnumbered them by three to one, and that their own intellectual backwardness would make their position even weaker than mere numerical considerations might suggest. It seemed to them that they could never hope to count in the government of a self-governing India and that they could not even form an effective opposition. In 1883 the great Muslim leader, Sayyid Ahmad Khan, thus gave utterance to these fears.

'The system of representation by election means the representation of the views and interests of the majority of the population.... In a country like India, where class distinctions still flourish and where there is no fusion of the various races, where religious differences are still violent, where education in the modern sense has not made an equal or proportionate progress amongst all sections of the population, I am convinced that the introduction of the principle of election pure and simple, for the representation of various interests on local boards and district councils, would be attended with evils of greater significance than purely economic considerations.... The larger community would totally over-ride the interests of the smaller community.'

When the Indian National Congress was founded in 1885 Sayyid Ahmad Khan advised Muslims to have nothing to do with it and founded a Muslim body to oppose its political aims and ideals. At the same time, he strongly urged Muslims to take to Western education and did much to provide them with the necessary facilities. Muslim fears were strengthened when the Indian Councils Act of 1892 increased the non-official membership of the Councils, since that seemed to be a step on the road to government by a majority. In 1905 the violent and successful Hindu agitation against the partition of Bengal dismayed the Muslims, confirmed them in the belief that their interests were separate from those of the Hindus, and led to the foundation of the Muslim League.

During the next decade the Muslim leaders gave much thought to devising methods for their protection as a backward, minority community. 'Weightage', or the allocation to them of more seats in the Legislatures than they could claim on a purely numerical basis, was one of the suggested methods. It would, however, avail them little if the Muslim members were to be elected by general territorial constituencies in which Hindus would also vote. They therefore began to put stress on the demand for separate electorates in which Muslims alone would vote for the Muslim members.

This principle had, indeed, been accepted in the field of self-government as far back as the 'eighties, when the various Municipal Acts provided for the separate representation of Hindus, Muslims and Europeans. When the Morley-Minto reforms were under discussion, the Muslims resisted all the attempts of John Morley to persuade them to abandon this claim. The Viceroy, Lord Minto, took a more realistic view than Morley and recognised that 'any electoral representation in India would be doomed to mischievous failure which aimed at granting a personal enfranchisement regardless of the beliefs and traditions of the communities composing the populations'.

Separate electorates were included in the new constitutional scheme, and the Muslims never afterwards showed the slightest sign of being ready to abandon them. The Hindus, on the other hand, being the majority community, could afford to stand on abstract, democratic principles and denounced communal electorates bitterly until 1916.

At that time, war between Britain and Turkey had created anti-British feeling amongst the Muslims in India and thrown them temporarily into the arms of the Hindus. The Lucknow Pact of 1916 provided that the Muslims would join the Hindus in demanding self-government, while the Hindus, for their part, agreed that the Muslims should have 'weightage' and separate electorates. At the end of the war, the Indian Muslims failed to persuade the British Government to adopt a lenient attitude towards Turkey and, in anger at their failure, launched the Khilafat movement. Gandhi skilfully exploited this movement and the somewhat unnatural alliance formed at Lucknow continued for several years.

In the middle 'twenties the alliance broke down and fierce antagonism flared up between Hindus and Muslims, partly as a result of growing Muslim fears of Hindu domination and partly on account of two highly militant campaigns known as the Suddhi and Sangathan movements conducted by the *Hindu Mahasabha*, or right-wing Hindu party. The Sangathan movement was the complete antithesis of Gandhi's non-violence, in as much as its most spectacular aspect was the training of Hindu boys in lathi play and gymnastics in order to fit them for the coming struggle. The Suddhi movement was concerned with the reconversion of Hindus who had become Muslims or Christians.

These two movements seriously alarmed the Muslims and permanently widened the breach between the two communities. In 1927 a committee set up by Congress, under the chairmanship of Motilal Nehru, to make constitutional proposals, repudiated the Lucknow Agreement regarding 'weightage' and separate electorates, and left the Muslims more than ever convinced that the Hindus were determined to secure power. The following decade was an unhappy one, marked not only by civil disobedience, and its inevitable offspring terrorism, but also by serious communal tension, which in many places led to rioting on a considerable scale.

An interesting illustration of the way in which the demand for independence led to communal trouble is provided by events in the East Bengal city of Dacca. In that city, the wealthy shopkeepers and moneylenders were almost exclusively Hindus, while the small stallholders, cab drivers and other lowly persons were mainly Muslims. Again and again these Muslims were forced by the powerful Hindus-to whom they were frequently in debt-to observe *hartal* that is to close down business, as a protest against some action taken by the Government against subversive or violent movements connected with the Congress.

The Muslim masses began to feel that they were hopelessly in the grip of the Hindus, and in 1930, resentment of this position and of their constant harassment by the Hindus, led to communal rioting on a considerable scale. Similar developments occurred in many arts of the country and in those areas where the Muslims, by their superior physical prowess and courage, terrorised the more highly educated, but timorous Hindus, the constantly maligned British official spent much of his time protecting those very Congressmen who were his chief critics.

At this time the question of the relations between the Federal Centre and the Provinces, when the next constitutional change took place, was in the forefront of the minds of educated men. The Muslims were in a strong position in certain Provinces, but were fearful of the overwhelming Hindu majority in the All-India Legislature. They demanded, therefore, that the Federal Centre should be limited in scope and power and that the Provinces should be the predominant element in the Federation.

Hindus, on the other hand, genuinely believed in the unity of India and were at the same time conscious of their own strength. They accordingly insisted on a strong Federal Centre. The Government of India Act, 1935, was perhaps a workable compromise between the two views, and though the Muslims were not happy about it, they would at that time have accepted it as a whole. Unfortunately, as we have seen, the princes held back and the Federal part of the Act never came into force. The remainder of the Act was put into operation and in 1937 Provincial autonomy was established.

It had been hoped that, in the mainly Hindu Provinces, Muslims would be included in the Provincial Cabinets. The Congress, however, declined to include in their Cabinets any Muslims who would not subscribe to the Congress creed, and at the same time they launched an intensive campaign to recruit Muslims to the Congress Party. They were fully entitled to do this, but the timing of their action was unfortunate and it inspired genuine apprehension in the minds even of reasonable Muslims. During the next two years the Muslims alleged that they had suffered injustice and oppression in the Hindu-majority Provinces, and at one stage their leader, M. A. Jinnah, demanded a Royal Commission to inquire into the oppression of the Muslims.

No such injury was ever held and it is impossible to judge as to whether the complaint was justified or not. The important practical point is that Muslims genuinely believed it. It may be that many Hindus in Muslimmajority Provinces had similar complaints, but their All-India strength made them less apprehensive. The upshot of all these transactions was to leave the Muslims convinced that their position under Hindu rule would be hopeless, and it was from the conviction that the Hindus would be all-powerful in any Central Government of undivided India that the demand for partition sprang.

Some years before the Muslims generally had begun to think of the partition of India, the idea of Pakistan was promulgated by four pamphleteers, of whom Rahmat Ali was the best known. In 1933 they issued a pamphlet asserting that the Muslims in India were a distinct nation from the Hindus, and demanding a separate State consisting of the Punjab, the North-West Frontier Province (Afghanistan), Kashmir, Sind and Baluchistan.

'The initial letters of those States were formed into the word Pakistan and it was then fortunately discovered that in Arabic this would mean the land of the pure.' Few at that time took the suggestion seriously, but as the years passed the idea of partition began to appeal more strongly to the Muslims, particularly in the Provinces where they were in the minority. In 1939 Sir Sikandar Hyat Khan, the Premier of the Punjab followed up this line of thought by putting forward a proposal for a loose federation of zones, which would, in fact, give a considerable measure of autonomy to the main Muslim areas. This proposal, however, was overtaken by events and Muslim fears soon passed beyond the stage when they could be allayed by half-measures.

In 1940 the demand for partition was formally made. The present writer has described elsewhere a dinner party just before the demand for Pakistan was officially formulated by the Muslim League. 'Mr. Jinnah declared that at the stage of imperial rule where self-government was not in sight the British were the finest administrators known to history, but that when politics and national feeling had begun to count they completely failed to understand the mentality of subject races.

"You talk," he said," of the unity of India, but you ought to know that it is a chimera, existing nowhere except in your own minds and in the external unity which you wisely forced on the country. You go on to talk of parliamentary democracy and you fail to realise that the assumptions on which it depends have no application at all to Indian conditions." He went on to develop, cogently and impressively, his two-nation theory and to expound the full Pakistan demand, which was to be adopted by the Muslim League formally in March 1940.

The writer and others present raised all the obvious objections-economic dangers, frontier problems, military and administrative difficulties. Mr. Jinnah brushed them all aside and completely refused to discuss details. This capacity for adhering to a clear-cut idea and ignoring all difficulties of detail and procedure was perhaps Mr. Jinnah's greatest source of strength. From this time onwards, he who had for long been the apostle of the unity of India set his face steadfastly towards partition and would not be deflected either by blandishments or by threats.'

In a general, political history of India, the eight years between the outbreak of the Second World War and the transfer of power would require extensive discussion. It would be necessary, in such a work, to explain why Gandhi's instinctive sympathy with Britain's war aims had to yield to the general Congress determination to exploit the war situation and to demand self-government under what they regarded as satisfactory conditions.

The failure of the Congress plan, the abstention of Congress from participation in the war effort, and the somewhat ambiguous attitude of the Muslim League, which gave no official co-operation, but nevertheless encouraged individual Muslims to join the armed forces, would all require consideration. Attention would then have to be directed to the magnificent contribution made by India to the war effort in spite of the Congress, and to the share of soldiers, artisans and industrialists alike in that contribution.

The Cripps Mission of 1942-which failed chiefly because the Congress was determined to drive a hard bargain and to surrender nothing to the Muslim League-and the Congress rebellion later in the same year, would all demand study and the historian would have to record how the Congress abandoned the theory of non-violence and embarked on a violent revolution at a time when the war situation in the East was at its worst.

It would be necessary, too, to describe how completely and firmly that rebellion was crushed and how it left the Congress Party so paralysed and impotent that if Britain had been anxious to cling to power after the war she could have done so. None of these matters is strictly relevant to an account of India to-day and we can pass them by.

After the war events moved rapidly. The attempts of the Viceroy to bring the parties together in Simla; the 1946 elections at which Muslims voted so solidly for partition that not a single Muslim constituency returned a non-partition candidate to the Central Legislature; the Cabinet Mission, which failed, chiefly because of the constitutional inability of Sir Stafford Cripps to believe in the reality of what he regarded as the irrational Muslim demand for Pakistan; and the unhappy handling by the

Viceroy, Lord Wavell, of the arrangements leading up to an interim Government including the Congress and the Muslim League-all these happenings were merely part of the process leading, step by step, to partition and independence.

It need only be noted that self-government in India dates in effect not from the final transfer of power on August 15, 1947, but from the formation of the Interim Government in 1946. From that time onwards, the Governor-General was little more than the Chairman of an Indian Cabinet, the members of which were not, like their predecessors, his personal nominees, but the representatives of the major parties. They were, in fact, the rulers of the country.

By the end of 1946 India was drifting rapidly to chaos. The real power had passed from British hands; senior officials, anxious about their own future, were conscious that they were caretakers under notice and were disheartened; Ministers, paralysed by the communal situation, seemed unable to come to grips with the problems of administration; and the unparalleled communal riots in Calcutta, together with serious disorders in many parts of India, made it clear that nobody was in effective control.

At the Centre, the Interim Government was proving unworkable and, in the spring of 1947, thoughtful men were shocked to see influential members of the Congress Party attempting to sabotage the Budget proposals of Liaquat Ali Khan, Jinnah's second-in-command, while still they composing the major wing of the Government in which he was Finance Minister. As a result of a genuine and praiseworthy desire on the part of the British Government to arrive at an agreed settlement of the communal problem and to avoid partition if possible, the transition had teen too long drawn out and chaos had resulted.

The situation in India at the beginning of 1947 was perhaps without parallel in history, inasmuch as Britain was determined to hand over power, but could find no generally acceptable transferee. Hindus and Muslims agreed that any long continuance of British rule was out of the question, but disagreed about almost everything else.

The Congress claim to represent the people of India was indignantly repudiated by the leaders of the Muslim League, who pointed to the solidarity of the ninety million Muslims of India in support of partition. Law and order had broken down in important areas and the present writer recorded about that time that 'life in Calcutta and the other big cities of India to-day is life on the edge of a volcano which is already giving the premonitory signs of a great eruption'. Effective power had, as we have seen, been transferred to Indian hands when the Interim Government was formed in 1946, but the complete disunity of that Government deprived it of all moral authority and heightened communal tension throughout the country.

The attitude of the major parties was mainly negative. The Congress would not have partition and the Muslim League would not accept a unitary Government. One reason for this negative attitude was the belief held by many Hindus that Britain would never completely part with authority, but would always reserve some measure of control. There was therefore no need for them to find a constructive solution. The resulting stalemate might have continued indefinitely, but for an act of great moral courage on the part of Attlee's Government, which, on February 20, 1947, declared that India must govern herself by June 1948, whether agreement as to the form of the constitution had been reached or not.

The wording of the announcement was significant. It stated that 'His Majesty's Government will have to consider to whom the power of the Central Government in India should be handed over on the due date, whether as a whole to some form of Central Government for British India, or in some areas to the existing Provincial Government, or in such other way as may seem most reasonable and in the best interests of the Indian people'.

The effect of this statement was electric. Hindus and Muslims alike now realised that the British Government was determined to end its responsibility for India, and for the first time for many years a sense of reality was introduced into Indian politics. The Congress leaders were forced to recognise that partition could no longer be dismissed as fantastic, while the Muslim League could not shirk the uncomfortable thought that power might even be transferred to the existing Interim Government in which they were in a minority. Of necessity, both parties now began to look for a solution to the political problem, and thoughtful men soon began to feel that, in view of the chaotic state into which India was drifting, the transfer of power ought to take place even before the stipulated date.

At this stage, Lord Mountbatten succeeded Lord Wavell as Governor-General and brought to the Indian problem his characteristic fondness for rapid action. This attitude may not always be suitable for the settlement of great political problems, but it happened to be what India needed at that moment. There was a danger that the sense of reality induced by the February announcement might disappear, and a stalemate might recur, with disastrous results.

If the whole issue as to partition had been open at that time, it is doubtful if Mount batten's forcing tactics would have assisted the deliberations of the leaders. In fact, however, by March 1947 it had become clear, even to the Congress leaders, that partition was completely unavoidable. Ninety million Muslims were determined not to accept a united India, and there was nothing that either the British Government or the Congress could do to resist this determination.

The task which faced Mountbatten was, therefore, the limited though difficult and vital one, of securing agreement as to what areas should be included in Pakistan and then ensuring that the Congress did not, at the last minute, shy away from a solution which their heads, but not their hearts, accepted as inevitable. This task he was supremely fitted to carry out, and within three months of taking office he was able to recommend complete self-government, accompanied by the partition of India, with effect from August 15, 1947.

The statement issued by the British Government on June 3, 1947, accepting this recommendation was the fourth great State pronouncement on India in thirty years, the earlier ones being the Montagu-Chelmsford Declaration, the Cripps Memorandum, and, of course, the announcement of February 1947. This succession of documents makes clear the continuity of British policy and the faithfulness of Britain, in spite of many causes of doubt and exasperation, to the ideal of self-government for India.

The Indian Independence Act did three things. It conferred on India, full independence; it provided in principle for partition, subject to local ratification; and it ended the relationship between the Crown and the Indian States, leaving them free to decide their own future. The first of these changes has already been discussed at length, and it is only necessary to add that India and Pakistan were to start with Dominion status, but would be fully free thereafter to decide whether they wished to remain within the British Commonwealth or not.

The second and third changes brought about by the Act require some consideration. Although the demand for partition was based on the two-nation theory, the Muslims were not prepared to be satisfied with a true ethnic frontier, but claimed whatever non-Muslim areas might be considered economically or strategically necessary to them. Broadly speaking, this meant that they demanded the inclusion of the whole of Bengal, Assam and the Punjab, besides Sind, the North-West Frontier Province, Baluchistan and the adjacent territories. This claim was clearly untenable. The further claim put forward at one stage by Jinnah for an eight-hundred-mile corridor between East and West Pakistan need, perhaps, not be taken seriously.

Under the Cabinet Mission Plan, a Constituent Assembly was set up towards the end of 1946, and the Provincial delegates were to meet in three groups. One comprised the Punjab, the North-West Frontier Province and Sind; a second was constituted by Assam and Bengal; and a third by the remaining Provinces. The first two groups were Muslim-majority areas, while in the third the Hindus were in a considerable majority. The Muslim League declined to participate in the Constituent Assembly and when the statement of June 3, 1947, came to be implemented, it was therefore necessary to ask the people of certain areas to choose whether they would enter the existing Constituent Assembly and ultimately join the Union of Hindustan, or join a separate Constituent Assembly and thereafter form a separate Union of Pakistan.

It is not necessary to describe the machinery by which this choice was to be registered, though it must be noted that in Bengal, as in the Punjab, the members of the Legislatative Assembly were summoned to sit for this purpose in two parts - those representing the Muslim-majority districts in one part and those from non-Muslim districts in another part. It was always clear that the North-West Frontier Province, Baluchistan, Sind, the West Punjab and the Sylhet district of Assam would opt for Pakistan, while it was equally clear that the East Punjab, a predominantly Hindu and Sikh area, would join India. Bengal presented a more difficult problem, and for some weeks before the final partition the issue was in doubt.

The population of East and North Bengal were mainly Muslims, while West Bengal, including Calcutta, was predominantly Hindu. During the course of the years, a genuine Bengali nationality had grown up and this, combined with economic considerations, made many educated Bengalis, Hindus and Muslims alike, averse to any idea of a second partition of Bengal. Some leaders of both communities even discussed the possibility that Bengal might remain united, but outside both India and Pakistan.

The great mass of Muslims of East Bengal, however, were determined to opt for Pakistan, and Bengali Hindus thus either had to preserve the unity of Bengal at the cost of being included in Pakistan, or to accept what they felt to be the vivisection of their mother land. They chose the latter alternative, and what Curzon had affected for administrative reasons was restored forty years later on political grounds. The partition of Bengal was perhaps the inescapable, logical consequence of the partition of India, but it was felt as a tragedy by many of the most influential and thoughtful Bengalis.

The third change effected by the Indian Independence Act was the release of the Indian princes from the ties which bound them to the British Crown. The fact that the princes had stood on their treaty rights and refused to join the Federation contemplated by the 1935 Act presented the British Government in 1947 with a serious problem. The treaties between the Crown and the States had in many cases been declared to be perpetual.

They laid on the British Government the obligation of protecting the State territories, while, either by treaty or by the doctrine of paramountcy, the relations of the State with other States and with the world outside were controlled by the Crown. If these relationships were to continue when British India became self-governing, Britain would in fact be committed to maintaining an imperium in imperio of the worst possible kind-562 outposts of Britain scattered throughout territories to which Britain had granted self-government. The independence of what had been British India would, in fact, have been a mockery.

There was also a more practical aspect of the matter. The Viceroy was able to protect the Indian States because he had at his command and army and an administration financed by British India. It could not seriously be suggested that Britain herself should finance and provide an army and a Civil Service in the Indian States for the express purpose of allowing those States to remain outside the new self-governing India. The proposition only needs to be stated to be immediately rejected. It was, in fact, clear that, with the transfer of power, the relationship of the Indian States to the Crown must come to an end.

This had indeed been stated in the pronouncement of February 20, 1947, but critics of Britain's policies can justly argue that on all occasions previous to 1947 the British Government had declared its intention of keeping faith with the princes and that this intention had been reaffirmed even as late as 1942. It is possible to maintain that these assurances should never have been given, but the more practical consideration is that it would have been impossible to implement them without gross injustice to British India. In the view of the present writer, when power was transferred there was no practical or defensible alternative to the annulment of all ties between the Crown and the Indian States-a procedure which left the States, in theory, free to decide their own political future. Many of them in practice found that freedom illusory.

On August 15, 1947, amidst scenes of great emotion, in which the colourful personality and capacity for friendship of Mountbatten displayed them to the full, the vision of the greatest British administrators of India was fulfilled and India became independent. Although the goal had long been clear, none of those concerned could have predicted the path to it. It is, indeed, interesting to notice that, in spite of the practical continuity of British policy in India, on the few occasions when Britain laid down abstract principles they were almost invariably abandoned.

The East India Company, for example, began by declaring that its servants must not meddle with the internal affairs of India; a hundred years later the company resolved to limit its territorial possessions to those already acquired; while a little later still the company laid great stress on the principle of non-interference with Indian customs, however inhuman they might seem to Western eyes. In due course, each of these principles was, in practice if not in theory, completely abandoned. The same process was seen at work in later years, when British statesmen declared that India must learn to govern herself.

'Four conditions were explicitly or implicitly laid down. They were that the new form of government must be based on agreement between Indian parties; that India must remain one and undivided; that minorities must be protected; and that India must remain within the Commonwealth. Not all these conditions were stated initially, and, indeed, some of them would have seemed obvious as to require no statement; but all were an integral part of the policy laid down by British statesmen in 1917.' Not one of these conditions has in fact been maintained.

The need for agreement was expressly rejected by the announcement of February 1947; India was partitioned; it was recognised that self-government was not compatible with imposed safeguards for minorities; and India was free to leave or remain in the Commonwealth. This empirical approach to the problems of India was in keeping with the English genius, and although it involved a long period of tutelage, which educated Indians naturally resented, few to-day would deny that it has been justified by results.

4

A Critical Decade

The unwillingness of the British Government to admit the necessity of partition until all hope of preserving Indian unity had vanished, had the unfortunate result that no detailed thought was given to the mechanics of division until June 1947, and all preliminary arrangements for the establishment of two independent countries then had to be made in a little over two months. Within this brief interval, three major problems had to be tackled-the settlement of boundaries; the division of the apparatus and personnel of civil government; and the division of military assets and formations. The first of these problems was mechanically the simplest.

The grouping of Muslim and non-Muslim districts in the Punjab and Bengal for the purpose of opting for India or Pakistan was made on a rough-and-read basis and a much more meticulous examination was required before the final partition. of the two Provinces could take place. A Boundary Commission, with Sir Cyril Radcliffe as Chairman, was appointed to make the demarcation, both in the Punjab and in Bengal. The Bengal problem was relatively simple, but the Punjab presented grave difficulties, particularly in connection with the district of Gurdaspur.

The Commission had been directed to demarcate the boundaries on the basis of ascertaining the contiguous majority areas of Muslims and non-Muslims, but was also to take other factors into account. These other factors loomed large in the case of Gurdaspur, partly because it would have been unsatisfactory to isolate Amritsar, the great centre of Sikh influence, from India and partly because, as Lord Birdwood puts it, 'it was a case of the needs of an area artificially created by a canal against the sentiments of a majority of the inhabitants'.

The matters soon assumed greater importance than would otherwise have been the case, since the award of most of Gurdaspur to India strengthened India's strategic position against Pakistan in the course of the Kashmir campaign. It is not necessary to discuss the award in detail. It was deeply and perhaps unfairly resented by the Muslims, and some of the leaders of Pakistan made the unworthy allegation that the settlement had been influenced by Mountbatten in India's favour. The present writer was in Delhi and in contact with all the chief personages concerned at about this time and he is entirely satisfied that there is no substance in this charge, and that the award was completely unbiased. Its soundness or otherwise will be a matter of controversy amongst historians to the end of time.

In spite of her resentment, Pakistan loyally accepted the award and the boundaries of India and Pakistan were finally settled. Recent boundary incidents are of no importance in them, but are merely symptomatic of strained relations between the two countries.

The second problem was the division of the assets and personnel of the civil government. A Partition Council, consisting of two representatives each of India and Pakistan and presided over by the Governor-General, was set up as soon as partition had been accepted in principle. It operated through a Steering Committee, consisting of two officials -H. M. Patel, now Finance Secretary of the Government of India, and Mohammad Ali, until recently Prime Minister of Pakistan-whose names deserve to be recorded in view of the signal service they rendered to both countries by reason of their fair-minded approach and their readiness to work together as old colleagues.

It is not necessary for us to follow the complicated details of their work and we need only mention two or three of its aspects. Muslim civil servants in India and non-Muslim civil servants in Pakistan were given the option to choose which Dominion they would join. The magnitude of the administrative difficulties which this presented can be realised from the fact that it affected not only a few senior officers, but all grades, and that in the Railway Department alone nearly 160,000 employees asked for transfer from India to Pakistan or from Pakistan to India.

The division of the physical paraphernalia of Government was perhaps less difficult-though Pakistan complained bitterly that she did not get her fair share-but a more complex problem was that of dividing the cash balances, as well as allocating the Public Debt. The attention of politicians was concentrated on the present rather than the future and the allocation of cash balances therefore attracted a good deal of notice. Pakistan claimed a quarter shares of the total cash balances of the Government of undivided India, but the Indian representatives maintained that only a small portion of the cash balances represented the real cash needs of the country and that the rest was held as an anti-inflationary measure.

Deadlock was reached, but Gandhi's personal intervention led to a settlement which, in spite of protests, was not unsatisfactory to Pakistan. The customs and excise revenue for the year in which partition was affected gave rise to serious disputes, but, on the other hand, a common currency and coinage was maintained until Pakistan set up its own State Bank in 1948. The division of military personnel and stores, which was the third problem arising out of the mechanics of partition, gave rise to much greater controversy than the arrangements with regard to the civil administration. Feeling between India and Pakistan was bad from the outset, and for a time the possibility of open hostilities-on a wider scale than those in Kashmir-could not be ruled out. Pakistan, as the new creation, felt strongly that it must receive its share of arms and ammunition without delay.

A joint Defence Council, with Auchinleck as its Supreme Commander under Mountbatten, was established and charged with the duty of completing the division of the armed forces and their plant, machinery, equipment and stores. The transfer was to take place in two stages. In the first stage, Muslim-majority units were to be transferred to the Pakistan area and non-Muslim units to India and this was to be done even before the transfer of power. The task in the second stage was 'to comb out the units themselves on the basis of voluntary transfer'.

While these processes were taking place, administrative machinery for the armed forces was to be set up in each Dominion and it was expected that all this would be completed by April 1, 1948, when the functions of the Supreme Commander would be at an end. During his term of office he was to have no operational control and no responsibility for law and order. The arrangements were well conceived, but the operations of the Joint Council gave rise to much bitterness and on December 1, 1947, a break-down was frankly recognised and the post of Supreme Commander abolished. In the state of feeling which then prevailed between India and Pakistan and between Muslims and non-Muslims, the task of the Supreme Commander had become completely impossible and the termination of the arrangement does not in any way reflect upon Auchinleck.

Pakistan has alleged consistently from 1947 onwards that India refused to send to Pakistan the arms and ammunition which it had been agreed that Pakistan should receive. Without access to confidential documents, it is impossible to pass judgement on this allegation, but it would not be surprising, in view of the tension between India and Pakistan and the dispute over Kashmir, if India did, in fact, keep back arms which she should have sent to Pakistan. The question has since become quite academic in view of Pakistan's remarkable success, with American aid, in building up adequate defence services, but it nevertheless rankles in Pakistani minds.

The difficulties arising out of the process of partition paled into insignificance before the appalling problems presented to the Governments of India and Pakistan by the communal massacres in the Punjab shortly after the transfer of power. To understand these developments it is necessary to recall that the Sikhs were, in origin, a puritanical sect which broke away from Hinduism at the beginning of the sixteenth century. Their founder, Guru Nanak, cared little for the things of this world, but the Jats, who were his principal converts, were a hard-headed and practical people who soon aimed at temporal power and determined to build their strength on military discipline, inspired by religious fanaticism.

They developed a remarkable cohesion and a highly militant spirit, which soon brought them into conflict with the Muslim rulers of India. The tenth and last Guru, Gobind Singh, was a great organiser who, as the writer has put it elsewhere, 'devoted his whole energies to the organisation of his followers as a great military community whose lives were dedicated to enmity to Islam'. Ranjit Singh consolidated the power of the Sikhs and in the early nineteenth century made them the masters of the Punjab until they were conquered by the British. Even under British rule they never lost their pride in their great past, or ceased to dream that they would reassert themselves if ever British power waned.

If the Sikhs had been concentrated in one particular area of the Punjab, the Sikh-Muslim problem could have been solved by the Radcliffe Commission, but unfortunately they were widely scattered throughout the Province. Wherever the partition line might be drawn, nearly two million Sikhs would find themselves under Muslim rule. The apprehension of this possibility caused tension some months before the announcement of June 1947, and fierce communal riots in April were followed by inflammatory speeches by Tara Singh and other Sikh leaders. The Muslim members of the Interim Government strongly pressed Mountbatten, after the June announcement, to arrest the Sikh leaders, and they could justify their demands by the fact that Tara Singh an Gyani Kartar Singh had frankly declared that they would raise the standard of revolt against Muslim rule.

Mountbatten apparently took the view that any such action would merely make a grave communal outbreak certain and that the only chance of peace lay in avoiding precipitate action. Responsibility for this decision must have weighed heavily on Mountbatten who had staked his reputation on a peaceful transfer of power and it is impossible to say that at this stage he was wrong. Nevertheless, preparations for an emergency had to be made and it was accordingly arranged that, while the division of the armed forces was taking place, a Boundary Force, consisting of units from both the Indian and the Pakistan armies and operating under British commanders, should be available to aid the civil authorities in keeping the peace.

The situation grew even more explosive a few days before the transfer of power, and critics of Mountbatten maintain that whatever might have been the prudent course of action in June or July, in the first few days of August he should have arrested the Sikh leaders who were intransigent and inflammatory. After August 15, 1947, violence on a scale previously unknown in modern India broke out. It is impossible to pronounce dogmatically as to who began the orgy of murder, but it seems probable that the Sikhs must accept this responsibility.

Within a few hours, however, the Muslims retaliated. Before long the cities of the Punjab were in flames, while armed bands of Muslims and Sikhs roamed the country committing unbelievable outrages. District Officers were powerless and the Boundary Force was unable to fulfil its functions, since its members refused to fire on their own co-religionists. The Force was disbanded a little later and few impartial observers will criticise this action.

It is, fortunately, unnecessary for our purpose to dwell on the horror and brutality of the next few weeks, when neither age, nor sex, nor condition offered any protection against murder or mutilation. Before long the common man, unaided and unadvised, realised instinctively that nothing could put an end to these horrors except the physical separation of the Sikhs and the Muslims. Towards the end of August 1947 there began one of the greatest and most tragic mass-migrations of history. Innumerable multitudes, from towns and villages alike, left their homes and all their worldly possessions, except perhaps what they could carry with them, and trekked wearily to the hoped-for safety of the west if they were Muslims or the east if they were Sikhs or Hindus.

They had no plans, no idea of how they would live and in most cases no known destination. The imagination is numbed in the attempt to conceive the suffering and the sense of helplessness of these wretched cavalcades. Nor did flight necessarily bring safety. Many groups of refugees were attacked on the road and put to death, while refugee trains were derailed and their passengers murdered. When the first news of what was happening reached Delhi and Lahore, both Governments not unnaturally believed that it was still possible to restore confidence and discouraged great movements of population.

Within a few days, however, they realised that this was now out of the question and they applied themselves with great vigour to the task of somehow feeding and protecting the terror-stricken refugees. That task might well have broken a long-established Government and it is to the eternal credit of India and Pakistan that their newly formed Governments succeeded, little by little, in bringing order out of chaos.

A Joint Military Evacuation Organisation was set up at Lahore. Every possible form of transport, including the air services, was laid under requisition to facilitate movement; composite Muslim-Sikh escorts were provided for convoys of refugees; and, where possible, evacuees were gathered together in temporary camps until they could be sent on to safety. The greatest of all these temporary camps was in Delhi, where it is said that 100,000 Muslims took shelter in the Purana Qila. The story of these operations is graphically told in a publication of the Government of India, and a short extract from it will give some idea of what was involved.

'Fleeing from towns and villages close to the Indo-Pakistan border, non-Muslims began to enter India in large numbers in small disorganised parties towards the end of August and the early part of September 1947. Later, when the Indian army began to help them, huge foot convoys, each 30,000 to 40,000 strong, started upon a 150-mile march from the fertile colonies of Lyallpur and Montgomery districts. Thus in forty-two days (September 18 to October 29), twenty-four non-Muslim foot columns, 849,000 strong, with hundreds of bullock-carts and head of cattle, had crossed the border into India.

'The movement of these columns raised problems of baffling complexity. When the supply of food failed, the Government of India had to drop cooked food as well as food grains and sugar by R.I.A.F. planes which flew from Amritsar and Delhi to Jaranwala, Lyallpur, Churkhana, Dhabhansinghwala, Balloki head-works and Bhai Pheru. Drugs, vaccines and doctors were rushed by air and motor transport. A field ambulance unit was sent to Raiwind to inoculate refugees before they crossed the border. On the way the columns were often attacked and sometimes suffered heavy casualties. Women and children were abducted, and unauthorised search deprived them of the few valuables they carried. The columns suffered at the hands of not only man but also nature. Exposure and devastating floods thinned their ranks. Nevertheless, the determined caravan moved on.'

The railways, in spite of the disorganisation resulting from the distribution of personnel between India and Pakistan, and the even greater difficulties caused by floods of unusual severity, also played a great part in the movement and, according to the publication just quoted, between August 27 and November 6, 1947, they carried 2,300,000 refugees inward or outward across the Indian frontier.

The failure of the Boundary Force to fulfil its proper function has already been mentioned, and from August 31 each Government took over separate responsibility for the maintenance of law and order in its own territories and used its own army for that purpose, as well as for the assistance of evacuees. This proved a much more satisfactory arrangement, and the magnificent part played by the armies from this stage onwards did much to atone for the break-down of discipline in certain units of the Boundary Force.

By November the main movement was at an end and it was estimated that eight million refugees had crossed the frontier. During the three months since partition, human nature in the Punjab and other affected areas had sunk to the lowest depths and risen to the greatest heights of which it is capable. There are nauseating but well-documented stories of troops and police of both communities who fired on the very convoys they were engaged in protecting. On the other hand, there were Sikhs who died defending Muslims and Muslims who gave their lives for Sikhs and Hindus-and there were British officers and women who cared only to protect the Indians or Pakistanis in their employ.

There can be little doubt that the instinct of the common man was right and that only the tragic process of segregation of Muslims and Sikhs could lead again to peace and security. Nevertheless, it provided the Governments of both countries with the appalling problems of housing, feeding, clothing and providing medical attention and sanitation for the vast numbers of refugees, who realised their helplessness more than ever now that the physical danger was over. When these more immediate problems had been solved by means of the construction of vast temporary camps, the Government of India had to take up the harder task of rehabilitation-or, to put it in more concrete form, of finding permanent occupation for the great army of now landless peasants or urban workers.

Agricultural lands left vacant by Muslims were allotted to the cultivating classes amongst the refugees, but loans also had to be given on a considerable scale for the purchase of implements and seeds, as well as for maintenance until harvest time. The urban classes were more difficult to settle, particularly as the occupational structure of the non-Muslim refugees was unlike that of the Muslim refugees who had migrated to Pakistan.

Industrial training classes were instituted; the All India Spinners Association organised cotton-spinning centres to provide work for 100,000 spinners; and public works were undertaken to furnish employment. None of these schemes was of much help to a man who had spent his life in an office, or to the small trader, and though the Government gave loans and grants to assist refugees of these classes to set up in business, many remained for long without any real occupation. They swelled the unhappy ranks of the unemployed and increased the magnitude of a problem which finds a prominent place in the national plan.

Every thoughtful Englishman must ask himself from time to time if this great tragedy, humiliating and painful to Britain as to India, could have been avoided, and three suggestions have been made in various quarters as to how the Punjab massacres could have been prevented. The first is that the Governor-

General should have arrested Tara Singh and his colleagues when they began to inflame the minds of the Sikhs in the middle of 1947.

Although it is reasonable to contend that they should have been arrested, to believe that action against a few individuals would have arrested the flood of communal passion in the Punjab at the time is gravely to underestimate its depth and intensity. The second suggestion, that a peaceful transfer of population should have been arranged before partition was affected, ignores the traditional attachment of the Punjab peasant to his land.

It is extremely improbable that any degree of persuasion or, indeed, anything short of the communal massacres which actually occurred, would have induced either the Sikhs or the Muslims to migrate, and there is also the possibility that propaganda directed to this end might have precipitated the very tragedy it would have been intended to prevent.

Thirdly, it is said that the British army should have been left with responsibility for law and order in the Punjab for a limited period after the transfer of power. This is an oversimplification of the problem. Under whose orders would the army have acted? Clearly, it could not have been under the control of two mutually hostile Governments and the only possible arrangement would have been one in which law and order had not been completely transferred by the British Government.

Neither India nor Pakistan would have accepted such an encroachment on their newly-gained sovereignty. The time had at length come when India and Pakistan had to govern themselves and no form of continued surveillance was compatible with that decision. Britain had discharged her responsibility by establishing in undivided India a reliable and well-trained administration, and it was because that administration was strong enough to stand the strain imposed on it by the events in the Punjab, that order was at length brought out of chaos.

We have already seen that, when the transfer of power took place, the treaties between the States and the Crown were annulled. At the same time paramountcy came to an end, for, in spite of pressure from Indian politicians, the British Government rightly took the view that 'it could not and will not in any circumstances transfer paramountcy to an Indian Government'. All political relationships with either British India or the Crown thus terminated in 1947 and a void remained. The 562 States were left in isolation from the new Union of India and, in theory, could have remained 562 separate kingdoms.

If they had formed a solid geographical block, a third dominion existing side by side with India and Pakistan might have been a possibility, but, in fact, the Indian States occupying 45 per cent of the area of undivided India and containing a population of ninety-three million people, were scattered all over the map. A few of them could perhaps have made out a case for remaining independent, but it was unthinkable that the States as a whole should stand aloof from the Union of India. As Coupland has put it, 'An India deprived of the States would have lost all coherence.

For they form a great cruciform barrier separating all four quarters of the country. If no more than the Central Indian States and Hyderabad and Mysore were excluded from the Union, the United Provinces would be almost completely cut off from Bombay, and Bombay completely from Sind. The strategic and economic implications were obvious enough. The practicability of Pakistan must be admitted, but the more the separation of the States from British India is considered, the more impracticable it seems: India would live if its Muslim links in the north-west and north-east were amputated, but could it live without its heart?'

One of the first tasks of the Union Government was thus to find 'a common centre for the whole country, including the Indian States, able to function effectively in the Provinces an States alike in matters requiring all-India action'. This task was taken in hand before the transfer of power and on July 15, 1947, Sardar Vallabhai Patel, the member of the Interim Government in charge of the States Department, invited the States to accede to the Indian Union in respect of defence, foreign affairs and communications, while preserving their sovereignty in all other matters. There was at that time a great deal of loose talk of a possible federation, outside the Union of India, of the great southern States of Travancore, Mysore and Hyderabad.

If this talk ever had any foundation at all, the Nizam of Hyderabad held the key to the situation, but fortunately for the Union of India, his vacillation, together with the relentless pressure exercised by Patel, destroyed any illusions that might have been entertained by the Government of Travancore, or its forceful Dewan Sir C. P. Ramaswami Aiyar as to the possibility of holding aloof. By the date of the transfer of power, all the States within the geographical limits of India, except Hyderabad, Kashmir and Junagadh, had acceded to the Indian Union.

Critics of India have declared that many of the States were dragooned into accession by that great administrator Vallabhai Patel, but the alternative would have been chaos and disintegration, and credit must go to the Sardar for having preserved the unity of India. The view held by most thinking Indians on this subject was thus expressed by a highly placed and acutely observant Indian friend of the present writer. 'Sardar Patel broke the revolutionary urge in the States by interposing himself between the ruler and the people.

He just put the people aside and settled with the Ruler.... Just as the Britise broke the revolutionary urge in 1946-47 by making a straightforward declaration that they would quit India, on the State front the Sardar would not allow any forces to gather in antagonism to the princely rule. With the exception of Hyderabad, where force had to be used, the Sardar was responsible for the fact that the changeover took place without violence.'

Hyderabad presented a more difficult problem. It was a province of the Mughal Empire until, early in the eighteenth century, the Viceroy Asaf Jah succeeded in making himself independent of Delhi, though he never formally renounced allegiance. Later in the century, after a defeat by the Marathas, the Nizam put him under British protection and the treaty then made placed the external relations of Hyderabad under the control of the Crown. In the nineteenth century the doctrine of paramountcy still further strengthened the authority of the Crown and attempts made by the Nizam from time to time to assert that his position was different from those of other Indian princes' *vis-à-vis* Britain, were unsuccessful. The supremacy of the paramount power was decisively affirmed by Lord Reading in a famous letter in 1926.

The old system of personal rule had continued in Hyderabad without much radical change from Mughal times and all important posts were held by relatives and friends of the ruling family who were, of course, all Muslims. In many ways the State was well run and progressive, though not democratic, but the Hindus, who formed 85 per cent of the population, were an insignificant minority in superior Government service.

When the transfer of power took place, the Nizam was in an indecisive frame of mind, but his real desire seemed to be to remain independent of the Indian Union. He had every legal right to do this and was urged to such a course by many of those closest to him. The arguments used in favour of it were threefold.

First, with a population of seventeen million, revenue of Rs. 26 crores and a highly organised administration, Hyderabad was fully capable of existing as a separate State and her special traditions demanded that she should do so. Secondly, it was likely that India would become a republic and the Nizam was not prepared, after an association of one hundred years, to dissociate himself from the Crown. Thirdly, accession to either Union would almost certainly provoke the communal strife from which Hyderabad had hitherto been free. A little later, a fourth argument was added to the effect that, with its mixed population, Hyderabad could not contemplate taking sides with either Union in the struggle for Kashmir.

The Government of India refused to recognise Hyderabad's claim and urged that India was an economic and political entity, that the Union Government was the natural successor to the Crown in respect of relations with the States and quoted Sir Reginald Coupland's dictum that 'an India deprived of the States would have lost all coherence'. Neither side seemed inclined to give in, but in November 1947 a stand-still agreement for one year was made to cover the period until the question of accession should be decided one way or another. Relations between the Nizam and the Government rapidly worsened and disorders, for which both sides were to blame, grew seriously in Hyderabad.

The State Congress Party, organised largely from Madras, advocated the overthrow by force of the Hyderabad Government and launched a mass civil disobedience movement which soon led to widespread violence. Meanwhile, the Muslims in the State had been equally ready to resort to the use of force. The Ittehad-ul-Muslimeen' with its semi-military organisation known as the Razakars, took a bitterly communal line. Each Razakar vowed to 'fight to the last to maintain the supremacy of the Muslim power in the Deccan'. Individuals who sought union with India were terrorised and arms and ammunition were smuggled into Hyderabad on a considerable scale ready for the impending struggle.

The Communists naturally made the most of this opportunity. They established themselves firmly in the two districts of Nalgonda and Warrangal and were, in the initial stages at any rate, welcomed by the State Congress authorities. According to the official Hyderabad report, 'Communists and Congress flags were hoisted together; violence, arson and murder increased; grain was looted or destroyed; attempts were made to prevent the collection of taxes by force and by promises that, with the advent of the Congress and the Communists to ower, taxation would cease and land be handed over to the peasants; those who refused to join were threatened with death'.

In fact, there was little to choose between Hindus and Muslims in the practice of violence and there was no chance that it would be brought to an end until the question of accession was settled. In the meantime great pressure was brought to bear on the Nizam by Sardar Vallabhai Patel. More than once negotiations seemed to be on the point of success and on at least one occasion there was some ground for thinking that the Nizam was about to agree to the Indian demands, but he was deterred at the very last minute by the threats of the Razakars. At another stage there was talk of the substitution for accession of an agreement giving India control of defence, foreign affairs and communications, but here, again, at the last moment the Nizam raised fresh stipulations and the discussions were infructuous.

While these discussions were going on, the Government of India steadily increased its pressure. An economic blockade was imposed and according to the special correspondent of the *Daily Telegraph*, the Reserve Bank of India 'closed down on Hyderabad's requirements of Indian currency. At length the negotiations finally broke down and India settled the question once for all by sending troops into Hyderabad to take posses. Their action in Hyderabad was ruthless and effective, though the complete restoration of order proved a long and difficult task.

It is difficult to feel that this long-drawn-out dispute reflected credit on any of those concerned. Razakars,

Congressmen and Communists showed an equal readiness to resort to violence; the Government of India exerted a degree of pressure which is difficult to justify in view of the undoubted right of the Nizam to remain independent if he so chose; while the Nizam, by reason of his vacillation and his inability or unwillingness to consider the long-term interests of his people, cut indeed a sorry figure. Whether India was justified or not in the action she finally took is a matter about which historians may well argue for generations to come, but the practical man is bound to consider that the inclusion of Hyderabad in India was the only satisfactory conclusion possible.

The accession of the States meant only that they had handed over to the Union responsibility for defence, foreign affairs and communications, while in all other respects they were autonomous-free even from the limitations which paramountcy had imposed on them before the transfer of power. The existence of these strongholds of autocracy presented a challenge to the new Congress Government of India. There were, it is true, some States in which Legislative Assemblies and Councils had been established, but in most cases these bodies were only advisory.

According to the White Paper on the States issued by the Indian Government, 'These institutions served to create an illusion of democracy while retaining the autocratic set-up with the help of large blocks of members nominated by the Executive.... The position on the eve of the transfer of power in India was that in most cases autocracy continued unmasked and in a few States it was covered by a thin veneer of democratic façade.'

The disparities between the different States in size, resources and stage of development were great. There were States like Travancore, which compared favourably with most parts of British India in education and other aspects of progress; while at the other end of the scale were small States which have been described as little more than the demesne lands of their rulers, where elementary forms of feudalism provided the only pretence at administration. There were sixteen States, each of which had a population of over one million, and at the other extreme there were in Saurashtra 222 States having a total population of three and a half million people.

Again, there were nineteen States, each of which had had a revenue of more than one crore of rupees a year, while there were, according to the White Paper, petty principalities which 'showed a revenue approximating to an average artisan's wage'. It was clear that it would be difficult, if not impossible, to modernise some of these small States and to introduce democratic forms into them, and yet the official view was that 'with the advent of independence the popular urge in the States for attaining the same measure of freedom that was enjoyed by the people of the Provinces, gained momentum and unleashed strong movements for the transfer of power from the rulers to the people'.

The present writer believes that this account of the popular movements in the States was exaggerated and that the urge for change operated in Delhi rather than amongst the peoples of the States. However this may be, the Government of India was determined to introduce popular government throughout India and for this purpose decided to merge the States, where necessary, into sizeable units.

Three different processes were involved, of which the simplest was the merger of 216 States into the neighbouring Provinces. This treatment was mainly applied to small units such as the seventeen Deccan States, with an average population of a hundred thousand, or the Orissa States with an average area of fifteen hundred square miles and an average population of less than two hundred thousand. There were also a few larger units, such as Baroda and Kolhapur, which for geographical and administrative reasons, were included in the Bombay Province.

The second process was that by which sixty-one States were consolidated as centrally administered areas. These States were in the main small, though some larger States were; included in this category for strategic or administrative reasons, or because there was no Province to which they could conveniently be attached. The important State of Bhopal was taken under central administration at the express wish of the Nawab.

Thirdly, there were five groups of States which 'with due regard to geographical, linguistic, social and cultural affinity of the people could be consolidated into sizeable and viable units existing entirely of States'. The numerous petty States of Kathiawar and the Rajputana States obviously lent themselves to this treatment and, in all, 275 States, containing a population of nearly thirty-five millions, were included in these five groups. Each group was to have at its head a *Rajpramukh*, who was to be elected by The Council of Rulers from amongst the former rulers of the States in the group.

The rulers of the merged and centrally administered States signed agreements providing for the cession by them to the Dominion Government of full and exclusive authority, jurisdiction and powers. They ceased altogether to be concerned in the government of their States and became pensioners who, on the whole, were well treated by the Government of India. It would be idle to pretend that in all cases the surrender of power was purely voluntary. A great deal of pressure was exercised on some States by the Government of India, and the freedom that Britain bequeathed to the States to decide on their own relationships with India was illusory.

The justification for the pressure was the plain fact that in many of the smaller States the rulers rendered no service to their people. They had become an anachronism and it was desirable that an independent India should sweep them away. It is, indeed, reasonable to maintain that the British Government should have abolished them before the transfer of power. These mergers and consolidations were all completed before the end of 1949 and the only princes then exercising authority were the *Rajpramukhs* and the rulers of Mysore, JammuKashmir and Hyderabad, which had not been affected by the integration.

The *Rajpramukhs* executed covenants transferring to the Union Government jurisdiction over all federal matters (except taxation, which was dealt with later), and their own position was at the same time assimilated to that of Constitutional Governors of Provinces. In June 1949, Mysore, which had hitherto only acceded to the Union for the purposes of defence, foreign affairs and communications, accepted the authority of the Centre in all Federal subjects, except taxation. Somewhat similar arrangements were made with Hyderabad.

After the constitution of India had been framed, these States executed further instruments accepting it, and from 1950 onwards all the States of India have been full members of the Federation, with their rights and status determined by the Constitution Act itself. It only remained to bring about the financial integration of the Indian States with the rest of India. This was done by a process too complicated to be described here, but of which the essential elements were the abolition of internal customs duties, the increase of income tax to the same level as in British India and financial adjustments between the Centre and the States by way of transitional payments to make up for loss of revenue.

With the enactment of the Indian constitution, the process of integration was complete. India now consisted of twentyseven States, namely nine Part A States coresponding to former Governors' Provinces, eight Part B States comprising the five Union States together with Hyderabad, Mysore and JammuKashmir, and ten Part C States or centrally administered areas. A little later, Parliament established a new Class A State, namely Andhra, and merged the Class C State of Bilaspur with another Class C State. There was also a fourth class of State described as Class D, consisting of a few backward territories.

However tidy the situation may have appeared on paper, in many parts of the new Union there was virtually no administration at all. The British Government had carried the policy of non-interference with the Indian States so far as not even to insist on the establishment of regular judicial machinery and in some of the smaller States only the crudest forms of feudal organisation existed. The personnel necessary for a modern administrative system did not exist, and in some States the people may even have been worse off as a result of the destruction of the old feudal forms, which could not yet be replaced by anything better. Steps were taken to fill the void, but the process is by no means complete yet.

The danger that the unwillingness of some of the princes to join the Union would lead to the disintegration of India had thus been avoided, but it was thought by some observers that a similar danger would arise from the demand for the formation of what were described as linguistic provinces. Until 1919 the Government of India was a unitary and undemocratic government and the division of British India into Provinces was mainly a mater of administrative convenience. It was of little consequence whether or not the Provincial boundaries corresponded with ethnic or linguistic or even geographical frontiers.

As political consciousness grew, the question became of greater importance, and both the Montagu-Chelmsford Report and the Simon Commission suggested that some redistribution of the Provinces on linguistic and ethnic lines might receive consideration. In its own organisation, the Indian National Congress made tentative advances in this direction in 1908, but it was not till 1920 that it accepted the linguistic redistribution of official Provinces as a definite objective. The Nehru Committee in 1928 declared emphatically that it was most desirable for Provinces to be regrouped on a linguistic basis.

Thenceforth this policy was uniformly followed by the Congress until independence and new responsibilities compelled a more practical approach. In 1948 a committee known as the J.V.P. Committee, consisting of Nehru, Patel, and Pattabhai Sitaramayya, said frankly that 'when the Congress had given the seal of its approval to the general principle of linguistic Provinces, it was not faced with the practical application of the principle and hence it had not considered all the implications and consequences that arose from this practical application'.

Nehru now set his face steadily against linguistic Provinces, on the grounds that if the units of the Federation corresponded too closely with ethnic and linguistic divisions, fissiparous tendencies might develop and indeed the Provinces might loom larger than India in the eyes of their inhabitants. This was indeed the crux of the matter. If Indian nationality was a reality, it was difficult to understand why people attached so much importance to provincial boundaries. If it was not yet an unqualified reality, linguistic Provinces might be dangerous. This was an over-simplification of the issue, however, for there were many Indians who were gradually becoming conscious of their Indian nationality, but who were more immediately aware that they were Bengalis, or Biharis, or Telugus.

Nehru might have been able to postpone this problem indefinitely if the Communists had not skilfully exploited the Telugu demand for an Andhra State in the elections of 1952. The Communists adopted 'Andhra for the Telugus' as their slogan in that area and romped home in the Telugu-speaking part of Madras. It was probably this fact, rather than the fast unto death of Shri Potti Sriramulu in support of the Telugu demand, that led Nehru to surrender and to agree, in 1953, to the formation of an Andhra State. This led inevitably to the opening of the larger question of State boundaries and to the appointment of the States Reorganisation Commission.

One of the most complicated of the problems with which the Commission was faced was that of the great Marathi-speaking people lying athwart India from Bombay to Madhya Pradesh and Hyderabad. The people of the eight Marathi-speaking districts of Madhya Pradesh, known collectively as Vidarbha, had long claimed separation from the rest of that

Province, and the Hindi-speaking inhabitants had more or less become reconciled to the idea of the bisection of the Province.

It was urged by important sections of the Maharashtrians that Vidarbha should be consolidated with Maratha areas in Bombay and Hyderabad to form a Samjukta Maratha State. Opinion, however, was divided about this in Madhya Pradesh, particularly in view of the fact that Vidarbha had a financial surplus which its inhabitants did not wish to see spent elsewhere. The States Reorganisation Commission was opposed to the splitting up of the Bombay State and accordingly abandoned the idea of a united Maharashtra, but recommended the formation of a separate Marathi-speaking State of Vidarbha.

The Maharashtrians would thus be almost entirely included in Vidarbha and Bombay. This proposal was overtaken by events in Bombay which will be described below. There remained the problem of how to deal with the Hindispeaking districts of Madhya Pradesh. It was ultimately decided to consolidate them with Bhopal, most of Madhya Bharat (old Central India) and the recently formed and rather unsatisfactory State of Vindhya Pradesh. The new State will be a prosperous and compact unit and will have Bhopal as its capital.

The Bombay State was in many ways the most advanced in India. Its literacy rate was high, the State was well administered and progressive, and civic-consciousness was perhaps more developed than in any other part of India. On general grounds, the case for leaving it unchanged was strong. Unfortunately, there was in Bombay a serious communal problem which led both the main elements in the population to clamour for partition.

The Maharashtrians, who form 44 per cent of the population in the Bombay State and about the same proportion in the City of Bombay, are an energetic, martial people who have for long urged the formation of a united Maharashtra comprising the Marathi-speaking areas of the State of Bombay, Madhya

Pradesh (the old Central Provinces) and Hyderabad, with Bombay as its capital. The other main element in the population of Bombay State consisted of the Gujeratis, who, for historical reasons, have long had great influence in the councils of the Congress Party. They have at times demanded a consolidated Gujerat State, including the States of Saurashtra and Kutch in the north, together with the Gujerati-speaking areas of Bombay.

When this matter was examined by the J.V.P. Committee, it was recognised that the cosmopolitan character of Bombay City, and its position as 'the hub of Indian financial and industrial activity', made it unthinkable that it should become the capital of a purely Maharashtrian State. 'It should continue,' reported the Committee, 'the meeting place of all communities, their source of pride and affection, and a convenient centre for their joint labour and enterprise. It will be incongruous to make this multilingual, cosmopolitan city the capital of a unilingual Province.'

This sentiment will be echoed by every impartial observer and there was therefore general approval outside Bombay for the recommendation of the States Reorganisation Commission that Bombay City and State should be left more or less in statu quo. The writer was in India when this recommendation was made and it seemed probable to him that, in spite of Maharashtrian agitation, the people of Bombay as a whole would accept it. Unfortunately, the Congress Working Committee took a hand and decided to make Bombay City into a separate State and to break up the rest of Bombay State into Gujerati and Maharashtrian areas.

Violence and disaster broke out at once, on such a scale that Delhi felt bound to intervene. The Government of India then made the astonishing decision that the City of Bombay should be administered from Delhi, while the residual Gujerati and Marathi areas should be formed into separate States. The greatest and most progressive city of India was thus to be treated in the same way as the backward tract of Manipur. It can only be assumed that this was a tactical move on Nehru's part, designed to bring the contestants to a sense of reality.

After some months' unrest, the Government of India ultimately decided to create a new State consisting of the whole of the old Bombay State-including alike Bombay City and the Maratha and Gujerati areas of the State-together with the Maratha areas of Madhya Pradesh and Hyderabad, and certain Gujerati areas to the north. In other words, the united State which the Maharashtrians had so long demanded is to be established, but it is to have included in it the commercially important Gujerati areas of the old Bombay Province, as well as Saurashtra and Kutch to the north.

It will have a population of over fifty million people and an area of more than 180 thousand square miles and it may well be regarded as too large for an administrative unit. The settlement naturally satisfied the Marathas, except for certain extremists, but profoundly disturbed the Gujeratis, who feared that their interests would be subordinated to those of the Marathas. Severe rioting broke out in Ahmedabad and elsewhere when the decision of the Government of India was announced, and the position remained uneasy for some time.

Hyderabad also presented special dificulties, since it consisted of the three areas of Telangana, Karnataka and Marathwada, the populations of which differed from one another in race, language and character. Advocates of the dismemberment of Hyderabad maintained that it had remained an artipicial unit, that 'the progress of the people who have remained backward cannot be accelerated unless its three component regions are attached to more advanced units', and that this step was necessary for the liquidation of the undemocratic position of the State.

As against this, it was urged that the area had been integrated for more than six hundred years, from the time of the Bahmani kings, and that a real cultural synthesis had taken place. It is not easy to weigh these conplicting arguments, but it is probable that Hyderabad's resistance to the pressure on it to join the Indian Union in 1947 had somewhat prejudiced its case. The Commission came to the conclusion that all organised parties in the State desired its disintegration.

It accordingly recommended that the Telangana area should be reconstituted as a new State to be called Hyderabad, and that the Maratha areas should be merged in Bombay, while the districts of Raichur and Gulbarga should be included in the proposed Karnataka State-which was to consist of the former State of Mysore and the Kannada-speaking districts surrounding it. Ultimately, the Government decided to merge Telangana into the Andhra State, and Hyderabad as a State ceased to exist. The decision may possibly have been right, but it is impossible for an Englishman not to regret the disappearance of what was once the faithful ally of the British Crown-a State which, though considered backward by those who equate progress with democracy, was of great cultural and historical interest.

In dealing with the problem of the Punjab and the Patiala and East Punjab States Union (which formed an *enclave* within the East Punjab), the Commission was confronted with what appeared to be a linguistic claim, but was in reality a demand for a separate Sikh-majority State. The Sikh organisation known as the Shriromani Akali Dal declared, in effect, that the Punjab could be divided into two areas, in one of which Punjabi was the principal language while Hindi was mainly used in the other area, and they demanded the formation of a separate Punjabi-speaking State. The Commission was not impressed with this demand.

It pointed out that there were many Hindus in the so-called Punjabi-speaking area who attached nearly as much importance to Hindi as to Punjabi and in any case the distinction between Punjabi and Hindi was far from clear cut. Punjabi was regarded by the best authorities as a dialect of western Hindi and, according to the Commission, 'the line of demarcation between the Punjabi and Hindi spoken in the State has become more theoretical than real'. It went on to say that the problem of language in the Punjab was primarily a battle of scripts and sentiments and it seemed to it that, however the State might be divided, Hindi and Punjabi would have to exist side by side.

Closely linked with the demand for a Punjabi-speaking State was the claim that the artificial unit known as PEPSU should, in view of the fact that 49 per cent of its population were Sikhs, be maintained as a separate State and not merged with the Punjab. The Commission did not consider that PEPSU could be regarded as administratively or economically viable and it recommended its merger. Similar treatment was proposed for the Himachal Pradesh and the Commission wrote enthusiastically in support of its proposal for these two mergers.

'The whole of the Punjab from the Sutlej to the Indus was obviously intended by nature to be a single natural area. Even after the division of the State, the areas within the Union of India commanded by the Ravi, Beas and Sutlej constitute a compact unit fertilised by a single river system. The central part of this unit consists of an area on both sides of the rivers Beas and Sutlej.

This central part, however, has vital economic links with the hill districts of Himachal, where the catchment areas of this river system are located; and the portion which is to the south also has important economic links with this central part, because the most important irrigation work which has been undertaken since partition is intended to serve this southern portion, either directly by means of new irrigation canals, or indirectly by means of augmenting the available supply in the old canals.... Apart from the fact that the irrigation system of the whole of the Indian Punjab is thus one and indivisible, the power potential of this region, which is also dependent on this system, is also immense; and the Uhl and Bhakra-Nangal electrical power grids together are intended to command the entire area of united Punjab.... In our opinion, the formation of a united Punjab will facilitate planning of the kind which seems to be so obviously indicated.'

There can be little doubt that this reasoning was sound. The Commission's proposals regarding the merger of PEPSU and West Punjab were accepted and in due course became law, but after much discussion it was decided to leave the relatively backward Himachal Pradesh under Central administration as a Part C State. The Government of India's rejection of the Sikh claim for a separate Punjabi-speaking State was a great disappointment to the Sikhs, but they appear to have accepted it with a good grace.

In the eastern portion of India the reorganisation of States presented no problems comparable with those of Central or Western India, but at one time relations between West Bengal and Bihar seemed likely to give rise to trouble. The real issue was as to the transfer of certain border areas from one of those States to the other, but Dr. B. C. Roy, the Chief Minister of West Bengal, threw a bombshell into the arena by announcing that he and the Chief Minister of Bihar had agreed to a complete merger of their States. For those who knew either State, it was difficult to take this proposal seriously.

There is little love lost, between the Bihari and the Bengali, and while the Bihari was naturally jealous of the superior wealth and education of the Bengali, the Bengali on his part resented the prospect of being swamped by the numerical strength of Bihar. The proposal was greatly disliked in both States and has been quietly dropped. It is not easy to understand why it was made, since Dr. B. C. Roy is perhaps the most astute and experienced Chief Minister in India, and is not likely to have made this proposal without good reason.

The Congress High Command presumably backed it out of anxiety to reverse the process of disintegration which they feared might set in as a result of the formation of linguistic

States, but it is unlikely that the Government of India expected the merger to go through. Apart from these territorial questions, the Commission found itself bound to deal with two matters of policy. In the first place it recommended the abolition of all the different classes of State and the organisation of the entire Union, apart from the Andamans and the Nicobars, on the basis of sixteen States and the two centrally administered territories of Delhi and Manipur.

Secondly, it abolished the posts of *Rajpramukhs*, apparently on the grounds that they would maintain undesirable loyalties to the past, and would ill-accord 'with the essentially democratic framework of the country'. In other words, all units of the Federation were to be assimilated to the uniform democratic pattern of the old Provinces.

At the end of the whole process of reorganisation the Government of India may in one sense feel that it has played its cards skilfully, since the ultimate result of all these protracted and complicated discussions has been a substantial reduction of the number of units in the Federation. Henceforth India will consist of thirteen Part A States and five Centrally administered areas, besides Jammu and Kashmir.

Nevertheless, many Indians regard Nehru's handling of the Bombay situation-as indeed of the whole problem of the States reorganisation-as his greatest failure. To the outsider it seems difficult to acquit the Government of India of the charges of vacillation and of failure to appreciate the strength of the emotions associated with the various communal and linguistic demands. Nehru himself is completely indifferent to local as distinct from India patriotism, and has regarded the question of States reorganisation as a matter mainly of administrative detail. His view is logical, but is not accepted by large sections of the Indian public.

The desire of the Government of India to put in reverse the centrifugal forces which seemed to be operating, led it to propose the establishment of five zonal councils, each comprising Ministers and other representatives from the various geographically contiguous States. The Councils will have no powers and are purely advisory and it is not easy to see that they will have many important functions. Their real value is psychological and, if Nehru's hopes are realised, they may in due course lead the people of India to recognise that State boundaries are purely matters of administrative convenience and that the only patriotism required or justified is of an allIndia character.

Even with the integration of the States, the unification of India still remained incomplete, in view of the existence of the French and Portuguese enclaves. After some hesitation, the French took a realistic view and their territories, of which Pondicherry and Chandernagore were the most important, were formally ceded to the Indian Union. The Portuguese have proved more intractable and Goa has continued to be a source of irritation in India. The Portuguese claim that Goa is, in fact, part of the metropolitan territories of Portugal and can, therefore, in no way be affected by the withdrawal of the British and the French from India.

The Government of India regards this approach as legalistic quibbling with no relation to reality. They claim that by all ethnic and cultural tests the people of Goa are Indians and that Goa is a natural part of India. They think of Goa as the one remaining outpost of colonialism and are determined to see it swept away. However much opinions may differ as to the merits of the conflicting claims, there can be little doubt that the Indian view will prevail in the long run, and the great purpose of unifying India will then be fulfilled.

5

India's Democratic Experience

In few countries of the developing world has the impact of the state on agricultural modernization been as pervasive as in India. Since independence, India's democratic state has intervened extensively in the countryside with a plethora of policy packages aimed at promoting rural development, advancing social justice, and improving the living standards of the vast majority of the its inhabitants-known in official parlance as the" weaker sections of society."

However, the achievements of some five decades of democratically planned economic development fall far short of the goals and aspirations. While the state in its ongoing role as modernizer, intervenor, and mediator has acquired an extensive administrative and institutional presence in the countryside, it has demonstrated a remarkable weakness in implementing its own proclaimed policy goals, especially reformist and distributive goals.

For example, land and tenure reforms that have been continuously on the government's agenda since independence have not led to any meaningful redistribution of land to the tillers. Similarly, the wealth generated in the agricultural sector through the extension of generous state subsidies and price supports, and the increased profitability of agriculture as a result of biological and technological innovations (i.e., the" green revolution" inputs), have disproportionately benefited the already well off, with little perceptible gain in the income and living standards of the majority of rural households.

On balance, the fruits of economic growth have not" trickled down" to the poor. Instead of mitigating the extent and incidence of rural poverty by providing security of tenure to small and marginal cultivators and improved employment and wage conditions for the landless, state policies designed to promote agricultural and rural development have often further exacerbated socioeconomic inequalities in the countryside.

Moreover, respectable average annual economic growth rates of 3.5 per cent between 1950 and 1975, over 5 per cent in the period from 1975 to 1990, and over 6 per cent since fiscal 1992, and an increase in food grain production at the unprecedented annual growth rate of around 2.9 per cent over the period 1950 to 1990-which has given India self-sufficiency in per capita food production (with current public stocks of over 30 million tons of food grain)-have not led to any perceptible improvement in the consumption patterns (or caloric intake) of the urban and rural poor. In fact, net aggregate consumption of food per head has remained remarkably constant since 1950.

Mukesh Eswaran and Ashok Kotwal (1994) note that this is due in part to growing income inequalities and the constrained purchasing power of the poor. The most recent available figures (for 1991/92) indicate that the top 20 per cent of Indian households have a share of more than 40 per cent of the total consumption expenditure (i.e., income minus saving), the top 10 per cent have a share of over 27 per cent. On the other hand, the share of the bottom 40 per cent of households is about 20.4 per cent, with the lowest 20 per cent having a share of only 8.1 per cent (World Bank 1996, 196). The distribution of income is even more skewed than that of consumption expenditure. As a result, the poorest in India are exceedingly poor.

All-India estimates indicate that the rural poor spend anywhere between 70 to 80 per cent of their total income on basic food items and that about 48.4 per cent of the rural population (roughly 300 to 320 million people) live under conditions of poverty because they do not have access to what Amartya Sen (1981) has called" basic entitlements" or an income that would cover their" subsistence minimum" daily caloric and nutritional requirements of 2,050 calories per adult per day. On the basis of the trend in per capita consumption of food grains, Sen creatively demonstrates how economic growth (measured on the basis of income) has failed to trickle down to the poor.

He notes that although the demand for luxury goods, in particular Western-made high-value consumer products, is the fastest growing sector in the Indian economy, the rate of growth of food grain consumption (including consumption of coarse grains such as sorghum and millet-the principal item in the poor's budget) increased from only 181.8 kilograms a year to 185.2 kilograms a year between 1954–1958 and 1976–1985, a trivial increase over a twenty-five-year period.

This suggests in a compelling way that the income gains from economic development are accruing to the top 20 per cent of households, while the poor lack incomes to purchase even basic food grains despite the growing accumulation of grain stocks. One of the cruel ironies of development in India has been that even some of the more ostensible measures adopted by the central and state governments to alleviate poverty through direct redistribution of land, assets, or income, and through the creation of state subsidized" self-help" Programmes and employment schemes, have at best been slow and piecemeal in their implementation and have seldom reached their target groups.

These measures include the "20-point garibi hatao" (i.e., abolish poverty) Programme, the Integrated Rural Development Programme, the Food for Work Programme, the National Rural Employment Programme, the Small Farmer Development

Agency, and the Jawahar Rozgar Yojana (probably one of the world's largest antipoverty Programmes), and numerous other such "propoor" Programmes. It is widely recognized that such Programmes have been a politically attractive palliative rather than an effective solution to the problems of rural poverty and underdevelopment.

POVERTY PROBLEM

Despite such compelling evidence, the debate on the nature and extent of the "poverty problem" in India continues to rage. Hence an overview on this debate is necessary. According to the estimates made by the Government of India Planning Commission report (GoI 1963) of 1960/61, over 50 per cent, or approximately 211 million people, were living below the poverty line in the sense they lacked the 15 rupees (Rs 15) per capita per month in the rural areas and Rs 18 per capita per month in the urban areas to maintain minimum subsistence needs.

The Planning Commission report (GoI 1972) for the early 1970s revealed that the percentage of people living in poverty had remained the same, but in absolute terms their numbers had increased to over 220 million. Estimates by the Planning Commission for 1977/78 placed the proportion of the population below the poverty line in rural areas at 51 per cent and in urban areas at 38 per cent. These estimates were based on a poverty line of Rs 65 per capita per month (1977/78 prices) for the rural areas, corresponding to a minimum daily caloric requirements of 2,400 units per person, and Rs 75 in urban areas, corresponding to a calorie intake of 2,100 units.

However, the Planning Commission's 1983/84 report (GoI 1985), including a World Bank study *India: Poverty, Employment and Social Services* (1989a), made a startling claim about poverty trends for the 1980s. The reports contended that since the beginning of the 1980s there had been a "clear trend" "toward" "greater" income redistribution and that the proportion of those living below the poverty line declined significantly-according to the *Seventh Five Year Plan* (GoI 1985) from 48.3 per cent in 1978 to 37.1 per cent in 1984. The Planning Commission's 1993 *Report of the Expert Group on Estimation of Proportion and Number of Poor* confirmed its 1983/84 findings claiming that by the early 1990s under 30 per cent of Indians were living below the poverty line.

This official claim has not gone unchallenged, resulting in heated debates and outpourings of published materials on the " poverty problem."

Several analysts have criticized the reports for their "exaggerated conclusions," arguing that the data have been based on the unprecedented assumption that incomes increased uniformly across all expenditure classes and on the "untenable assertion" that all families enrolled in the major antipoverty Programmes benefited sufficiently to cross the poverty line. Others have pointed out that the poverty ratio fluctuates and that the 1983/84 *National Sample Survey* (*NSS*) took place in an exceptionally good year for agricultural production, which largely explains the lower incidence of poverty.

The critics add that at any given time poverty levels reflect the variability in individual incomes, and although the transient component may be large, there also exists a substantial core of the chronically poor that has not changed much over time. B. S. Minhas (1991, 1673) aptly notes:

> The massive reduction in the incidence of poverty in 1987–88, as reported by the Planning Commission is again largely a consequence of the peculiar statistical artifacts used by the Commission. Just as it did with the 1983 NSS data, the Planning Commission has continued to indulge in mindless tinkering with the observed NSS size distribution of consumer expenditure for 1987–88 also. Appropriately computed incidence of poverty in 1987–88 comes to about 48.7 for rural and 37.8 per cent for urban India, rather than the artificially low estimate of 32.7 and

19.4 per cent reported to parliament by the Planning Commission.

It should also be noted that poverty estimates by the Planning Commission and the World Bank are based on requirements of minimum caloric intake only, to the exclusion of the other basic necessities of life such as clothing, shelter, access to safe drinking water, sanitation, and health facilities. By excluding these variables the official data grossly overstate the so-called improvements-the overall per centage" decline" in poverty levels reflects not only the changes associated with measurement techniques (changes in what is considered an acceptable minimum level of consumption) but also the normal fluctuations in poverty levels between a poor person and someone who is even poorer.

Granted, even though precise data on how much poverty is transient and how much is persistent are difficult to gather as poverty levels vary over time (reflecting the variability in family employment and incomes), the fact is that in India there exists a substantial core of chronic and persistent poverty. Interestingly, using three different measures of poverty-the headcount index, the poverty gap index, and the squared poverty gap index-in an attempt to capture alternative dimensions of poverty corresponding to its incidence, depth, and severity, the *NSS* for 1993/94 reported that approximately 37.0 per cent of the rural and 30.5 per cent of the urban populations live in poverty.

The *NSS* implied a national average of 35 per cent living in poverty and sharp regional disparities in poverty levels. In Bihar, for example, the proportion of poor in the rural population was estimated to be 64 per cent, in Uttar Pradesh 42 per cent, and in the Punjab and Haryana 25 per cent. Finally, a recent World Bank report (1997, iv–v) claims that some five decades of growth in India clearly refutes any presumption of "immiserizing growth"-that is, growth that tends to marginalize and impoverish large sections of the population.

This report's statement that" it is only through rapid growth that India will be able to reduce poverty and generate the resources to invest in the health and education of its people" sounds rather hollow in light of the sustained economic expansion of 5 to 6 per cent per year since 1992. This growth, the result of the Indian government's ambitious macroeconomic liberalization Programme (introduced in mid-1991) has failed to ameliorate the poverty problem. In fact, earlier World Bank studies by Gurav Datt and Martin Ravallion (1995; 1996) reported that the Indian government's stabilization and structural and reform measures have led to sharp rises in the prices of such key commodities as rice, sugar, cotton, and gasoline, hurting the poor and increasing the incidence of poverty from 36 to 41 per cent of the population.

To reiterate: the stark fact is that India's major developmental challenge, the poverty problem, has not been mitigated despite efforts by some to wish the problem away (at least statistically). According to the World Bank (1999), roughly 40.9 per cent of India's population continues to live under variously drawn poverty lines, a proportion that has not changed since independence. India, the world's largest constitutional democracy, also has the dubious distinction of being the largest single-country contributor to the pool of the world's poor.

POVERTY PERSISTS: ECONOMIC EXPLANATIONS

Why is poverty so persistent in a country where "abolishing poverty" has long been the proclaimed goal of the democratic state and an indelible part of the developmental discourse? Is the problem the result of misguided and poorly implemented policies and the resultant insufficient "trickle down," or is it due to bureaucratic log rolling and incompetence? More fundamentally, is India's democratic state up to the task (i.e., does it have the capacity and resolve) of implementing its own professed reformist and distributive policies and Programmes?

If so, how can India's national development, to reiterate Rajni Kothari's (1989, 10) poignant words, be "made just and humane ... where each individual can achieve their true potential under the general constraints of a democratic-capitalist model of development?" These questions, which constitute the core in the study of political-economy of development, have long puzzled researchers, generating a lively scholarly debate and a prodigious volume of literature. The following sections provide a brief critical review of the various perspectives.

Analyses of the poverty problem by development economists have tended to adhere to a number of competing, if not overlapping, positions. According to one view the persistence of mass poverty and underdevelopment is mainly the result of rapid (and uncontrolled) demographic growth. Specifically, rapid population growth has a deleterious effect on the disadvantaged because it reduces employment opportunities and the flow of monetary benefits to the wider society. Hence, significant reduction in population growth is a prerequisite to economic development and poverty alleviation.

No doubt, the sheer size and rapid increases in human population in many developing countries have simply overwhelmed the employment generation and social welfare Programmes and exacerbated the poverty problem, but it is now widely recognized that such a narrow Malthusian hypothesis is flawed. While acknowledging that rapid population growth poses a serious constraint to development and poverty alleviation, critics argue that the negative demographic impact can be significantly reduced with greater levels of labour absorption in agriculture and by the creation of employment in the tertiary sectors of the rural and urban economy.

Others have put forth the view that the problem of underdevelopment and poverty is essentially the result of low levels of economic growth, in particular, of domestic savings and investment in the developing world. For example, Simon Kuznets (1955), in his celebrated essay "Economic Growth and Income Inequality," concluded that given the close correlation between levels of industrialization, economic growth, and equity, the problem of underdevelopment and poverty is largely a sequential one. He argued that the poverty problem would automatically be alleviated over time as maturing industrialization generates increases in national productivity and incomes-a process that in turn would result in "trickle down" to the wider society.

Kuznets's arguments were later elaborated by Walt W. Rostow (1962), who argued that like the industrial North the less developed nations would undergo the same sequence or "stages of economic growth"- evolving from the "low-level equilibrium trap" "of traditional society to the critical" "take off" stage, and "then progressing under" "the virtuous circle of "self-sustaining growth" to the age of "high mass consumption"- as did their developed and modern Western predecessors. Rostow believed that the Indian economy, given its "healthy savings," investment, and a growing "consumer" "middle class was ready for" "take off."

However, he cautioned that to facilitate "take off," the role of the state should be neutral and minimal (the role best performed by democracies), at best aiding the process of development by occasionally intervening to ensure social quiescence and removing the structural barriers to the percolation of self-generating wealth. To Nobel Laureate W. Arthur Lewis (1954), underdevelopment and poverty were rooted in the inherent "dualism" of developing nations' economies. Dualism, or the "Lewis two-sector model," viewed the economy of poor nations as divided into the "traditional and modern sectors."

The traditional or subsistence rural sector is characterized by zero marginal labour productivity that is, producing surplus labour that can be gradually transferred (without any loss to the agricultural sector) to the modern urban industrial sector. To Lewis, this labour transfer and the simultaneous growth of output and employment in the modern sector are key to solving the problems of poverty and underdevelopment.

The Lewis development model has been criticized for its implicit assumption that the rate of labour transfer and employment creation in the modern sector is proportional to the rate of modern sector capital accumulation, and that a competitive modern sector labour market guarantees the continued existence of constant real urban wages up to the point where the supply of rural surplus labour is exhausted.

Theodore Schultz (1964) provided an alternative to the Lewis model. He makes the case that labour is efficient within traditional agriculture; it is the farmers' aversion to technological innovation that explains the general failure to raise agricultural productivity. There are several reasons for this: modern agricultural technology is expensive for most farmers, the diffusion of new technology is slow given the low educational levels, and technological diffusion is often stymied by the farmers' inadequate motivation. Schultz's policy prescription was for governments to promote technical modernization of agriculture. Implicit in Schultz's arguments was the assumption that market-friendly democratic governments are the most likely to create environments where individual farmers are able to fully maximize their" economic rationality and utility."

By the late 1960s, the concerns of development economics shifted as some of the early optimism about "trickle down,""stages of growth," and the promise of the capital-centered industrial approach to development failed to materialize or produce the desired results. Some concluded that there was an inevitable trade-off between growth and equity and that the "cake" had to first grow in size before it could be better distributed. Others, however, while agreeing that higher growth rates are necessary, posited a complementarily between the twin objectives of economic development (i.e., growth and equity) because of the belief that higher equity levels actually reinforce the growth-promoting process.

According to those taking the latter position, the problem was not so much that the "cake" was small but that poorly conceived and haphazardly implemented policies, by squandering the fruits of economic growth, were ultimately responsible for preventing benefits from "trickling down" to the poor or the underprivileged sectors of society. Over the years a number of these scholars/policymakers, some affiliated with the World Bank and other international agencies, have put forward various policy prescriptions for reconciling "growth with distribution" in the developing world. The" solutions" have ranged from calls for a more open market (i.e., the policy of " comparative advantage") to strategies for "getting the prices right."

To Robert Bates (1981) and Deepak Lal (1985) intrusive statism must give way to a wider role for markets and private entrepreneurship, freed from the depredations of rent-seeking *dirigiste* regimes of diverse ideological stripes. Moreover, cutting government spending and streamlining public agencies will promote more efficient production and distribution of collective goods. Others have argued that accelerating growth in agricultural production and productivity is the key to solving the poverty problem. For example, in the Indian case, after noting a close inverse correlation between growth in foodgrains and the incidence of poverty, these experts have claimed that the trick is to raise the growth rate of agricultural production and productivity.

According to the noted economist, K. N. Raj (1973), a sustained 3.5 per cent growth rate for a period of "several years" will force the trickle-down mechanism to work efficiently in Indian agriculture. Hence, the proponents of this view maintain that although in the short run the reduction of poverty will depend on keeping food prices low and by generating rapid growth in rural and nonagricultural employment, the long-term solution will lie in a broad-based rural development strategy centered around market-guided and productivity-enhancing "green revolution" technology.

To policy advisers like Montek Ahluwalia (1986) and John Mellor (1985; 1988) the extension of such "scale neutral" modern inputs as improved or "high yielding" seed varieties, chemical fertilizer, irrigation, and energy as well as price, credit, and market incentives to "progressive farmers" is essential to achieving sustained agricultural growth. This growth, they add, will be followed by related spinoffs, such as secure and remunerative rural and" off-farm" employment, lower food prices, and resultant decline in poverty levels.

However, as Terence Byres (1988a) notes, the literature may analytically support the validity of" growth with distribution" and trickle-down arguments, but the empirical reality is not so clear. First, the causal relation between higher levels of agricultural growth and decreased levels of poverty is problematic, at least in the case of India. Evidence from different regions of the country shows that, the skewed patterns of income distribution (that became fixed during periods of rapid growth) are extremely resistant to subsequent change.

This explains why the rural poor have not benefited from a greater abundance of food-that is, the increases in grain production have not forced down the price of food, nor have they led to a significant transfer of incremental incomes that accompanied agricultural growth. Given such evidence, Atul Kohli (1987, 12) aptly notes that "the burden of proving the proposition that higher growth rates will automatically percolate down and alleviate poverty in the near future now more than ever, rests squarely on the shoulders of the believers in trickle down."

There is yet another group made up of the "reform-oriented" economists, who are less sanguine about the technological and market-oriented prescriptions. They have called for the establishment of a new international economic order, with equitable participation in the world economy by the poor nations as a necessary precondition for "humane and equitable" development. They have forcefully argued that poverty alleviation must be treated as an explicit objective of national development and that development strategies must be consciously structured to achieve this objective. For example, Paul Streeten (1981) has long advocated a "direct frontal assault" on the problems of poverty and underdevelopment via massive state-sponsored "poverty alleviation Programmes."

He and others have outlined an agenda for radical institutional reforms, namely, the redistribution of wealth, the adoption of more "integrated" development Programmes, and investments in human capital through improved nutrition, public health, education, and family planning in order to provide" basic needs" to the poor. Even though the preceding literature provides important insights into the problems of development and poverty, its failure to adequately take into consideration the political determinants has left significant gaps in the debate. The "basic needs" literature suffers from political naiveté based on the belief that enlightened policy packages by themselves can overcome the entrenched socioeconomic and political structures.

There is substantial scholarly consensus around the" procedural minimum" that defines liberal democracy as a form of government under which citizens, via open and free institutional arrangements, are empowered to choose and remove leaders who vie for the people's vote. Democracies are based on the principles of popular sovereignty and competitive political participation and representation.

An independent judiciary, regular elections, universal suffrage, freedom of expression and conscience, and the universal right to form political associations and participate in the political community ensure that the government in power adheres to the constitution and the rule of law. Moreover, a democratic state is seen to be responsive to the demands and pressures from members of the citizenry since its right to rule is derived from popular support manifested in competitive elections-or, as Robert Dahl (1971) argues, that government responsiveness to citizens' demands is built into periodically held electoral contests guaranteed by juridically protected individual rights.

Given this, classical political theorists of the seventeenth through the nineteenth centuries, including John Locke (1988), John Stuart Mill (1961), and Alexis de Tocqueville (1966), not only viewed democracies as the embodiment of reason and advancement, but also assumed that liberal democracies would greatly empower the labouring and disadvantaged sectors of society to press successfully to redress the gross socioeconomic and political disparities.

The quintessential democrat, Jawaharlal Nehru (1948; 1958) also echoed similar convictions, arguing that the fate of India's "toiling and downtrodden masses" is inextricably tied to the countries "democratic ethos and idea." He argued that India's democratic government, constantly pressured by the formidable political resource of the masses with their numerical strength manifest through the ballot box, would willy-nilly compel the governing political elites to promote public policies that directly or indirectly benefit the poor and the underprivileged.

Analysts such as T. H. Marshall (1964), Seymour Martin Lipset (1959), Karl Deutsch (1961), and Albert Hirschman (1970) have argued that economic modernization and the concomitant structural differentiation, emergence of the urbanized middle and working classes, and expansion of rights and privileges of citizenship give civil society an avenue to advance its material interests through organized collective action.

According to Marshall, the great distributive measures of the postwar welfare state, including measures introducing health services, social security, unemployment insurance, and new forms of progressive taxation, have been the result of a" modern contract"-the very foundation of democratic citizenship. Some of these themes have been elabourated in the recent writings of Larry Diamond, Juan Linz, and Seymour M. Lipset (1990), Stephan Haggard and Robert Kaufman (1995), Carole Pateman (1970), and Adam Przeworski (1991; 1996), among others, who have argued that the granting of formal rights of citizenship and the expansion of civil-political liberties under liberal democracies make the preservation of the political and socioeconomic status quo problematic because democracies motivate political leaders to be responsive to the preferences of the majority rather than to a small proportion of the citizenry.

Gabriel Almond and Sidney Verba (1963) examine the relationship between democracy and development from a slightly different angle. Focusing on citizens attitudes and values in five countries, they conclude that citizens in stable democracies are characterized by a particular set of widely shared attitudes and values or" civic culture." That is, the citizens possess a relatively common set of understandings about the appropriate boundaries of government, the sanctity of political rights, and the fundamental duties of citizens to preserve them. Hence," if there is no consensus within society, there can be little potentiality for the peaceful resolution of political [and economic] differences that is associated with the democratic process."

Robert Putnam (1993) elaborates the arguments of Almond and Verba-reflecting a return to the study of citizen values, norms, and traditions and their implications for political stability and economic development. Putnam demonstrates that an active associational life complemented with "networks of civic engagement," or communitarian ethic, translates into "social capital" that helps to resolve dilemmas of collective action and to smooth economic and political negotiations.

In the Tocquevillian tradition, Putnam argues that a vibrant political culture is based on trust, compromise, reciprocity, and egalitarian values that are central to promoting economic development and social-cultural advancement. Societies endowed with appropriate democratic norms and traditions (namely, dense "networks of civic engagement and generalized reciprocity") can sustain and promote socioeconomic and political cooperation more effectively, as reflected in northern Italy. In sharp contrast, less civic regions reflect a "Hobbesian equilibrium" characterized by "mutual distrust and deflection, vertical dependence and exploitation, isolation and disorder, criminality and backwardness."

However, such sanguine views of the relationship between democracy and development with equity are not universally shared, because, as Robert Dahl (1995, 46) writes, "In practice democratic systems have always fallen considerably short of the criteria and values that justify democracy." David Apter (1965) warned of the possible incompatibility between democracy and development in the "newly emerging nations."

Apter suggested that the formidable task of nation building necessitates self-discipline and societal restraint, hence a free-wheeling and potentially divisive Western style democracy may not be the most appropriate, especially in economically weak and fragmented multiethnic societies. Samuel Huntington's (1968) classic *Political Order in Changing Societies* and Huntington and Nelson (1976) noted more explicitly the "cruel choice" between democracy and development. According to Huntington, since socioeconomic modernization increases the political participation of citizens without ensuring that their demands can be met, economic development is best promoted under conditions of "a high degree" of political stability and order.

In settings where elites lack in the "art of associating together" and institutions are unable to channel the chaos that accompanies modernization, democracy can be counterproductive because it has the potential to open and destroy the already fragile political institutionalization. In such settings popular participation makes democracies ungovernable because pluralism tends to create more divisions and encourage consumption at the expense of investment. Hence, contrary to the "assumptions of liberal, technocratic and populist models ... in the early stages of development, the expansion of political participation tends to have a negative impact on economic equality".

In a similar vein, political philosopher C. B. Macpherson (1965) stressed the need to conceive "democracy" in terms of "liberal," "communist," and "underdeveloped" variants. According to Macpherson the last variant was distinct insofar as the relevant society was, as a whole, culturally "not attuned to competition and political pluralism." In such environments, Macpherson (1965, 29) argued that a single dominant regime was not only necessary, but also essential to achieve the goals of modernization.

> To call it democratic is to put the emphasis on ends, not means. It is to make the criterion of democracy the achievement of ends which the mass of people share and which they put ahead of separate individual ends. This of course is the classic, pre-liberal, notion of democracy. The classic formulation of this democratic doctrine was Rousseau, and there are strong echoes of Rousseau in many of the theoretical statements made by leaders in the underdeveloped countries.

Other analysts have also posited an inherent "cruel choice" between democratic governance and economic development, especially in the early stages of modernization, claiming that the "trade-off" renders democracies incapable of promoting sustained economic development or reconciling growth with distribution.

For example, Guillermo O'Donnell (1973) aimed to explode the "optimistic equation" that democracy was a natural concomitant of development by forcefully arguing that authoritarian coercion acted as a functional requisite to "economic deepening." O'Donnell presumed an inevitability, arguing that the association between democratic governance and the early import-substitution stage of industrialization in Latin America was premature and would give way to the" new authoritarianism "during the later stage of" industrial deepening."

The deepening, or expansion, of domestic intermediate and capital goods industries imposed painful economic restructuring, including repression, of the popular sector, necessitating the maintenance of stability and order by "new" bureaucratic-authoritarian regimes led by an alliance of assertive civil-military technocratic elites. Since the new authoritarianism did emerge in the most modernized countries of Latin America, O'Donnell argued that an "elective affinity" exists between industrial deepening in capitalist peripheries like Brazil, Chile, and Argentina and repressive "bureaucratic-authoritarian rule."

Elaborating O'Donnell's thesis, some scholars have stressed the significance of regime characteristics for understanding the capacity of governments to promote economic development-repeatedly linking authoritarianism with successful economic modernization and democracy with failure. With illustrations from Latin America, James Malloy (1987, 249) states that "present economic policy ... demands decision-making centers able to impose policies resisted by almost all segments of society. This is a task that prior cycles show is beyond the capacity of open democratic regimes in Latin America."

Authoritarian rule, which implies efficient technocratic management, less dependence on popular support, and more capacity to override political dissent, is consequently seen as more compatible with economic development than democracy. Jack Donnelly lucidly summarizes the various arguments put forth by the proponents of the "cruel choice" thesis:

The exercise of civil and political rights may disrupt or threaten to destroy even the best-laid development plan, and must therefore be temporarily suspended. For example, elected officials are likely to support policies based on short-run political expediency rather than to insist on politically unpopular but economically essential sacrifices. Freedom of speech, press, and assembly may be exercised so as to create or inflame social divisions, which an already fragile polity may be unable to endure; free trade unions often merely seek additional special benefits for a labour aristocracy; elaborate and punctilious legal systems on the Western model may seem to be extravagant anachronisms.

Drawing on the archetype derived from the developmental success of East Asia's high-performing economies, some of these analysts have argued that market-oriented" developmental dictatorships" or" soft authoritarianism" as practiced in South Korea during the Park Chung Hee and Chun Duo Hwan regimes, Taiwan under the Kuomintang, and Singapore may hold the secret of rapid economic development with redistribution. Chalmers Johnson (1987), a most astute observer, argues that regimes embodying autonomous growth-oriented political and technocratic elites are more able in rehabilitating or forging state capabilities and judicious" developmental alliances" than open democratic ones that simply retrench cumbersome and profligate governing structures.

As Johnson states:

Since 1947, despite its adoption of a formally democratic constitution and the subsequent development of a genuinely open political culture, Japan seems to have retained many "soft authoritarian" features in its governmental institutions: an extremely strong and comparatively unsupervised state administration, single-party rule for more than three decades, and a set of economic priorities that seems unattainable under true political pluralism ... it has seemed to some that the coincidence of soft authoritarianism in politics and capitalism in economics had something to do with economic performance.

While casual empiricism and the experiences of Japan, South Korea, Taiwan, and Singapore suggest that bouts of hard and soft authoritarianism were critical for growth with redistribution, the question of whether authoritarianism is a *necessary* precondition is open to debate.

Finally, rational choice theorists building on Anthony Downs's (1957) and Mancur Olson's (1971) seminal studies have added yet another dimension to the debate. They ask why, since individual actors are inherently "rational maximizers" who constantly make "self-interested choices," the many underprivileged members of the electorate have not utilized the leverage of democratic governance to demand and extract more material benefits from public officials and the state-the entities with a vested interest in serving their constituents?

To rational choice theorists, the related "free-rider" and "collective-action problems" prevent the masses from improving their conditions even under responsive democratic regimes. Specifically, although smaller groups may reach binding agreements to cooperate, collective action becomes progressively more difficult as the number of potential actors increases. According to this logic, members of the majority cannot get their voices heard because they are unable to band together in collective action.

The debate on the relationship between democracy and development in the developing world has resolved little. Rigorous empirical testing to compare economic growth under democratic and authoritarian regimes has produced, at best, inconclusive and contradictory results. Some have questioned the analytical underpinnings of such comparisons, arguing that the "exclusionary" or "inclusionary" nature of a regime is more significant than its authoritarian or democratic underpinnings.

For example, Karen Rammer (1985/86; 1990) has noted that exclusionary authoritarian governments tend more toward economic predation than "developmentalism"; hence, democracy per se may not be incompatible with reformist and distributive reform, but exclusionary types of formally democratic rule may be incompatible. Writing in the context of advanced democracies, Peter Gourevitch (1986) and Peter Katzenstein (1984) have also compellingly refuted the facile maxim that democracies are poor managers of the economy: rather, they have lucidly argued that democracies have tremendous built-in resilience, flexibility, and developmental capacity.

Gourevitch argues that in hard economic times (he uses the example of the Great Depression) the institutional problem-solving mechanism in democracies allowed for mediation between labour and business. By becoming part of the larger" social coalitions" (that soon included the middle classes and farmers), and eventually becoming embedded in political parties and state institutions, these coalitions were able to ride through the hard times without the institutional breakdowns typical of former authoritarian and totalitarian experiments.

Similarly, Katzenstein highlights how the *modus vivendi* (what he calls "democratic corporatism") established between labour and capital in Austria and Switzerland has enabled these countries to enjoy pragmatic business cycles. Perhaps these complex issues are best understood through detailed country case studies-which recognize each case's unique experiences and distinctive challenges-yet situate each case in broader cross-national comparative perspective-the aim of this study.

THE INDIAN EXPERIENCE

Considering the high mortality rate of democracies in most post-colonial settings, democracy in India has long appeared something of an anomaly. At the time of independence it was widely believed that India was among the least likely of the newly emergent nations to sustain democratic governance. Liberal democracy and the practice of representative government, the skeptics argued (reflecting the hubris of the small Westernized elite that had led the independence struggle), was too alien a system to survive in a subcontinent nostalgic for "imagined traditions" and compromised by irreconcilable fissiparous and centrifugal forces. Indian democracy, they believed, imposed from the top and lacking enduring roots in society, would eventually succumb to the inertia of traditionalism and the divisiveness of oriental despotism.

Indeed, the bloody communal riots that followed partition, and the subcontinent's ancient enmities sustained and abetted by a myriad of competing traditions and interests, each with its crosscutting layer below layer of entrenched inequities and resentment, lent credence to the view that India lacked the basic requisite" preconditions" in which the values, norms, and institutions of liberal democracy could be expected to survive and flourish. Yet, this rigidly hierarchal and excruciatingly poor agrarian social order, whose population will cross the billion mark in less than a decade, has so far defied the odds.

Not only has India maintained its national and territorial integrity, but for much of the five decades since independence has shown remarkable political stability. It stands virtually alone among the new nations in preserving a relatively open system of parliamentary government and holding (on balance) free, fair, and competitive elections on the idea of a secular nation-state in which all groups and communities may aspire to cultural-religious dignity and ultimately share in economic prosperity and political power.

It was this remarkable "Indian exceptionalism" that led Barrington Moore (1966) to devote an entire chapter to India in his influential study. According to Moore agrarian societies with the entrenched" feudalistic type" of social, economic, and political inequalities stood as an impediment to the rise of capitalism and democracy; in contrast, a vigorous class of town dwellers or bourgeoisie was indispensable to democratic development. In his words, "no bourgeois, no democracy". He concluded that since India lacked these basic requisites, "peaceful stagnation" was the ultimate price of democracy in India.

It was his frustration with the linear, "positivist" theories (particularly the narrow economic growth models) that led Gunnar Myrdal (1970) to advance an alternative "broad institutional approach" to the study of the problems of economic development in poor nations. In his magisterial three-volume study that is "mainly about India," Myrdal (1970, 229) attributed India's inability to reconcile economic development with redistribution to the exigencies of the nation's" soft state":

> The soft state is characterized by a general lack of social discipline, ... signified by deficiencies in ... legislation and, in particular, in law observance and enforcement, lack of obedience to rules and directives handed down to public officials on various levels, often collusion of these officials with powerful persons or groups of persons whose conduct they should regulate, and, at bottom, a general inclination of people in all strata to resist public controls and their implementation. Within the concept of the soft state belongs also corruption.

Thus, to Myrdal, the "soft states" of the newly emergent nations (India being the classic example) simply lacked the institutional capacity and political resolve to promote urgently needed economic development. However, instead of linking the state's "softness" to the political and socioeconomic configurations, Myrdal attributed it to the peculiarities-cum-idiosyncrasies of India's cultural-religious traditions, in particular to the "obstructionist Brahmanical institutions" and to the inherent immobilism of the Hindu caste system.

The "preconditions" for development that logically followed Myrdal's reasoning were that the erstwhile religious attitudes and the panoply of cultural idiosyncrasies had to be neutralized, if not destroyed, before economic modernization and more equitable sharing of the fruits of development could take place. In the 1960s and the 1970s, a new generation of India scholars radicalized by the "paradigmatic revolution" in Western social sciences (i.e., the emergence of the dependency approach) and troubled by the "twin crisis" of India's development (i.e., the failure to achieve sustained growth and growth with distribution) began to search for new ways of analyzing India's political economy.

These radical critics (some claiming to be neo-Marxists) provided trenchant criticism of the" modernization perspective," regarding not only the substantive interpretations of the problems of developing countries but also the methodological and ideological grounds-challenging what they considered to be the teleological, unilinear assumptions of the various modernization and developmental approaches.

Some of these critics viewed India's democracy as a cruel hoax, a system that perpetuated the hegemonic rule of the dominant classes through periodic elections. Others denounced the Indian state as a tool of neocolonial domination. Specifically, the critics claimed that "development" carried out under the auspices of a "comprador-bourgeois regime" (hiding behind the facade of democratic politics), headed by an alliance of the "imperialist metropolitan bourgeoisie," the local comprador classes (i.e., the feudal landed classes), and a weak national bourgeoisie, is inherently incapable of promoting growth with redistribution because it is designed to serve the interests of imperialism and its local allies.

The first significant attempt to transcend the rigidities of modernization and neo-Marxist approaches to the study of India's development experience was Francine Frankel's *India's Political Economy, 1947–1977: The Gradual Revolution* (1978). Her 600-page study revolves around two key questions: (1) Why have reformist and distributive efforts failed in India despite strong commitment by the national political leadership to guide the country toward a "socialistic pattern of society"? (2) Can India's democracy reconcile the goals of economic growth and the reduction of disparities without unleashing the social chaos of a violent upheaval?

In a nutshell, Frankel's central argument is that the constitutional and administrative frameworks of democratic India were designed in the interests of the powerful propertied classes. In the case of rural India, the assignment of significant powers to the dominant-class-controlled state governments over "key subjects as land reforms, agricultural credit, land revenue assessments and taxation of agricultural income" put severe brakes on the possibilities of any "sweeping changes of the social order by action from above". But, why did the Indian government succumb to the propertied classes?

Here, Frankel provides a quintessentially "pluralist" answer. She argues that the predilection of Mohandas Gandhi (and a large section of the Congress elite) for nonviolence and an ideological preference for class conciliation and accommodation with the propertied castes and classes served to greatly limit the post-independence state's capacity to fundamentally reform the hierarchal social structures or successfully implement reformist Programmes. Frankel carefully documents that government policies were determined by the political compromises made by influential political leaders with the powerful interest groups and factions that made up India's ruling coalition.

In the case of rural India the relative power of the propertied interests in bargaining, negotiating, and marshaling votes for political support, and the political victory of the "conservative" forces over the "Gandhians" and "Socialists" in the ruling Congress Party early in the post-independence period, virtually guaranteed that the new policies and institutions would favor the interests of the powerful landowning interests. Frankel's focus on the ideological underpinnings of the Congress Party and the political elite's coalition with the various interest and factional groups sheds much light on the nature of elite political activity in India.

Her detailed discussion of the intra elite and governmental struggles over allocations and over turf lucidly shows that politics in a democracy is often the stuff of forced compromises and squalid bargains-the best deals salvaged in the political agreements made by the various factions that made up India's ruling coalition. Also, her discussion of elite decision-making in terms of the organizational interests pursued by competing leaders, ministries, bureaus, and other agencies within the party/state apparatus is highly informative.

However, there are gaps in Frankel's analysis. Specifically, it fails to adequately capture the complex articulation between the democratic state and society. Frankel's study provides a detailed analyzes of elite political activity and the upper level policy process, but it does not provide much understanding of evolving relationships between the multi-tiered structures of state and society or why the weaker sections of society-empowered through the" gradual revolution"-failed to make the state promote their collective interests.

Two other studies that make a concerted effort to analyze the relationship between democracy and India's development are by Lloyd and Susanne Rudolph (1987) and Atul Kohli (1987). In directing attention to the centrality of the polity, these studies not only provide correctives to the reductionism of modernization and neo-Marxist approaches but also craft an innovative approach for the analysis of India's political economy. Yet, the studies' excessively "statistic" orientation, with its asymmetrical and" absolutistic" view of political power, is not without problems.

To the Rudolphs "India is a political and economic paradox: a rich poor nation with a weak-strong state ... [that has] alternated between autonomous and reflexive relations with the society in which it is embedded." India's democratic state is simultaneously " weak" and "strong." It is strong because it controls the commanding heights of the economy and because it's political "centrism" (a posture seen as functional for the dominant interests in society) has enabled it to minimize (or better manage) socioeconomic and political conflicts.

Its growing weakness, or incapacity "to govern wisely and well," stems from the personalization and centralization of power that occurred during the seventeen-year rule (1969–1984) of Indira Gandhi. Specifically, under Mrs Gandhi, the systematic "deinstitutionalization of the Congress Party and state structures, [the erosion] of professional standards, and procedural norms of the Parliament, courts, police, civil service and the federal system", greatly eroded the autonomy and organizational capacity of state and effectively eliminated the channels through which society's many "demand groups" had long articulated and expressed their interests.

The consequence of such destructive actions (carried out to enhance "personalistic rule") was to diminish the state's legitimacy or" moral authority" and compounded the crisis of "govern ability"-or the state's ability to mediate and reconcile conflicting interests, generate consensus, and deal effectively with the pressing problems of law and order and economic development. Even though the Rudolph's agree that the Indian state's autonomy and capacity have declined since independence, they reject Birdman's claim that the decline is rooted in the nature of the dominant class alliance.

Instead, they see the problem as stemming largely from the" wasting of political assets" and from the dismantling of Congress Party institutions by self-serving and unscrupulous leaders. For the Rudolph's, the solution to the problems of economic stagnation and the growing crisis of govern ability is to rebuild the legitimacy and effectiveness of the democratic state. That is, the currently weak state can once again regain the relative autonomy (or the centrist posture it enjoyed during the Nehru years) by reintroducing "principled politics" and by rebuilding institutional and political structures along the lines of the Nehruvian state.

Only a polity with responsive leadership and strong grassroots organization committed to liberal-democratic parliamentary norms and procedures of governance, and accommodating the political aspirations and economic needs of all the groups in society, can promote political stability, the *sine qua non* for growth with development. The Rudolphs' *In Pursuit of Lakshmi* has been the subject of much critical review. Rather than provide a comprehensive review I will draw attention to three relevant issues. First, one of the key criticisms leveled against the Rudolphs is that their study is excessively "state-centric and elitist ... essentially seen from the viewpoint of elites and managers of the system at the apex".

To the critics, the Rudolphs' thesis is both methodologically and empirically flawed because it overlooks the role of the "vast social peripheries" by treating society as some residual category in the process of change. In reducing society to a mere aggregation of "fragmented social forces" made up of either sectorally oriented " demand groups" or caste and *jati* clusters, the Rudolphs underestimate the power of the dominant social structural forces, namely how the forces' control over a formally democratic polity has enabled them to legitimize accumulation and dominance.

The second and related criticism is that in viewing Indian politics largely in terms of the roles and actions of individual leaders, for example, devoting much intellectual energy in denouncing the role of Mrs. Gandhi, the Rudolphs underestimate the socioeconomic determinants of politics. To be sure, Mrs. Gandhi's actions weakened the Congress Party and left a deep imprint on the country's political landscape, but it is also important to note that Mrs. Gandhi came to preside over a party that was already deeply factionalized at the top and rapidly losing its old coalitional base on the ground.

The decline of the Congress Party has occurred in tandem with significant socioeconomic changes and the emergence of social groups and classes no longer willing to be passive" vote banks" for the elites and eager to assert their interests in an open democratic polity. Finally, at the conceptual level, the Rudolphs overemphasis on powerful leaders and intraelite power struggles (reminiscent of the" plural state" approach) and their deliberate eclecticism in their characterizations of the political system as "strong" or "weak" fails to capture the deeper determinants of state-society relations.

Kohli's valuable study not only avoids many of the analytical pitfalls of the Rudolphs' study but, to date, is the most coherent exposition of India's developmental problems presented from a statist viewpoint. Kohli argues that in theory democratic states, through their claim to legitimate control of the representation of various social interests, have considerable potential to determine and shape political and socioeconomic relationships between the state and society. Moreover, given the state's control over public resources, its capacity to mobilize interests and intervene actively through coercion, legitimating, and to co-opt or accommodate, it has the potential to enjoy a high degree of continual autonomy from any given class or interest.

However, Kohli is cognizant of the fact that in reality complete state autonomy is hardly the norm. He argues that the ideological orientation of the state leadership, the organization of state power or "regime types," and the composition and structural relationship between the state and the dominant classes are some of the important varying conditions that affect the state's capacity to act autonomously vis-à-vis society.

As these variables are continuous and vary in degree, so does the capacity of political authorities to define and implement state goals. But, for Kohli, in the final analysis the variations in state autonomy and capacity depend fundamentally on "the type of regime wielding state power". He argues that in the case of India the "nationalist-democratic regime" that took power in 1947 (and has ruled the country since) was too closely tied to the dominant classes and thus did not have the political nor the organizational capacity to confront and "tame" the powerful propertied interests.

Specifically, "as anti-colonial nationalism falls into the background and interest groups compete for state resources", the capacity of states governed by nationalist-democratic regimes to extricate themselves from political and socioeconomic ties so as to restructure the economy and society declines. The state and regime lack the will and capacity to confront the propertied classes, and this political weakness "is, in turn, not merely a function of the omnipotence of the propertied groups. It is in part related to it, but it is also independent of it".

Thus, for Kohli the failure to achieve growth with distribution in India is rooted in the weakness of the democratic regime. He argues that only a strong autonomous developmental state, or a state with strong and stable leadership, a pro-poor ideology, and a closed organizational structure with disciplined cadres (such as the CPM [Communist Party–Marxist] regime in West Bengal) can facilitate economic development with redistribution in India.

Kohli's analytical emphasis on the state and regime type as important independent variables has great merit. Indeed, a considerable body of comparative research has shown that the varying regime types that control state power can significantly condition the patterns of socioeconomic development. Kohli makes a strong general case to illustrate that India's political arrangements have been singularly unsuited for distributive intervention.

His analysis of the reformist performance of the Indian state in comparison with that of three provincial governments in

India, namely, the governments of Karnataka, West Bengal, and Uttar Pradesh, with each functioning under a different regime type "within the larger constraints of democratic capitalism," is highly instructive and further reinforces his position that the organization of politics (i.e., the regime characteristics of the state) do matter in shaping the patterns of national development.

Yet, the overemphasis on regime type has its problems, however. In the case of India, where a wide array of ideologies, economic interests, and political coalitions are encompassed by the broad category of "nationalist-democratic regime," regime types as an independent variable offers only a limited basis for understanding how and why particular policies are chosen and the implications for development and reform. Also, in devoting too much attention to the organizational structure of the state and regimes, Kohli often undervalues the role of non state actors in the formulation and implementation of public policies.

That is, although the state may be the single most consequential actor in most polities, it does not act in a vacuum; more often than not what it does is conditional upon society. Thus, what counts in the formation and implementation of policy is not only the regime characteristics but also the political-institutional linkages between the state and society. As the critics of statism have argued, the degree of state autonomy cannot be derived solely from regime types without weighing the independent organizational, political, and economic resources of social groups and classes.

Karen Remmer (1990, 316) notes that a growing body of research has generated considerable skepticism about the importance of regime variations for understanding policy performance. Not only are policy choices constrained by socioeconomic realities, but the similarities and differences among nations appear to be far too complex and multifaceted to be captured by simple distinctions of types of regimes. As a result, knowing that a regime is civilian rather than military, democratic rather than authoritarian, or even inclusionary rather than exclusionary establishes only a limited basis for making predictions about policy outcomes.

Moreover, Akhil Gupta has aptly noted "a deep-seated elitism ... in conceptions of political-economy that does not systematically integrate the lowest levels of the political system ... [therefore] denying agency to the subaltern." This point is particularly relevant in the Indian context, where the state is far from strong and autonomous but imperfectly consolidated, weak, and retreating. In such an environment, a preoccupation with the upper reaches of the state (i.e., "regimes types") may obscure or at best reveal only a part of the complex and multifaceted drama of socioeconomic change.

This problem is vividly highlighted in Ross Mallick's (1994) recent study. Mallick criticizes Kohli and others for portraying a false epistemology of the "Left Front regime" that has governed the state of West Bengal for some two decades as a" developmental success" in terms of promoting growth with redistribution. To the contrary, Mallick argues that West Bengal's "progressive" Left Front regime has failed most egregiously in three core reformist and distributive areas.

First, in the failure to enact land and credit reforms, Mallick compellingly shows that the Left Front's Land Reform Act netted only 184,049 acres in excess of land ceiling in its major phase, and that the area redistributed as a per centage of cultivable land by 1985 was only 0.55 per cent, well behind a number of states in India. Second, the regulation and protection of tenants under Operation Barga ("Sharecropper Protection") is a farce. Marshaling a wide array of evidence (some based on official surveys), Mallick notes widespread intimidation and eviction of poor and small tenants, including the payment of illegal rents to the rich peasantry and their backers, even in the Left Front strongholds of Burdwan and neighboring districts. Third, minimum-wage legislation designed to help the rural majority and the "poorest of the rural poor" (i.e., the landless agricultural workers) has remained ineffectual.

Mallick writes that in fact wage demands have been suppressed (*NSS* data indicate that the prevalence of bonded labour in West Bengal remains among the highest in India), and that pro-poor Programmes are rife with corruption and patronage and are poorly implemented by the state. Overall, the "exploitation of agricultural labour under the Left Front appears to be the worst in India". Finally, Mallick adds that the most oppressed strata of West Bengal (indeed Indian) society, the low castes and "untouchables," who represent over 12 million people, or 22 per cent of the state's population, have received low priority.

Allocations to special "uplift" Programmes to help the untouchables are among the lowest in all-India terms, and even blatant atrocities against the untouchables have not produced official outrage or punishment of those responsible. But why have Kohli and others have failed to see the seemingly obvious?

According to Mallick the problem lies in their narrow analytical focus. By focusing exclusively on "states," " regime types," and "political elites," and ignoring the lower reaches of the polity and the weaker social constituencies, these researchers have been duped by state officials-in large part due to the analysts' own uncritical acceptance of the official story. The state-society approach outlined in the next section hopes to avoid these problems.

CONCEPTUALIZING THE STATE-SOCIETY RELATIONS

In the social science literature there is no consensus on the definition of the "state." In fact, over a hundred different conceptualizations have been suggested by scholars representing various ideological and epistemological persuasions. According to Theda Skocpol (1979), who speaks for many, the state as a set of administrative, legal, and coercive organizations is the principal institutional locus of political power in most settings.

Through its nationalist-populist and/or organic-statist ideologies and manifold structures and institutions, which include *inter alia* the central executive branch, the legislature, the bureaucracy, the judiciary, the army, and the police, the state tries to formulate, implement, adjudicate, and enforce the laws and policies, not to mention engage in "revenue extraction" from its society, to promote and enhance the calculus of its power: territoriality, nationality, sovereignty, and regime longevity.

Despite the state's assumed pivotal position, recent research has compellingly shown that the focus on the "state" may not be universally valid. In most developing world settings, where states are imperfectly consolidated, with diminishing capacities, and increasingly disengaged from the economic realm, states can no longer claim to have sole and universal jurisdiction or be seen as the final arbiters of economic and political authority. This is particularly the case in societies with a large agrarian social base.

Rural communities firmly embedded in a textured web of familial, kinship, caste, community, and clientage relationships, with deep historic ambivalence toward the state, are tenacious defenders of individual and collective interests-what James Scott (1976) has referred to as the "moral economy of peasant society"-and not easily "captured" despite repeated interventions by democratic, or authoritarian, or even the " all-penetrating" totalitarian regimes to bring them under control. To the contrary, traditional nexuses of power and dominance in the countryside (even in an attenuated form) have remained resilient despite the "modernizing" and coercive thrusts of states.

In fact, states have found their capacity as claimants limited by the strategic negotiating strength of societies, some of which have remained substantially outside the authoritative reach of their states. Nowhere is this more evident than in India. The foundations of the new Indian state were intensely debated in the Constituent Assembly (elected indirectly from the various provinces in 1946) during the years 1947–1950. The result was the Constitution of India, adopted on 26 January 1950, proclaiming India a sovereign federal democratic republic under a parliamentary system of government.

The 395 articles and ten appendixes (known as schedules) in the constitution make it one of the longest and most detailed in the world. Following a British parliamentary pattern, the constitution embodies the Fundamental Rights, similar to the United States Bill of Rights. The Fundamental Rights guarantee to all citizens basic substantive and procedural protections. These civil rights take precedence over any other law of the land and include individual rights common to most liberal democracies, such as equality before the law; freedom of speech, association, assembly, and religion; the right to constitutional remedies for the protection of civil rights such as habeas corpus; and the right to property.

In addition, the constitution outlaws the traditional Indian system of social stratification based on "casteism" and "untouchability" and prohibits discrimination on the grounds of religion, language, race, ethnic background, sex, or place of birth-and includes the right of" minorities" to establish and administer their own educational institutions and to conserve a distinct language, script, and culture. An interesting feature of the constitution is the Directive Principles of State Policy, which delineate the obligations of the state towards its citizens.

The precepts of the Directive Principles are not justiciable; that is, they are not enforceable by a court, as are the Fundamental Rights. The Directive Principles' admirable goals (some say vague platitudes) such as the injunction that the state "shall direct its policy towards securing ... that the ownership and control of the material resources of the community are so distributed to subserve the common good" or that "the state shall promote the interests of the weaker sections of society" are there to guide the government in framing new legislation.

The key institutions of national governance are the executive, composed of the president, the Council of Ministers (headed by the prime minister), the Parliament, and the highest judicial system in the land, the Supreme Court. It is important to note that although the Indian constitution formally vests executive power in the president (also the head of the state), the president exercises these powers on the advice of the Council of Ministers headed by the prime minister. Hence, power in both theory and practice is concentrated in the hands of the prime minister, the de facto head of the Indian executive.

Theoretically (and in practice), it is the prime minister who determines the composition of the Council of Ministers and assigns departmental portfolios to the "inner circle" or the cabinet, made up of between fifteen to twenty individuals. In India the nature and composition of the Council of Ministers and cabinet has varied according to the prime minister in power. The prime minister's office is also supported by a "secretariat," a large body (currently over 300 strong) headed by a principal secretariat, senior bureaucrats, technocrats, economists, politicians, and their assistants.

India's Parliament, the country's supreme legislative body, consists of a bicameral legislature made up of the Lok Sabha and the Rajya Sabha (the Council of States, the upper house of the national Parliament). The Lok Sabha in 1995 constitutionally had 545 seats, and with the exception of two members that are nominated by the president as representatives of the Anglo-Indian community, all seats are popularly elected on the basis of first past the post, similar to the system in the United States. Seats in the Lok Sabha are allocated among the states on the basis of population, each state divided roughly into several electoral districts made up of around 1.5 million people.

The usual term for an elected Lok Sabha is five years, and under the rules of the constitution it must meet at least twice a year with no more than six months between sessions. However, the president may dissolve the house and call new elections if the sitting government loses its majority in Parliament. The Rajya Sabha, on the other hand, like the United States Senate is a permanent body and meets in continuous session. It has a maximum of 250 members, and all but twelve are elected by the state legislative assembly for six-year terms. The Rajya Sabha (like the British House of Lords) permits more extended debates.

Home to a large number of India's elder states people, it is designed to provide stability and continuity to the legislative process (that is, it is not subject to dissolution as is the Lok Sabha). Nevertheless, since it rests on the confidence of the popular assembly, the authority of the Rajya Sabha in the legislative process is subordinate to that of the Lok Sabha. Decision-making on public policy in India is concentrated at the highest levels of authority, with the prime minister, his inner cabinet, and high-level officials and bureaucrats, via their control of the various ministries of government, taking the initiative.

The government of the day has primary responsibility to draft legislation and introduce bills in Parliament-in either house-albeit financial bills for taxing and spending (known as money bills) can only are introduced in the Lok Sabha. The central government is aided in its activities (known as Public Services) by some 17 million central government employees, 5,000 of whom are officers of the elite Indian Administrative Service. Finally, the Supreme Court as the highest legal tribunal is the ultimate interpreter and guardian of the constitution and the laws of the land.

Headed by a chief justice and twenty-five associate justices, the Supreme Court ensures that all legislation passed by the central and state governments are in conformity with the constitution, and the constitutionality on any enactment is determined under the power of judicial review by the Supreme Court, which has original as well as appellate jurisdiction. While India's federal system has vested many powers of legislation in the central government, the constitution has also provided for enumerated powers divided among the union or central government, the provincial or state governments, and the so-called local governments.

Below the central government are twenty-five state governments and six union territories, with populations ranging from 400,000 for the union territory of Sikkim to 140 million for the largest and most populous state of Uttar Pradesh. Although states do not have their own separate constitutions, they are governed by the provisions of the constitution, which specifies that all the states have similar governmental structures and provides for a popularly elected bicameral or unicameral legislature in each state and territory, headed by a chief minister responsible to the legislatures.

A governor for each state and territory is appointed by the central government, and has the power to dissent from a bill and refer it to the president of India and to appoint, with the approval of the legislature, the state's chief minister. The strength of the central government relative to the states is further apparent in the constitutional provisions (laid down in the seventh schedule of the constitution) for central intervention into state jurisdictions.

The center has exclusive authority over matters of national importance-the ninety-seven items includes defense, foreign affairs, transportation, communications, interstate trade and commerce, and finances. Moreover, article 3 of the constitution authorizes Parliament, by a simple majority vote, to establish or eliminate states and union territories or change their boundaries or names. The central government can dismiss any state government through the president's rule. The center also exerts control over state governments through the financial resources at its command: in a real sense it" acts as a banker and collecting agent for the state governments".

Under the rules of the constitution, financial resources flow from the central government to the states through a system of discretionary divisible taxes and grants-in-aid-making the states dependent on the center for their regular budgetary needs as well as their capital expenditures. The central government also allocates and distributes substantial" development funds and grants" through its five-year plans. The resources available under the plans are substantial, given the center's exclusive control over taxable income and foreign financial flows.

India's democratic federal state exhibits all the features of a highly institutionalized modern unitary government. However, despite the constitutional powers of the central government, the provincial governments are not without significant constitutional powers. In the words of B. R. Ambedkar, the chairman of the constitution-drafting committee, "The states of the union of India are as sovereign in their field which is left to them by the Constitution as the Center in the field which is assigned to it".

Under the constitution states have exclusive authority of sixty-six items, including public order, welfare, health, education, local government, industry, agriculture, and land revenue. In regard to the agricultural sector and land revenue, the constitution, in assigning primary responsibility to the state governments (while placing constitutional and legal limitations on the powers and jurisdiction of the central government), reduced the center to providing guidelines, leaving the actual task of translating rural development policies into legislation, including their implementation, to the state governments. In other words, the development of the rural sector has depended in large measure on the actions of the state governments.

In fact, Paul Appleby (1953, 21), who at the request of the government of India conducted a comprehensive review of the country's administrative system, was astounded to discover how much the center was dependent on the states for the actual implementation of major national Programmes and how little real authority the center seemed to have in the vital areas of policy and administration. He has lucidly captured this paradox: "No other large and important government ... is so dependent as India on theoretically subordinate but actually rather distinct units responsible to a different political control, for so much of the administration of what are recognized as national Programmes of great importance to the nation."

Below the state governments exist an array of formal and informal governance structures known simply as "local self-government"-ordinarily understood as the administration of a locality (a village, town, city, or any other area smaller than a state) by a body representing the local inhabitants. The idea behind local self-government, articulated most forcefully by the 1957 *Mehta Study Team Report*, argued that local self-government, or "democratic decentralization," could play a vital role in the process of political legitimation and offer a means for developing a sense of participation in the citizenry.

The report claimed that so long as we do not discover and create a representative and democratic institution, which will supply the local interest, supervision, and care necessary to ensure that expenditure of money upon local objects conforms to the needs and wishes of the locality, invest it with adequate power, and assign to it appropriate finances, we will never be able to evoke local interest and excite local initiative in the field of development.

The district is the principal formal subdivision within the states. In 1990 there were 476 districts in India, varying in size and population, the average running at about 4,000 square kilometers and containing an average population of approximately 1.8 million. The district collector, a member of the Indian Administrative Service, and the state-government appointed district judge (who is in no way subordinate to the collector) are the most important government officials in district administration. Districts are further subdivided into *taluqs* or *tehsils* comprising anywhere between 200 to 600 villages.

The *taluqdar* or *tehsildar* and the occasional village *patwari* (accountant) are the most important government (state) representatives at this level, responsible for overseeing government Programmes, maintaining land records, and collecting revenue. Finally, to provide effective channels of political and economic participation article 40 of the constitution directs all levels of government to engage in the" democratic decentralization of Indian administration" by reviving and creating" traditional village councils for self-government" or *panchayati raj*, and to" endow them with such powers and authority as may be necessary to enable them to function as units of self-government".

Most states have since introduced a fairly institutionalized system of *panchayatiraj*, a three-tiered system that has vested extensive responsibilities for community and rural development in three locally elected bodies. At the base of the system is the popularly elected village council or *gram panchayat;* followed by village council chairs (the second tier), elected by the village council, who serve as members of the block council or *panchayat samiti* ; and the third tier, the *zila parishad*, congruent with the district, that includes all the *samiti* chairs in the district. The *panchayati raj* received constitutional status following the passage of the seventy-third amendment in 1992. The amendment stipulates that all *panchayat* members be elected for five-year terms in elections supervised by the state election commission.

India's federal arrangement is a political paradox: it is no doubt unitary, seemingly highly centralized and autonomous. However, behind the state's imposing pyramid lie complex networks of competing institutions and structures that cut across formal lines of authority, making the seemingly monolithic Leviathan also weak, decentralized, and easily permeable from within and outside. More appropriately, "the degree of stateness," the nature and extent of centralization or decentralization, state strength or weakness, varies markedly.

That is, the Indian state is highly centralized and autonomous vis-à-vis foreign policy or national security but decentralized and fragmented vis-à-vis the vast countryside. In concrete terms this means that while the broad objectives of national rural development are determined at the political center, the form and the prospects of such strategies are negotiated and laid down in the numerous district and village communities.

This is not to imply that the competition for political power and authority among the center, the states, and the localities necessarily results in a zero sum. After all, India's nation builders viewed the state and local governments not as rivals but as aids and extensions of central authority. Rather, the nature of India's democratic federalism and the vastness and complexity of the agrarian base-which at its core retains a certain imperviousness to central penetration-make the central government, on the one hand, quite capable of impressive initiatives in land reclamation, rural infrastructural development, water and irrigation control, and expansion of green revolution technologies, and, on the other, quite inept in implementing reformist and distributive measures.

The Indian state reflects features that Anthony Giddens (1985) in another context has associated with "traditional states." Such states are very different as "social systems" from modern ones. These traditional states are able to generate both authoritative and allocative resources through the intersection of city and countryside, but they are fundamentally segmental in character and can sustain only limited administrative authority. Such states have frontiers rather than boundaries (given their relative weak level of system integration); they do not actually "govern," if this means to provide regularized administration of the territory they claim as their own.

At best, such polities are mainly limited to governance of conflicts in dominant interests within society. This became apparent to me during my fieldwork. I realized that beneath the veneer of a rational constitutional order, legal procedure, and formal bureaucracy, India's democratic polity operates in the countryside essentially along neo patrimonial lines-with a shifting mixture of traditional and modern idioms of socioeconomic and political organization enjoying discretionary control over broad realms of public life.

Specifically, around the political core (or the so-called center), with its supposedly higher degree of administrative institutionalization and bureaucratic coherence (stateness), the state looks authoritative, with its pronouncements seemingly well calibrated and its bureaucratic regulation and demands garnering wary acquiescence and feigned compliance. However, beyond the political center and the state's realm of control its jurisdiction gradually diminishes, and the "borders" between the state and society become increasingly permeable and indistinct, with sovereignties flowing imperceptibly into one another.

At the heart of the sprawling rural universe-states, districts, and villages-the state becomes almost indistinguishable from the informal hierarchies of power and dominance. Over the course of my fieldwork, I came to appreciate that behind the state's imposing pyramid there are complex networks of competing institutions that cut across the state's formal lines of authority. In other words the state, as it spreads out from the political center, tends to dissolve or taper off sharply at the levels below the district.

As the reach of the state declines and its overarching structures and institutions become gradually intertwined and embedded in the traditional, informal hierarchies of power and authority, there is a simultaneous diminution in the degree of its autonomous capacity, authority, and influence. In the village, block, and district (and even in some states), the formal and informal structures of rule and governance become woven into the same tapestry, a process that over time has further reduced central authority and eroded its efficacy in the countryside.

Under these conditions, local notables and seasoned political brokers (some located ambivalently between state and society) have been able to extend their powers, actively pursuing the interests of their constituencies as well as their own individual imperatives by deflecting or delaying certain central directives and demands made against them, in particular, demands to implement reformist and distributive Programmes.

Through stratagems of collaboration, patronage dispensation, building of supportive coalitions with clientele groups, and opportunistic manipulation of the formal apparatuses of the state (e.g., the courts, bureaucracy, police, and various political and administrative structures), the local notables and power brokers have legitimized their power and authority and enhanced their rent-seeking capacities. Beyond the pale of law there are also stratagems of control centering on the blatant manipulation of cleavages within the village society, ranging to outright violence against the poor.

Given the preceding, this study suggests that India's rural development experience can be fruitfully understood by disaggregating the state, viewing it as one more organization within society rather than as some omnipotent agent standing above and apart from it. While states help mold their social surrounding (sometimes dramatically), they are also continually molded by societies in which they are embedded. The boundaries joining the two are often blurred, and the nature of the interaction frequently cuts across that boundary in the form of multilevel alliances and coalitions climaxing in periodic domination by the state, and at other times results in temporary and reluctant accommodation.

Therefore, highlighting the permeability of the boundaries between state and society-in particular, how the patterns of segmentation or structural differentiation within the state and society have evolved and impinged on each other-allows a nuanced understanding of the complex embroidery of forces linking the polity and the sprawling rural communities. Such highlighting also shows how these overlapping structures of power and dominance have worked, often in tandem, to undermine distributive and reformist efforts.

6

Democracy and Development

The complex society that inhabits the vast land mass today known as the Indian Subcontinent has never been easy to govern. The recurring theme in South Asian historiography-from the pre-colonial times, through colonialism, independence, and beyond-is one of an unending struggle by ambitious central authorities to extend their dominion over the heterogeneous and differentiated socioeconomic and political constellations in their midst.

The actualization of a unitary sub continental state has varied over the millennium as power and control shifted back and forth between the various constituents of state and society. The sub continental polities such as the expansionist Mauryan Empire (ca. 321 B. C. to 184 B. C.), the absolutist state of the imperial Guptas (ca. 300 A. D. to 540 A. D.), and the lofty empire of the Moghuls in the sixteenth and seventeenth centuries stand out as important epochs during which despotic and dynastic states established their hegemony over much of the subcontinent.

However, governing a vast and diverse region with all its heterogeneity and contradictions was not easy, and even during the best of times central control over the sub continental polity and society remained tenuous and constrained. To consolidate their power and expand their control, the early state builders (like their modern counterparts) were constantly engaged in what can be best described as coercing, manipulating, accommodating, and integrating the complex web of provincial loyalties, local jurisdictions, and traditional sovereignties that simultaneously collaborated with, resisted, and challenged the political center.

The Moghuls' efforts to weave their imperial order into the fabric of society are an excellent illustration of such a process. The Moghuls (like their Mauryan and Gupta precursors) established with Machiavellian cunning elaborate means of penetration and control of society. The highly centralized fiscal, administrative, and bureaucratic apparatus (the *mansabdari* system) and the imperial doctrine of *sul-i-kul* that stressed the role of the emperor, if not the state, as indispensable to order and prosperity were products of deliberate state policy aimed at integrating the diverse communities of the subcontinent into a common economy and polity.

However, despite the Moghuls' considerable powers of coercion and calculation, maintaining durable central control proved largely abortive, if not illusory, as the centralized instrumentalities eventually succumbed to the centrifugal tendencies of the various constituents of state and society. State decline was followed by interregnums during which power and control reverted decisively to the regional kingdoms and to the patchwork of local village *panchayats* that since antiquity had constituted the basal units of South Asian society and polity.

STATE AND SOCIETY UNDER COLONIALISM

By the early eighteenth century, on the eve of British conquest, the Moghul state was already rapidly disintegrating. The political vacuum was filled by the officials of the British East India Company, who amid the social and political chaos were able to establish themselves as the undisputed rulers of the subcontinent. Acknowledgment of the changed political realities came in 1765 when the Moghul emperor transferred the right of *diwani* or revenue administration and collection of Bengal, Uttar Pradesh, Bihar, and Orissa to the British.

The colonial regime was a fortuitous amalgam of what Judith Brown (1985) has described as the" traditional" and the" modern." That is, it built on Moghul rule, incorporating many of the institutional, personnel, and infrastructural legacies of the Moghul state with British ideas and institutions of control and governance. Moreover, by collaborating with and coopting regional and local notables, namely the *rajahs* (native princes), the *zamindars* (a hierarchy of landed interests), and a host of more predatory parvenus, the colonial regime was able to enhance its authority, extending its reach into the levels of society that lay outside the grasp of its formal structures of rule.

Also, the colonial state's impulse toward bureaucratization and" rationalization" and its relentless drive to increase revenues for colonial administration and pay for the costly" home charges" to the imperial metropolis forced it to penetrate society more deeply than its precursors. According to Christopher Bayly (1988), colonial rule was able to establish far more durable political and administrative institutions-and in so doing profoundly influenced state formation and state-society relations in the subcontinent.

Specifically, under the vice regal state of the British *raj* South Asian society and economy underwent significant realignments. For example, in an effort to gain the support and cooperation of the native princes and the hierarchy of landed interests who had earlier served as intermediaries cum-tax collectors for the Moghuls, the colonial state instituted its own revenue and land tenure" settlements" with these powerful groups.

The "settlements" varied from region to region, as prototypes of systems for the exploitation of land, labour, and resources, but they shared the common characteristic of introducing" private property rights" in land by vesting full rights of ownership including those of mortgage and sale in the *zamindars*. In return the *zamindars* were to pay fixed installments of revenue to the colonial state and collaborate in maintaining law and order in the countryside.

The introduction of private property rights in land did not transform the landed or *zamindar* classes into enterprising peasant capitalists or "junker-type" landlords. On the contrary, the policies of the colonial state only served to perpetuate and exacerbate rural disparities by further entrenching what Sumit Sarkar has aptly called" parasitic landlordism" and" feudalistic exploitation. "For example, the vesting of full rights of ownership, including those of mortgage and sale in individual holders and the growth of a market in land, led to the expropriation of the actual tillers and paved the way for land ownership to become concentrated in few hands.

Further, the high and rigid tax revenue demanded by the colonial state forced the *zamindars* and a host of other intermediaries (e.g., moneylenders, speculators) to maximize their incomes (to meet the revenue demands and maintain their opulent lifestyle) by intensifying the "squeeze" on the actual tillers of the land, ultimately driving many into debt and bondage. Moreover, the commoditization of land and labour, the rapid expansion of commercial agriculture, and the resultant closer linkages with urban centers and dependence on metropolitan markets not only made the rural society and economy greatly susceptible to the boom and bust cycles that characterized primary-commodity export systems, but also severely disrupted (and destroyed) the" corporate unity" and self-sufficiency-what James Scott (1976) has called the" moral economy"-of rural society.

Thus, under deleterious colonial economic policies the structure of agrarian society and economy underwent significant changes. As agricultural production became oriented toward commercial crops and foreign markets, the residual pool of grain and other basic foods available to support the needs of the growing peasant population declined precipitously, worsening the conditions of hunger and poverty and sinking large areas of the subcontinent into "a vicious cycle of hunger and famine." Moreover, colonial agrarian policies further cemented the highly unequal landholding systems and rural power relations by promoting increased concentration of wealth and power and differentiation among the landed classes, the cultivating peasantry, and the landless.

At the apex of a multilayered pyramid stood the traditional upper caste elites of native princes and the "big feudal *zamindars*" who controlled large landed estates and virtually monopolized productive (and much unproductive) land, labour, and capital and other agricultural resources. These "parasitic elites," as the support base and embodiment of the basic props of Pax Britannica, owed their position to the colonial rulers, with whom they jointly maintained "law and order" in the countryside.

Next in the agrarian hierarchy were many intermediate layers of landed interests with varying rights to land and resources, ranging from a class of rich peasantry, usually the dominant local landowning and cultivating castes and classes, with control over substantial landholding, to a group of prosperous "tenants," often identified in the literature as "middle peasants," who enjoyed legal protection in the form of fixed rents and permanent and inheritable rights to the land they occupied. Below this class were a mass of small-holding or poor peasants with claim (often tenuous) to a plot of land barely sufficient to provide daily subsistence needs.

At the bottom of agrarian society, totaling about 25 to 30 per cent of the populace, and drawn disproportionately from the "untouchable" scheduled castes and *adivasis* (tribal peoples) were the class of impoverished poor peasants, sharecroppers, and landless agricultural labourers. In contrast to the largely export-oriented and stagnant agricultural sector, a limited amount of manufacturing and industrial development took place during colonial rule.

Although the colonial state consistently favored British over Indian capital by insulating British trading and manufacturing interests from the pressures of international and local market forces, a small indigenous capitalist class did emerge out of the traditional mercantile communities (especially among the Parsis, Gujaratis, Marwaris, and Chettairs) in the mid-nineteenth century. But systematic discrimination (in both official and unofficial state policy) against indigenous entrepreneurs kept them not only in an unfavorable trading position vis-à-vis foreign capital but also highly fragmented and concentrated among particular families and regions of the subcontinent.

It was only after the end of World War I that the nascent indigenous capitalist-industrial classes were given a measure of fiscal autonomy and protection from the "one-way free trade" that enabled them to gain a firmer foothold in the financial, manufacturing, and industrial complexes. Eminent Indian historians, notably, Amiya Bagchi (1982), Sumit Sarkar (1983), and Bipan Chandra (1966; 1988), have argued that the incipient Indian bourgeoisie could never establish a strong and enduring "organic link" with colonial capitalism and thus developed a long-term "contradiction" with it.

According to Chandra, the Indian capitalist classes became the chief financial backers of the nationalist movement because the nationalist strategy of reversing the "underdevelopment and de-industrialization of India" and the nationalist commitment to the goals of *swadeshi*-which called for a total boycott of foreign, principally imported, goods-were quite consistent with that of India's nascent capitalists. Moreover, Indian capitalist classes realized that without freeing themselves from the "shackles of colonial subjugation" they would never develop their full expansionist and accumulative capacities.

The other significant class to emerge from colonial rule, or the class that first articulated the idea of "English rule without the Englishmen," was the indigenous Western-educated intelligentsia. Drawn from the traditional high-caste literati and the urbanized middle classes (also disproportionately upper caste), this anglicized urbane elite functioned as doctors, lawyers, and journalists, but mostly as "brown sahibs" (civil servants and petty bureaucrats) in the complex infrastructure of the British *raj*.

But limited opportunities for advancement, often open discrimination and exclusion from senior posts, and their overall subordinate position in the colonial hierarchy, gradually changed this class from being what Anil Seal (1968) has described as "collaborators to competitors" for power. Disillusioned with the slow pace of socioeconomic and political reforms, members of these elite were ultimately to spearhead the nationalist movement- first demanding administrative reforms and then *Hind swaraj* (or self-rule) and the end of British rule of the subcontinent.

MAKING OF THE MODERN INDIAN STATE

From its inception in 1885 to the early 1920s the embodiment of the nationalist movement, the Indian National Congress (also the INC or the Congress) remained in the words of Barrington Moore (1966, 372) "an essentially upper class club ... of timid English-speaking intelligentsia." Controlled by urban-based elite whose advanced education, cosmopolitan travel, and westernized culture had much in common with the colonial rulers, the INC leadership was content to agitate peacefully for political and constitutional reforms within the framework of continued British rule.

As is well known to specialists the INC underwent a decisive change in the 1920s. Under the formidable leadership of Mohandas Gandhi (later canonized as the *mahatma* or "great soul"), the INC was rapidly transformed into a mass-based political movement with the aim of achieving *swaraj* for India. Gandhi's sharp *volte-face* from the earlier INC strategy was a tribute to his political acumen. His sensitive intellect discerned with great clarity that for *swaraj* to be achieved, the anglicized nationalist elite had to first accommodate and politically mobilize the nation's" toiling and unemployed millions, "the numerous" "little traditions," the "provincial cultures," and the diverse social communities and classes for the cause of Indian nationalism.

Gandhi and his political lieutenants (who included such stalwarts as Jawaharlal Nehru, Subhas Chandra Bose, Vallabhbhai Sardar Patel, and J. P. Narayan) initiated an extraordinary campaign to raise social consciousness and mobilize the masses. They decentralized the Congress Party's organizations and structures and labouriously built its political units at the grass roots by carefully weaving together what Judith Brown (1985) calls the moral and cultural fabric of the world of the peasant with that of the urban-based Western-educated elites.

Specifically, the introduction of an annual four-*anna* (cents) membership fee per person, Gandhi "towering personality," personal austerities, extraordinary rapport with the masses, and novel mode of social action-which required that Congress Party workers at all levels alternate their political activities with *sarvodaya* (or social welfare and "village uplift" Programmes) and visibly identify with the masses by adopting the traditional *khadi* (homespun clothes) and conversing in the vernacular-enabled the INC to reach out successfully "to the tens upon millions" and bring the variegated communities and classes into a broad-based nationalist alliance.

In 1921, the year Gandhi launched his famous *satyagraha* (the nationwide civil disobedience campaign against British rule), Congress membership had skyrocketed to around two million, with a core circle of party activists and sympathizers in almost every provincial town, district, and village of the subcontinent. Yet, ironically, even while the INC's strategy of popular mobilization broadened its political base and transformed it into a formidable anti-imperialist force, it also produced countervailing tendencies that significantly weakened it as a political organization. This resulted in part from the INC's virtually open recruitment policy that did not exercise any real checks on those who joined; in fact, groups and individuals even vaguely sympathetic to the goals of *swaraj* could join the Congress.

A lack of established mechanisms of norms and procedure and institutional structures to check the motives or ideological orientation of those who signed on (the only" requirement" being sympathy or support for the anti-colonial cause) opened the INC to penetration by a multitude of organized vested interests, including, in Anil Seal's (1968) provocative words, "opportunists," " careerists," and "mercenaries." Some of these had little, if any, commitment to the announced egalitarian goals of the nationalist movement, but moved into the "Congress system" when it became clear (especially after the mid-1930s) that the INC was the most likely successor to the British raj.

Whatever the full extent of the vagueness and deliberate obfuscation of the INC's mobilization and organization strategy, the most critical factor that weakened the INC as a political organization, simply put, was bad politics. Specifically, even as the INC broadened its support base, the party leadership failed to knit together the mobilized social forces into a cohesive and disciplined political organization. This failure, as D. N. Dhanagre (1975) has noted, stemmed from the fact that in spite of the mass character of the nationalist movement, Gandhi and the Congress leadership remained conservative in political practice.

This conservatism was manifest in both the INC's mobilization strategy and the policy positions adopted by the party leadership. In particular, the Congress leadership's strict adherence to the strategy of class reconciliation and to the principles of "moral politics" based on the Gandhian doctrine of "trusteeship" prevented the party from taking firm and consistent political decisions because it feared that such actions might precipitate class warfare.

Indeed, as Myron Weiner (1967) and Paul Brass (1965) point out, the politics of accommodation and compromise practiced by the Congress elite only tended to reinforce and legitimize the strategic position of the dominant classes and castes. According to Weiner, "party building" involved little more than adapting to local power structures. In the countryside the Congress relied primarily on the support and cooperation of the local landowning interests, in particular the village landlords and the rich and upper strata of the middle peasantry, to organize the party cadres and mobilize the grassroots support for the Congress Party.

Weiner (1967, 15) notes that "in its effort to win, Congress adapts to the local power structure. It recruits from among those who have local power and influence. ... The result is a political system with considerable tension between a government concerned with modernizing the society and economy and a party seeking to adapt itself to the local environment to win elections."

As these links of dependence grew stronger the wider district, state, and national party organizations came increasingly to represent a complex pyramid of hierarchical alliances between the dominant rural interests and the Congress Party. In effect, from very early on the party in structure, process, and policy came to represent the dominant landowning class and castes. Such a political-organizational strategy, what historian Gyanendra Pandey (1978) has called the "politics of imperfect mobilization," not only precluded a challenge to the normative and institutional foundations of the traditional social, economic, and political hierarchies, but also undermined the pressures from below that could have effectively challenged the hegemony of the powerful groups and classes dominating the Congress system.

Not surprisingly, throughout the nationalist struggle the INC leadership, while demanding acquiescence from the popular classes and lower castes, nevertheless tended to respond to the initiatives and grievances of the mobilized *kisan* and *mazdoor sabhas* (peasant and worker associations) with a mixture of distrust and vacillation, seeing a situation to be managed and controlled" from above" by the Congress" high command." Frankel and Rao (1989/1990, 493–494) notes:

The leaders of the nationalist movement, in following Gandhi, carried out political mobilization from the top down. They relied on rich peasants as intermediaries in the rural areas, and professionals and the trading community in the towns and cities, to reach down to the poorer classes.... [Thus] the nationalist leadership not only failed to build links between the diverse religious, caste and tribal communities on the agrarian issue, but they withdrew support from leaders who took up peasant grievances in the name of Gandhi so that the movements were localized as unrelated agitations and petered out.

On a similar vein, D. N. Dhanagre (1975) and A. R. Desai (1966) have noted that even Nehru (the most influential advocate of socialism inside the INC), in placing a higher priority on class accommodation and preserving party unity, even if it meant significant concessions to the dominant class interests, failed effectively to utilize the mobilized peasant/worker political associations to build a dedicated and disciplined party cadre at the grass roots.

By not institutionalizing the interests and aspirations of the subordinate classes/castes and communities within the "Congress system" the INC leadership, and especially Nehru, whom Barrington Moore called the "gentle betrayer of the masses," failed to utilize this valuable political resource to build and enhance the party's political autonomy and institutional capacity vis-à-vis the dominant propertied classes.

As a consequence, even as the Congress broadened its political base, it grew not into a unified and disciplined political organization but a precarious and loose, elite-dominated, multiparty coalition-what Anil Seal (1968, 2) provocatively characterized as a "ramshackle coalition" of numerous shifting, crosscutting, competitive (and often hostile) centers of power, with conflicting ideologies, petty jealousies, and competing ambitions and interests, unamenable to organizational unity, party discipline, or a cohesive ideology.

During the long years of the nationalist struggle, the fragile unity of the Congress Party was barely held together by the "moral authority" of Gandhi's leadership and the efforts of leading nationalists-men like Jawaharlal Nehru, Vallabhbhai Patel, Maulana Azad, M. M. Malaviya, and Rajendra Prasad-whose substantial experience in politics enabled them to play a balancing act and arrange compromises among the INC, various social forces, and disparate groups and classes that made up the unruly coalition.

Numerous commentators have observed that it was the INC leadership's ability at conflict mediation, bargaining, and consensus building with competing interests that laid the groundwork for the creation of a consensual and democratic polity in independent India. They correctly note that it was the collective wisdom and political perspicacity of men like Nehru and Patel, as well as Rajendra Prasad, Babasaheb Ambedkar, and C. Rajagopalachari, that gave life to the Indian constitution, which not only enshrined the principles and ethos of parliamentary democracy, but did much to augment and transform the rudimentary political and institutional scaffolding of late colonialism into tools for democratic reconstruction.

In practice the founding fathers remained committed to the operative principles of parliamentary democracy, rules of civility, political accountability, and respect for constitutional and judicial procedures of governance. This ultimately enabled the founders to forge a united political community, arouse popular passion and allegiance, and assert solidarity with the masses-providing the capacity to reconcile differences without precipitating political-institutional decline.

Beyond this, the Indian founding fathers helped forge awareness about India that had not existed earlier: that the Indian union was greater than the sum of its parts, its sociopolitical pluralism and religious diversity the source of its strength, and its multitudinous problems best resolved through representative institutions and mediated politics.

As valid as these arguments are, it needs to be recognized that the Congress strategy and the exigencies of democratic politics created its own set of contradictions. That is, while the Congress system's pluralism expanded its power and made it representative, what is often overlooked and needs to be emphasized is that the Congress Party's" promiscuous accommodation" and its open, inclusionary style of politics (that often out of political expediency indiscriminately compromised with the powerful political and societal interests) made the party into a weak political organization with minimal capacity to confront those interests.

As so-called revisionist analysts such as Dhanagre (1975), Frankel (1978), and Kohli (1987) point out, the politics of compromise and accommodation that the Congress elites mast ere "to [the] highest degree" served fundamentally to sustain old inequalities and legitimize emergent ones. The revisionists argue that the accommodations, bargains, and compromises made within a rigid and hierarchical socioeconomic order not only reduced the Congress Party to a partisan political machine, distributing goods, services, and resources to a carefully selected array of powerful interests, but also made the INC "incapable of generating an autonomous political force to confront and reform [the] social structure" in the post-independence period.

According to Kohli (1987, 56–58) the INC, from the 1920s onward, can best be conceptualized as a quintessential political movement whose "inclusive ideology, open recruitment, and a weak internal control structure made it into a weak political force suitable for accomplishing only a limited range of goals." Thus, even though the INC's political organizational form "proved eminently suitable" in mobilizing anti-colonial sentiments into a broad-based nationalist movement, these same institutional and organizational characteristics "diluted the capacities of the INC as a tool of social transformation."

As the formal structures of the INC became intricately enmeshed in the traditional structure of dominance, its capacity to formulate and implement policies independent of the powerful classes and castes in society declined.

Unlike some other nationalist movements, such as the" reformist nationalism" of Lázaro Cárdenas in Mexico in the 1930s or the" revolutionary nationalism" of the Sandinistas in post-Somoza Nicaragua, which show that there is nothing inevitable about nationalist movements' compromising with and protecting the interests of the dominant classes, the leadership of the Indian nationalist movement (which from the beginning made the politics of class compromise with the dominant interests its *modus vivendi*) failed to translate its extensive popular support into a well-institutionalized and disciplined political organization.

Being institutionally weak and fragmented, and increasingly co-opted by the dominant propertied classes, "the INC was not designed to challenge the dominant social interests" and therefore "found it expedient to compromise with the powerful groups and classes in society".

Thus the INC, which had loudly proclaimed its goal of creating a socialistic pattern of society, and professed to be the guardian of the interests of rich and poor alike, betrayed early on its tendency to adopt a populist ideology and posture, while in practice compromising with the propertied classes. In consequence, since India did emerge from colonialism under the leadership of the Congress Party, some of these acquired tendencies and incongruities continued to exercise a decisive influence on the country's post-independence political economy.

STATE-SOCIETY RELATIONS

At the stroke of midnight on 15 August 1947, Prime Minister Jawaharlal Nehru proclaimed independence as the nation's "tryst with destiny," a quest to redeem over two centuries of colonial humiliation and to build a modern and prosperous nation guided by the principles of secularism, central planning, and democratic socialism. The nationalist elite maintained that such objectives could only be attained under the guidance of a strong democratic state that would be an exemplar and social arbiter and play the key role in maintaining political stability and spearheading the nation's strategy of "self-reliant" economic development.

In the immediate post-independence period the political elite's major priority was to consolidate the new democratic state. Despite many constraints that had to be faced, the early years after independence created conditions that momentarily "freed" the new state from established socioeconomic and political entanglements, thereby offering it a greater degree of maneuverability to redefine coalitions, alliances, and policies. In other words, as the rising tide of nationalism swept away the legitimacy and authority of the British raj, the buoyancy and enthusiasm of the times also offered an opportunity, a "breathing space," to use Theda Skocpol's (1979) term, to India's emergent democratic state to enhance its powers and autonomy by transcending dominant structural boundaries.

Specifically, the peaceful transfer of power made for a continuity of political and institutional structures. As the legatee and bearer of the anticolonial struggle, the Congress Party and its leaders such as Nehru and Patel, enjoyed enormous prestige and popular support. They capitalized on their popularity and legitimacy and enhanced their position by institutionalizing a "top-down" democratic system that further strengthened the legitimization of the new state and gave it greater room to "regulate" the competing interests in civil society and to mobilize popular support for the new regime.

Second, with the major divisive issue of the so-called "Muslim problem" solved by the creation of Pakistan, the Congress Party stood politically unchallenged as the lead player in the "one-party dominant system," and the only major nationwide political organization. Third, the so called steel frame of the British raj, the highly professional and technically efficient bureaucracy, the Indian Civil Service (later the Indian Administrative Service), along with a functioning independent judiciary and parliament provided the new state with the necessary vehicle for administering and maintaining political stability and order, especially during the tumultuous first decade after independence.

Furthermore, after independence the new state inherited such key investments as transportation, communications, defense, and some basic industries, notably in the vital sectors of steel, energy, and mining, that only served to enhance national economic power in the society and reduce immediate dependence on foreign capital and expertise. Equally important, the propertied castes and classes, despite their influence and wide representation in the Congress Party, were not always unified enough to make common cause or to effectively challenge the power and legitimacy of the new state.

The national bourgeoisie did not directly challenge the new state because as a class it was small in size (and dispersed), and its overall capacities were quite modest. Influential capitalists, including J. R. D. Tata, Purushotamdas Thakurdas, Kasturbhai Lalbhai, G. D. Birla, and A. D. Shroff, who had agreed after the signing of the famous "Bombay Plan" of 1944 to actively support Nehru's strategy of "planned industrialization," were willing to give the new state "a chance" to prove itself. In fact the indigenous capitalists, who had suffered through decades of discrimination at the hands of the colonial state, looked to the new state for protection and economic stimulation.

Moreover, the powerful classes of "feudal" native princes and *zamindars* who had collaborated with the colonial regime and had lost their colonial patrons were in retreat. Such analysts as Dhanagre (1975), Frankel (1978), and Kohli (1987) have noted that in the euphoric days after independence even the power and influence of the rich landowning peasantry (well entrenched in the state-level Congress political machine) could have been curtailed, or at least moderated.

The new democratic state, with its powers now endowed with legitimate authority, and the force of nationalism and potential political power of the mobilized lower peasantry behind it, could have undermined, or at least chipped away at, the vertical political and economic structures and replaced them with new political institutions at the village level-what Frankel (1978, 25) has called "new forms of horizontal class organization among the peasantry." By "utilizing the quintessential political resource-legitimate compulsion," the state could have stood above society instead of compromising with the dominant societal interests.

The cumulative effect of these post-independence conditions (both real and potential) produced at a crucial juncture in independent India's history a sort of "hegemonic crisis" (to use Cardoso's term) providing the state some autonomy to "tame" the dominant propertied classes and an opportunity to build and consolidate its social base among the less privileged castes and classes. Indeed, in the immediate post-independence period the state elites embarked on an aggressive attempt to construct and consolidate the instruments and institutions of the emergent democratic state.

STATE BUILDING AND THE DEVELOPMENTAL ALLIANCE

State building and consolidation are complex processes and do not automatically translate into greater state autonomy and capacity for reformist development. In India, despite the apparently favorable (though by no means sufficient) conditions that existed in the early post-independence period, the inheritors of the Indian state once again failed to utilize the conditions history and circumstance had provided to establish the bases of an autonomous democratic developmental state-that is, one capable of transcending, or at least "standing above," the dominant social-structural boundaries and guiding political and socioeconomic development to facilitate economic growth with distribution.

The reasons behind what Atul Kohli (1987, 227) has appropriately called "India's great political failure" are complex. Neo-Marxist analyses have generally viewed the INC (and India's democratic state) as essentially a "bourgeois-landlord organization" designed to preserve and perpetuate the capitalist mode of production. While the influence and powers of the rising national bourgeoisie were not inconsequential but in overemphasizing the powers of the industrialists and "capitalist classes" in general (which as a group were both unable and unwilling to seize control of the state), neo-Marxist analysis tends to be unduly reductions.

Similarly, the pluralist viewpoint simplistically argues that the proclivity of such important leaders as Gandhi and Nehru for accommodation with the dominant interests, their faith in incremental and peaceful approach to socioeconomic change, and the victory of the "conservatives" within the INC served fundamentally to retard national development in India. Even explanations provided by scholars such as Kohli, who attribute the failure of modern state building to India's weak "nationalist-democratic regime" and its incapacity to utilize "legitimate compulsion" to institutionalize the interests of the subordinate classes within the state structures, are problematic.

The Indian case amply illustrates that there were specific conditions simultaneously favoring and limiting state and regime autonomy in the formative post-colonial period. What, then, explains why a more autonomous democratic developmental state failed to emerge in India? In other words, why were the conditions facilitating relative state autonomy-conditions that existed during the immediate post-independence period-not prudently seized upon and utilized by the state elites?

No doubt, the legacies of colonial rule, the privileged position occupied by the propertied classes and castes within the INC, and the ideological predisposition of the Congress leadership toward class compromise with the rich and well endowed are important elements of any explanation, which, however, needs to be complemented. This study suggests that although the Nehruvian state elites actually envisaged a strong centralized federal government out of "necessity" they readily agreed to a decentralized "parliamentary federalism."

As will be discussed, such an agreement was a necessary precondition before the state could strike a tacit "developmental alliance" with the dominant urban and rural socioeconomic and political interests. But what were the forces that propelled the wily custodians of the state to give away so much and agree to preside over a spatially and politically fragmented institutional-administrative governing structure?

The usual references to Gandhian ideals of decentralized development notwithstanding, this study claims that, more than anything else, it was the convergence of interests between the political elites and the industrial and business classes (with the economic interests of the latter and the development goals of the former closely coinciding) that provided the impetus for the *first* "developmental alliance" between the state and the industrial and capitalist interests.

After all, the convergence and collusion of shared interests and, at times, complementary "development ideologies" between the political and economic elites were nothing new. Ever since Gandhi's rallying cry for *swadeshi* (economic nationalism) in the 1920s, the Congress elite and the industrial and business classes had shared "cordial interests," with the economic elites actively bankrolling the INC during the long anticolonial struggle.

During the rapidly changing political and economic circumstances in the post-independence period, particularly as the imperatives of national economic development took precedence over everything else, the state and the industrial classes were inclined to seek even closer cooperation and linkages with each other. But mutual suspicion and distrust persisted on both sides. The national bourgeoisie was still relatively weak as an "organized class" and geographically concentrated, remained leery of Nehru's socialist predilections, especially his fascination with Soviet-style state guided development, and needed reassurance, if not guarantees, from the new state.

Suffice to say, one way of curbing the powers of the center was to create a more decentralized parliamentary federalism-and such an arrangement would suit the economic interests of the national bourgeoisie. As early as 1948, the new state complied. As will be discussed, the Industrial Policy Resolution of 1948 and, less than two years later, the constitution not only gave the propertied interests a privileged position but also vested the state governments with an important constitutional role in the formulation and implementation of industrial policy. Industry was to be jointly developed by the center and the states, with primary responsibilities falling to the state governments.

What is important to note is that the closer linkages-cum-alliance between the state and the industrial classes and the subsequent development strategy adopted by the state did not simply result from class domination of the state by the emergent industrial and commercial bourgeoisie. Rather, India's chosen development strategy, though determined to a considerable extent by the state, was nevertheless a shared enterprise evolving from a shared vision that this strategy was the most desirable and feasible means of achieving rapid national economic development.

INSTITUTIONALIZATION OF THE FIRST DOMINANT ALLIANCE

First, it is important to reiterate that the task of socioeconomic development facing India at the time of independence was overwhelming. India had inherited an impoverished economy that was both extremely poor and stagnating. Under British rule the growth of food production had been negligible. In George Blyn's (1966) careful estimation, from 1890 up to 1947 the output of staple food grains per capita actually declined by roughly 26 per cent despite the relatively low population growth of 1 per cent per year.

Not surprisingly, an Indian could on average expect to live for no more than thirty-three years. Further, the almost total absence of growth of per capita income, low levels of capital formation in the public sector, and a technologically backward industrial sector that could barely produce basic goods such as cotton textiles, sugar, soap, matches, and salt (and with an almost nonexistent capacity for the production of basic capital and intermediate goods) stood as major obstacles to national economic growth and development.

Against this backdrop of economic backwardness and stagnation, and faced with the daunting task of economic reconstruction, India's new political leaders declared that the goal of building "national economic self-reliance" was the government's foremost priority.

The national political and economic elites agreed that the quest for national self-reliance could best be achieved through a "planned" strategy of modernization of the economy via rapid industrialization and import substitution in which the state would play the central role via its ownership and control of the "commanding heights" in the economy; the indigenous private sector would be guided in the desired direction by the state; and foreign economic interests would play, at best, a marginal and subordinate role, with minimal reliance on foreign capital inflows other than grants and concessional aid.

Prime Minister Nehru, the chief advocate and architect of the strategy of economic nationalism, argued that without industrialization India's economy was doomed to suffer from its peripheral status in the global capitalist economy, and perpetually remain poor and underdeveloped. He gave the modernization-cum-industrialization plan his imprimatur, arguing that the nation's pursuit of self-reliant development was a carefully thought-out strategic plan designed to make India industrially strong and economically self-reliant-which he argued was entirely consistent with the principles and goals of a "socialistic pattern of society."

However, he pointed out that because of India's colonial legacy of "deliberate deindustrialization," the process of industrial modernization would be different from that experienced by the early industralizers. Specifically, in India the state would have to assume much of the role that private capital had performed in other settings: the state should have control over important industrial infrastructures like public utilities and basic industries and strict control over the importation of all commodities in order to exclude those not considered central to industrial expansion.

The Industrial Policy Resolution of 1948 went to great lengths to outline a preliminary blueprint for future industrial development, as well as clarify the role of the public and private sector in the planned "mixed economy." The resolution gave the central and state governments a virtual monopoly in railroads and the exclusive right to develop minerals and the iron and steel industry, and specified eighteen key industries of "national importance" to be developed under the direct control and regulation of the central government.

However, the need to promote India's industries was so great that, in effect, the eighteen key industries the government undertook to develop were industries "in which private enterprise [was] unable or unwilling to put up the resources required, while the rest of the economic arena could be left free for private enterprise". In effect, the Industrial Policy Resolution of 1948 was a document of compromise between India's political and economic elites.

In March 1950 (shortly after India's constitution went into effect), a quintessential top-down expert committee, the Planning Commission, was established under the general guidance of the provision in the constitution. With Nehru as chairman, the Planning Commission was given the explicit task to further articulate and implement via the five-year plans (the first introduced in 1951) the national leadership's policy directives and developmental objectives.

Critics have noted that in spite of the political leadership's vocal commitments to the reformist or socialistic dimensions of "self-reliant" economic development, the "crash industrialization" strategy adopted by the government was not consistent with the goals of balanced economic development, or the goals of reform and redistributive justice. For example, Ayesha Jalal (1995, 127) argues that" it is hardly surprising that the early fruits of Indian economic development were reaped mainly by the privileged social groups. Committed to rapid industrialization ... Nehru compromised his socialism and endowed it with the logic of a mixed economy. Nehruvian socialism was perfectly consistent with indirect state support for private enterprise."

The harsh reality was that the new state simply did not have the necessary political-institutional capacity or the economic resources at its disposal to facilitate an ambitious industrial transformation. Presiding over a state still in the process of consolidation (and increasingly penetrated by the dominant propertied interests) and with only modest bureaucratic, political-institutional, and economic capacity-and yet desirous of rapid economic modernization of a "backward economy"-the Nehruvian state elites concluded that the state had few options other than entering into a tacit accommodation with the industrial and business/commercial classes in hopes of releasing the forces of economic dynamism "from above" via public support of private enterprise. Thus, in the end, the compulsions of production won out over the goals of distribution.

The "developmental alliance" between "modernist" state elites and the industrial and business classes that began with the Industrial Policy Resolution of 1948 became more firms during the First Five Year Plan, only to be consolidated with the proclamation of the Industrial Policy Resolution of 1956 and the Second Five Year Plan. The Second Five Year Plan and the Industrial Policy Resolution of 1956-heavily influenced by Nehru's close confidant and the Planning Commission's statistical adviser, P. C. Mahalanobis-spelled out the details of the government's development strategy.

The plan's heavy-industry bias was clearly evident as industry's share of the total investment was almost tripled (from 7.6 to 18.0 per cent out of a total outlay of Rs 48 billion), while agriculture's share was slashed by nearly half that of the first five-year plan. Overall, the second plan called for "planned industrialization" to be carefully guided in a "mixed economy" involving both public and private ownership. In practice, while the plans greatly expanded the scope of public-sector development they also allocated extensive areas to the private sector, in addition to protecting it from foreign competition.

Moreover, private-sector facilities were excluded from expropriation and nationalization, and the state even agreed to provide economic resources for their expansion. Three categories or "schedules" of industries were created. Schedule A, consisting of seventeen industries, reserved for development by the public sector most of the basic and heavy industries. Schedule B contained a list of twelve industries in which public-sector investment would supplement (in the form of equity capital) private-sector development. All other industries, including much of the lucrative consumer goods sector, were open to private-sector development.

Hence, it was the twin imperatives of building national power and rapid economic development via industrialization-what Baldev Raj Nayar (1972) has evocatively called the Indian state's "modernization imperative"-that inclined and, to some extent, necessitated the Nehruvian state elites to compromise, and form a developmental alliance, with the industrial and commercial classes. Moreover, it is important to note that "planned industrialization" did not represent a "movement toward social justice" as some have argued. To the contrary, it laid the foundations for state-guided capital-intensive industrialization.

Such an arrangement suited the needs of both the state elites and India's budding industrial and business houses. It not only allowed the state to harness the domestic wealth and the managerial and entrepreneurial talent but also buttressed the legitimacy of the political leadership as "progressive modernizers." Furthermore, private capitalists (fully aware that they were not strong enough to promote economic development without massive inputs of public investment and aid) welcomed involvement by the public sector, especially since the state had agreed to operate in risky, capital-intensive industries and provide the much needed financial and infrastructural support to private enterprise.

The first two five-year plans (1951–1961) committed the lion's share of the government's financial investment to modernizing the national railroads and related infrastructure, and included insurance, loans, tax breaks, investment opportunities, and, occasionally, even price supports- "services of tremendous importance to private capital".

Also, the state's commitment to establish a viable national market and its determination to push for import substitution and strict regulation of foreign capital and multinationals in the "national interest" (in practice, dislodging foreign investments and capital from their existing market positions) found strong support among India's rising industrialists, who had much to gain from these nationalistic economic policies.

For example, the Foreign Exchange Regulation Act, passed in 1973 to "regulate foreign investment," defined foreign firms as those with over 40 per cent of foreign equity. These firms' entry or expansion into most areas was restricted, except for 100 per cent export-oriented operations or those that brought advanced technologies into the country. Expansion, in effect, required dilution of foreign equity to under 40 per cent, resulting in the virtual halt of foreign direct investment into India. As Pranab Bardhan (1984, 40) has insightfully noted:

> The industrial capitalist class, mainly under the leadership of some of the top business families...supported the government policy of encouraging import-substituting industrialization, quantitative trade restrictions providing automatically protected domestic markets, and of running a large public sector providing capital goods, intermediate products and infrastructural facilities for private industry, often at artificially low prices. Since the mid-fifties, the government created several public lending institutions, loans from which form the predominant source of private industrial finance.

Thus, the first dominant alliance between the democratic state and the industrial and business classes was forged to industrialize India. To achieve this goal the state actively pursued a set of policies designed to release the forces of economic dynamism from above, "by public support of private profitability" (Kohli 1987, 64). Under this partnership the state greatly expanded its economic base by creating a public sector that, beginning almost from scratch, grew in a decade to dominate the "commanding heights of the economy."

By insulating the private sector from external market competition and providing improved infrastructure and financial incentives, the state helped transform the incipient capitalist classes into a well-organized and powerful social force. Indeed, in the decade after independence the twenty largest business houses controlled over one-third of all corporate assets in the country; a decade and half later, by 1976, these leading twenty houses had substantially expanded their operations to control nearly two-thirds of the total productive capital in the private corporate sector. Moreover, the small-scale industrial sector was by no means ignored.

Over the years it has also grown substantially, and its linkages through subcontracting and ancillary relationships with the big private-sector companies have become stronger. The simultaneous pursuit of private and state capitalism under the umbrella of economic nationalism and an open democratic polity, therefore, has served the interests of both the state and private capital, further consolidating the tacit but mutually beneficial developmental alliance. Stanley Kochanek has noted that "the decade from 1950 to 1966 proved to be the golden age of private sector development based on close business-government co-operation."

However, as the tacit alliance had matured, so has the conflict, with the state's emphasis shifting from development of the private sector to greater regulation of it. From the mid-1960s (until economic liberalization in 1991), the weak democratic state did what it could "legally" do: incrementally erect a whole series of complex and overlapping regulatory rules, orders, and laws designed to better "control" and " manage" the private sector. However, like the genie out of the bottle, India's industrial capitalists had grown too hefty to be easily controlled and regulated.

While these regulatory measures have resulted in some "tensions" and "conflicts" within the dominant alliance, the state and the private industrial/business sectors have on balance adjusted to the new "exchange relationship" of give and take. In Kochanek's lucid description of this relationship: "Business (the buyer) went to government (the seller) for benefits, and in return paid in the form of resources such as campaign contributions, political donations, and jobs for relatives. The political leadership came to depend very heavily on the system as a quid pro quo for securing campaign contributions, and the bureaucracy depended on it for payoffs, employment, power, prestige and patronage."

The state elites, particularly at the national level, enjoy a degree of relative autonomy as they preside and arbitrate over a plurality of contending interest groups and classes, but it should be noted that the industrial and business classes have been able to set in place an elaborate network of formal and informal mechanisms of access to the state. Thus, in practice, regulatory measures have promoted "private interests rather than vague notions of the public interests". As Pranab Bardhan lucidly elaborates:

Even the ostensibly adverse government policy of an elaborate scheme of industrial and import licenses has been allowed to be turned to the advantage of the industrial interests they were designed to control: the richer industrialists, having better connections and better access, have got away with the lion's share in the bureaucratic allocations of the licenses, thus pre-empting capacity creation and sheltering oligopolistic profits. The controlling interest of the public financial institutions in companies has been used more often to take over "sick" or marginal units saddled with large losses. Thus the government not merely finances private industry, it also acts as the risk-absorber of the last resort and a charitable hospital where the private sector can dump its sick units.

Overall, the growth record of India's import-substituting industrializing (ISI) strategy was modest (if not disappointing), in comparison with those of South Korea and other high-performing East Asian states. South Korea's GDP growth rates were 8.7 per cent, 9.1 per cent, and 9.7 per cent in the 1960s, 1970s, and 1980s, respectively, and 10 per cent over 1965–1980.

Its per capita GDP growth rate was 7 per cent over 1960–1981 and 8.5 per cent over 1980–1992 reaching $1,700 in 1981 and $6,790 by 1992. Korean industry grew at an astounding 17.2 per cent in the 1960s, 17.4 per cent in the 1970s, and slowing to a still high 12.7 per cent (World Bank 1993). India's growth rate of net domestic product (NDP) from 1956–1957 to 1965–1966 was only 2.9 per cent, with industry and manufacturing growing more rapidly at 6.4 and 6.0 per cent, respectively. Growth rates from 1966–1967 to 1981–1982 were 4.0 per cent, 4.5 per cent, 4.3 per cent, and 1.3 per cent for NDP, industry, manufacturing, and agriculture, respectively. Over 1980–1990, GDP growth picked up to 5.3 per cent, while manufacturing growth rate increased to 7.1 per cent (World Bank 1996).

THE POLITICAL FOUNDATIONS OF THE DOMINANT ALLIANCE

Besides laying the economic foundations necessary for planned rapid industrialization, the Indian state also created a legal and administrative framework for economic activity. To use a Weberian term, it established a "property regime" that over the years has been progressively adapted to the distinctive needs of the state and the dominant socioeconomic interests. Beginning with the judicious integration of the princely states into the Indian union, and the Machiavellian political tactics used to oust such opposition groups and parties as the Gandhians and socialists (who split from the Congress in 1948), the state reassured the industrial and commercial classes of its commitment to "nation building" and the ability to provide a stable and predictable political-economic environment, a *conditio sine qua non* for planned industrial-capitalist development.

By far the most important political initiatives aimed at protecting the interests of the propertied classes and castes were those incorporated into the legal, administrative, and institutional framework of the new democratic political order. The Constitution of India offered a complex coverage of legal protection regarding control and ownership of private property, with rights to private property occupying a privileged position in the constitution as a basic and "fundamental right."

Article 19 guaranteed the right to "acquire, hold and dispose of property," and article 31 of the constitution stipulated that no property could be acquired for public purposes unless the central government paid full and fair compensation. Even the *zamindars* and the former native princes and their successors were also given constitutional guarantees, recognizing their rights to receive tax-free privy purses from the central government, including the "personal rights, privileges, and dignities of the Ruler of an Indian State."

This was in sharp contrast to the more egalitarian sections of the constitution, such as the right to "an adequate means of livelihood to all citizens; distribution of ownership and control over the material resources of the community to best subserve the common good; operation of the economic system in order to avoid concentration of wealth and means of production; and the promotion the educational and economic interests of the weaker sections of the people, in particular, the under-represented Scheduled Castes and Tribes." Such sections of the constitution were confined to the non enforceable Directive Principles of State Policy.

Furthermore, as discussed earlier, the legal and constitutional provisions placed strict limitations on the powers and jurisdiction of the central government, particularly on the central government's powers over the rural sector, by assigning primary responsibility of the agrarian sector to the provincial and local governments. Under the new arrangement the central authorities were reduced to providing guidelines, while the actual task of translating policies into legislation and implementation was left to the state and local governments.

These "concessions" reflected, in part, the significant political and economic clout of the landowning castes and classes, their representatives in the local, district, and state (*pradesh*) Congress committees, and their ability to control and effectively manipulate the political and constitutional process to their advantage. It is also important to note that this division of powers reflected the growing linkages between the political authorities (especially at the provincial level) and the landed castes and classes.

The "vertical alliances" between the Congress Party and the dominant landowning castes and classes forged during the nationalist struggle became even more binding after independence. The Congress Party, lacking a strong political and organizational base among the cultivating peasantry and having only a modest administrative presence in the countryside, continued to rely on the established and emergent hierarchies to organize, on the party's behalf, the rural support base.

Specifically, under the arithmetic of the new electoral politics, the Congress leaders further accommodated themselves to the existing hierarchical power structures in order to win votes. Rural notables, who invariably were members of the dominant landowning classes and castes, enjoyed considerable local discretion and a base of support virtually independent of the Congress Party and increasingly became political intermediaries between the countryside and the outside authorities in the local, district, and national administration and government.

These notables became what F. G. Bailey (1963) has termed "brokers" in the rural constituencies, often pursuing particularistic local interests with extra vigor inside (and outside) the state institutions. Their support was courted by the Congress Party because these notables-cum-politicians, through their extensive caste, kinship, and economic ties and their ability to manipulate what Jayant Lele (1981) described as "strategies of patriarchalism and patrimonialism," controlled the rural "vote banks" for the Congress political machine in return for preferential treatment and tangible rewards.

Moreover, the landowning rich peasantry (including *zamindars* and former princes) successfully exploited the wide network of traditional vertical ties based on rank, caste, and tradition, not to mention their considerable economic powers, to become powerful "political bosses" with a firm grip on their constituencies. Under such conditions, the Congress Party could only win elections through a deliberate effort to accommodate, cajole, bribe, and reward these power holders into joining the Congress political machine. Indeed, this is how many local notables formally joined the Congress Party.

According to Rajni Kothari (1964, 1170) "the Congress system," as a vast, well-greased, hierarchically structured party, attracted "a plurality of elites, sub-elites and groups [that] could both voice their claims and attempt to realize them." Thus, through a complex weaving of the formal and informal structures of governance, the overarching apparatus of the Congress system was able to encapsulate even the most distant hinterlands in its political-institutional orbit.

The cumulative effect of all these sociopolitical and economic changes was to reinforce the strategic socioeconomic and political position of the dominant classes/castes in rural society and tie the Congress Party into a intricate web of "transactional linkages" with the traditional authority groups in the countryside. Clearly, then, the "power-sharing" arrangement worked out between the provincial and central governments "acted as a brake in preventing sweeping changes of the social order from above".

Dominated by the landed interests, the provincial governments were not only able to acquire significant powers of administration over law and order, local government, education, and communications, but were also assigned "virtually exclusive control over the governance of the vast rural sector, including such key subjects as land reforms, agricultural credit, land revenue assessments and taxation of agricultural incomes". This was of considerable consequence: it not only significantly reduced the central government's control over provincial policies, Programmes, and implementation, but the constitutional division of power was to become a permanent obstacle to the implementation of land and tenure reforms.

INDIA'S WEAK-STRONG STATE

In their seminal works, Barrington Moore (1966) and Alexander Gerschenkron (1963) illustrate that capitalist industrialization has historically required some sort of an" alliance" between the state and the emerging industrial and commercial/business classes. This was particularly true for "late bloomers" such as Bismarckian Germany and Meiji Japan.

Gerschenkron noted that "late industrializers" confronting an established, competitive, and hegemonic international industrial order faced complex problems of economic development and therefore required pervasive state intervention to overcome the political and socioeconomic impediments. In late-industrializing Germany, for instance, capital accumulation and industrialization were spearheaded by an alliance led by a strong interventionist state, private banking, and industrial capital. The state not only harnessed the resources for industrialization but also assumed firm political control over the dominant socioeconomic interests and a direct, coordinating role in economic management and decision-making.

Chalmers Johnson's study of Japan's Ministry of International Trade and Industry (1982, 17–25) also provides an excellent account of an "autonomous developmental state" in action. He argues that the Japanese state's "embedded autonomy," exemplified by its institutionalized and centralized decision-making structures, its emphasis on" performance" and "plan-rational" technocratic solutions, and the "existence of a powerful talented and prestige laden economic bureaucracy" allowed the state to act as a surrogate for weak indigenous capitalism, set "substantive social and economic goals," and implement a strategy of rapid economic development based on "industrial rationalization."

Similarly, a growing body of comparative scholarship reveals that postwar East Asia's rapid transition from ISI to export-led growth strategy and the relatively egalitarian pattern of income distribution cannot be attributed to untrammeled market-oriented policies alone, but rather rests on a combination of peculiar social historical conditions and strategic or" targeted" government interventions in the economy.

First, East Asia's smooth transition from ISI to export-promotion industrialization was not simply the result of responses to market signals; rather, the foundations of export-led growth was laid in an earlier period of business and entrepreneurial maturation that dated back to the interwar period under Japanese rule in Korea and Taiwan. Second, while it is true that the impressive performance of East Asian newly industrializing countries (NICs) with respect to rising real wages and income equity is due to its rapid expansion in labour-absorbing (hence, employment-generating) export-oriented manufacturing industries, it should also be noted that the socioeconomic structure and the patterns of income distribution in South Korea and Taiwan were relatively egalitarian even before the transition to export-led growth.

This is largely because extensive business/commercial restructuring and comprehensive agrarian reforms had been undertaken in these countries in the 1940s and 1950s by the Kuomintang (KMT) in Taiwan and the Syngman Rhee regime in South Korea. Third, the East Asian states performed functions that went far beyond the norms of prescribed free-market policy: the market-oriented policies were accompanied by discretionary state intervention that complemented and directed rather than negated market forces.

Despite some variations in the patterns of state intervention, the East Asian states through discrete and targeted interventions created an environment supportive of competitive market forces. For example, in the early phase of ISI the states not only acted as surrogates for missing capital markets by procuring domestic and foreign savings and protecting infant domestic industries through tariff barriers and quantitative restrictions, but later played a key role in identifying potentially lucrative niches in the global economy and quickly orchestrating incentives (including tax breaks and subsidies) to encourage domestic firms and export cartels to diversify, invest, expand, and modernize.

Moreover, the states, by assiduously following market signals, were able to respond (often preemptively) to externalities, provide crucial market information, and broker relations with foreign investors and creditors. By assuming a catalytic role in the areas of information processing and dissemination (including specialized research and development) and acquisition of technologies, the states were able to foster local mastery (rather than simply transfer) of modern technologies. Also, throughout the different stages of modernization these states provided (i.e., subsidized) the needed infrastructure to industries and businesses by creating a number of industrial parks and export-processing zones.

Finally, the activist developmental states, by heavily investing in education (especially vocational training), created a large pool of technically skilled and disciplined workers indispensable to economic modernization, especially export-promotion manufactures. These generalities will resonate better with a more detailed commentary on the role of East Asia' "interventionist, developmental state" in the process of economic development.

The "embedded autonomy" of the Chiang regime in Taiwan and the Park Chung Hee and Chun Doo Hwan regimes in South Korea enabled those states to achieve a relatively high degree of insulation from the dominant interests in civil society and actively shape their economies and societies.

A system of elaborate corporatist organization of interest groups- a strategy that granted considerable operational space to market-oriented technocrats and policy elites, and allowed paternalistic collaboration with the powerful business conglomerates (e.g., the Korean *chaebol*) in the private sector- enabled these states to pursue market-conforming methods of state intervention in the economy without precipitating organized opposition from the powerful vested interests.

For example, the Park regime's policy of "guided capitalism" launched in 1962 gave the state, via the newly created Economic Planning Board (EPB), chaired by the deputy prime minister, direct management over the nature and pace of industrial development. As Cumings notes:

The EPB ... took over from a previous ministry and entire budgeting functions: it decides which industries and firms to promote, which to phase out; it closely supervises both the development and the implementation of planning, along with an official trade promotion agency ... it surveys the world for needed markets, capital and technology.

Through careful manipulation of financial incentives and disincentives (including regulation), therefore, the Park regime protected infant industries and aggressively promoted exports of labour-intensive light manufactures. The state not only picked winners, it actually made them. Alice Amsden (1989, 18) notes that "to qualify as a regular customer of the government for long-term subsidized credit [and for all other forms of state benefits], objectively necessary, if not sufficient, conditions had to be met. ... Big firms and small firms, young firms and old firms, *chaebol* and non -*chaebol* had to export."

Moreover, the Park regime (like the KMT in Taiwan) by carefully responding to market signals shrewdly devalued the currency in 1964 and adopted a pragmatic floating unitary exchange rate in March 1965. The establishment of a unitary floating rate and liberalization of import controls, a classic example of "getting the prices wrong," created profitable investment opportunities in targeted export industries, resulting a few years later in an export boom.

These states further supported would be exporters by establishing the compulsory quality inspection of export goods (so the few bad apples could not damage the reputation of the other Korean or Taiwanese exporters) and provided exporters with information on foreign standards, tastes, and distribution and marketing systems. In fact, it was the state that placed Korean-made goods in international trade fairs-a strategy that proved useful in checking the problem of product and technological obsolescence, as well as helping Korean firms gain entry to the global marketplace.

As if all this was not enough, the states also guaranteed exporters exemptions from business and commodity taxes, easy access to foreign exchange, and assurance of high initial profits, thereby further reducing the manufacturers' reluctance to invest in export industries. Over the course of the 1960s and 1970s these states repeatedly intervened in their economies to enhance firms' competitiveness in the global marketplace by imposing moderate import protection-for example, the effective protection rate for manufacturing was nearly 30 per cent in South Korea well into the 1980s.

Complementing this, the states' well trained, efficient, and "meritocratic" bureaucracy (a product of "hard" developmental states' "business-like" institutional and decision-making structures) reduced intra bureaucratic log rolling and conflict, and the corporatist control of organized labour and students (and the states' ability to create manufacturing jobs) enabled the states to co-opt and subordinate groups (namely organized labour) from the popular sector.

Robert Wade (1990) essentially concurs with Amsden, Cumings, and Johnson. Wade articulates a "governed market" theory claiming that the East Asian developmental states are not merely "market conforming" in their intervention but "market governing." In other words, there exists a" pragmatic synergy" between East Asian governments and markets that explains their economic and developmental success.

Focusing on Taiwan with comparisons with South Korea, Japan, and Hong Kong, Wade provides detailed accounts of how these states have utilized their policy instruments to maintain macroeconomic growth and stability to spearhead export-promotion industrialization. Painstakingly tracing the state's role in different industries and sectors over time, Wade shows, for example, how Asian governments encouraged both high levels of investment and sectoral composition of investment (that could not have been supplied by the market) by managing their financial markets and maintaining control over both the interest rates and the allocation of credit through the state-owned banking system.

Further, he provides a detailed account of the "trade regime" (the core of the neoclassical account of export-led growth), arguing that although exporters enjoyed a free-trade regime for inputs, the domestic markets for final products were protected by governmental regulations well into the mid-1980s, and exporters were granted supports (such as relaxed enforcement of income tax payments) that went far beyond a favorable exchange rate.

For example, Wade notes that subsidies to Taiwanese exporters in the 1960s were tied to export targets and administered by industry associates that were monitored by state agencies. These associates, which acted as cartels, collected members' dues out of which bonuses were paid to successful exporters. That is, firms were allocated export targets and penalized if they fell short of their performance targets. It is enough to note that under such a demanding state regulatory system, most firms had to perform well, and many did.

Through the use of such detailed empirical evidence in the form of case studies and exhaustive reviews of the instruments of government policy, Wade demonstrates how market-guided state intervention-mobilizing domestic and foreign savings for "productive investments," targeting lucrative niches in the global economy, providing incentives to ensure technological and financial innovations, and deliberately responding to market signals to allow firms to minimize risk and exploit comparative advantage-have been central to the economic success of the East Asian NICs.

However, India's disaggregated and weak federal state, which also acted as a demiurge, failed to produce the economic achievements of the East Asian NICs because it lacked the embedded autonomy of the latter. This greatly limited the state's ability to calibrate linkages and forge dynamic symbiotic relationships between civil society and markets.

Therefore, although the Indian state continued to expand its role as regulator, producer, and distributor throughout the 1960s and 1970s, including sheltering producers (in both the public and private sector) from market competition, unlike the South Korean or the Taiwanese states it did not have enough leverage to facilitate global market competition by encouraging private capital flows or by expanding export-processing zones and foreign investment-while at the same time gradually removing itself from speculative and unproductive economic activities.

In the end, the Indian strategy of import substitution became more than a policy of protecting infant industries; it became a way of protecting inefficient and monopolistic producers. The Indian state, in adopting what Jagdish Bhagwati (1993) has termed "proscriptive economic policies" (unlike the "prescriptive policies" of the economically successful East Asian countries), failed to direct the economy through market signals. Proscriptive policies grant politicians and bureaucrats the power to say no to most private initiatives and create opportunities for self-aggrandizement, thereby spawning quasi-monopoly rents (in forms political contributions and black money), licenses, and inbuilt inefficiencies.

Although the economic crisis of the mid-1960s laid bare the inadequacies of India's ISI strategy, rather than shift to an outward-oriented export-led industrialization, the Indian state intensified import substitution. The failure of the Indian state to reorient macroeconomic strategy away from ISI to export promotion was rooted in the nature of the country's governing arrangements and the developmental alliance between the state and industrial-commercial interests.

This alliance only served to enhance the powers of the propertied classes, while at the same time eroding the political capacity of the state. Specifically, two core constituents of the dominant coalition, industrial capital and the political-bureaucratic state elites, had vested interests in the maintenance of state-regulated import substitution. Since ISI had created a substantially large as well as small scale protection-dependent private industrial sector, these interests had a stake in the state-controlled ISI model.

Similarly the state elites, both politicians and bureaucrats, had strong vested interests in maintaining their discretionary powers in industrial and import licensing and foreign exchange allocation. Furthermore, India's organized labour enjoyed legal protection (while its counterparts in East Asia faced repression), assurance of" permanent employment" under ISI, and the backing of the left wing of the Congress Party that was strongly opposed to even closing chronically unprofitable industrial units, let alone making the shift to export promotion.

The Congress Party split in 1969, which saw the defeat of the potentially free-enterprise (right) wing of the party and the victory of left leaning Indira Gandhi–led Congress, ensured the continuation of the pro-ISI and pro-public-sector strategy of the state. It was the complex and mutually conditioning mesh of forces from both the state and society that served to dilute the autonomy and capacity of India's state. Specifically, by failing to construct strong and durable institutional and structural capacity of the new state, by failing to "incorporate lower-class bias institutionally within the state", and by compromising with and accommodating to the needs of the propertied classes, the state elites weakened the polity over which they presided.

Moreover, the "top-down" developmental alliance, forged by political expediency and the imperatives of building national power, was from the beginning biased in favor of the dominant economic interests. The "development" policies of the state, justified largely in terms of the sole criterion of achieving maximum increases in production, benefited those better situated to exploit profit-making opportunities, namely, the propertied classes.

Moreover, as the interests of the propertied classes became incorporated institutionally into the constitution and state structures, these classes not only benefited disproportionately from state intervention but were also able to enhance their political and economic leverage over the state. The Indian case suggests that a state (whether democratic or authoritarian) lacking overall cohesion and discipline, and with weak and fragmented political and institutional structures of administration, cannot provide the necessary "administrative guidance" because the structures are easily penetrated by organized and powerful social and clientelistic forces that then confine the state to operating within an ever narrowing range of choices.

7

Democratic Governance and Globalization

POST-COLONIAL POLITICAL ECONOMY

Globalization, in the sense of the interweaving linkages of the factors of production, consumption and lifestyle across the territorial boundaries of sovereign states, is at least as old as the global expansion of European civilization through conquests, proselytization, trade, commerce, mass migration, industrial capitalism, and colonialism. All of South America, Australia, and New Zealand are among the various versions of globalization through mass migration; North America, particularly the United States and Canada, are among its most finished versions.

The colonial mode of production structurally linked Europe with Asia. In South Asia, including India, transfer of capital to, and migration of indentured labour, and soldiers, across the global British Empire have left their trail of complexities which have long survived, reinforced by the cold war. For example, the unresolved Kashmir dispute between India and Pakistan, and the ethnic conflicts in Sri Lanka as well as in most other countries of South Asia, are historically rooted in the distortions of the colonial process of globalization and the cold war, still surviving beyond its end in Europe. That may explain why what is often claimed in the Western hemisphere as the" end of history" has little resonance in much of the third world.

Admittedly, the end of the cold war-rather than the collapse of the Soviet Union-eliminated the most organized military, economic and ideological challenge to the unfettered expansion of postwar globalization of the United States' "power élite" through the world capitalist market. This reality, along with the quantum leap in technology and communications, has brought the spatial limits of the entire universe within this homogenized version of globalization through the world market, with one hegemonic power now also encompassing the cultural domain.

This is historically unique. So that, historically, while the process of globalization is not a new phenomenon, what is new in the post-cold war era is its pace and scale, range and sweep; also, its techniques of enforcing the rules of the game. This is important, because while globalization has always been within the terms and conditions of the dominant player laying down the rules of the game, the absence of any single hegemonic power provided enough space for diversity in the overarching process of globalization in the earlier phases.

For example, within the colonial phase of globalization, the British, French, Dutch, Portuguese, Spanish versions, or the American version of globalization of the "Banana Republics," the Japanese colonial globalization in East Asia, or the globalization of Central Asia and Eastern Europe under Soviet domination all were significantly different in terms of the techniques and instruments of dominance and impact. But in the post-cold war era, the existence of a single hegemonic power has meant its impact is of a globally homogenizing type.

Obviously, this version of globalization has asymmetrical levels of impact and resistance in different societies, varying with levels of asymmetry with the hegemonic power. This may explain partially the abiding resistance against globalization in its many historical versions in societies with long continuous civilizations, for example India. But Europe, more familiar with its own globalization in the colonial era, and with the hegemonic power in the period after the cold war, is more receptive to the new rules of globalization than countries like India and China, the historical targets of the process.

For India, by the time the post-colonial sovereign state emerged at the cost of partition of the Subcontinent, the overarching cold war process of globalization through military alliances was vying for space in South Asia. The objective priorities of India's post-colonial nation-building agenda were at sharp variance with the goals, instruments and techniques of the process. For example, the distortions on India's political economy of two centuries of the colonial mode of production had to be corrected, along with economic development. These distortions were at various tiers, political, economic and sociological.

In politics, the colonial political economy spawned multiple tiers of duality. First, between the relatively developed state apparatus created by a modern industrial power like the British colonial government, and the predominantly traditional, deeply segmented, indigenous, civil society. Second, within the state apparatus, between its relatively developed coercive components compared with the democratic instruments of conflict resolution. Political democracy in the absence of a civil society, linking these dualities through universal adult suffrage, from its inception spawned a range of problems in sharp variance with the historical trajectory of Western liberal democracies.

In fact, many of these variations distinguished the structural attributes of "post-colonial democracies" like India from Western liberal democracies despite their comparable formal institutions of governance. Third, since the colonial liberation struggle was concerned with the right to self-determination of nations as communities, the social base of democratic consciousness around the rights of citizens as individuals was relatively limited in most such "post-colonial democracies."

Fourth, in the specific case of India, the democratic state emerged in the midst of a massive communal upsurge within civil society (the result of partition and mass migration on communal lines), and an adversarial relationship with neighboring, theocratic, Pakistan, soon under military dictatorship, underwritten by the cold war era's dominant economic and military power. In the sphere of economics, along with underdevelopment there was the more daunting problem of distorted development during the colonial era: the duality between the relatively small modern sector linked with international trade-predominantly, plantations, minerals, low-technology consumer products and services, overwhelmingly owned and/or catering to the needs of colonial rulers-and the large agrarian sector with its primitive tenurial, technological and managerial structure.

Also a problem was the wide-ranging regional diversity between the coastal areas and around port towns, and the vast hinterland of landmass and population still derisively referred to as India's "cow-belt." The existence of an urban-rural sociological disparity between the metropolitan centers, hill stations and cantonments, and the rest of the country, a contradiction referred to by some modernized peasant leaders as the "India versus Bharat" syndrome. Many of these sociological disparities encompassed almost all components of the contemporary indices of human development, such as literacy, income, life expectancy, health care, environment and human rights, with long-term impact on democratic governance in the post-colonial era.

There were also the historical "untouchables" within the caste structure of India's predominantly Hindu population, now called the *Dalits* (oppressed); the tribals, now called *Adivasis* (original inhabitants), and the *Vanavasis* (forest dwellers); the disparate diversity of ascriptive identities, such as religion, language, caste, ethnicity, part of the inheritance of a long and continuous history. The developmental complexities of such wide-ranging diversities continue to have considerable salience for modern India's democratic governance, more so in the present phase of globalization.

The developmental imperatives of India's post-colonial state were shaped by the mass struggle for national liberation. Consequently, the economic development agenda under universal adult franchise had a built-in bias in favor of the social transformation of the overwhelming majority of the rural people, as well as the traditionally deprived and the socially oppressed, irrespective of its impact on the overall rate of growth.

These goals were to be pursued within the secular, democratic institutions of governance, a structural imperative of nation-building given India's demographic diversity. These and the institutions of nation-building constituted the core concern of India's national security, alongside external threat. But such goals were also at sharp variance with the aims and priorities of postwar reconstruction of Europe, Japan and the United States, the dominant players of the global market in the postwar era.

It was the United States that spawned the "realist paradigm" of national security, with its emphasis on military deterrence against an identified external threat. Whilst this version of national security conformed to the structural imperatives of postwar reconstruction of the industrial societies of Western democracies, it did not tally with those of post-colonial democracies such as India. The contradictions manifested themselves in many ways within India's developmental politics, including through its foreign policy of nonalignment.

India's emphasis on economic development through "self-reliance" and substitution through foreign imports, in sharp contrast with the export-led growth strategy advocated for the third world by Western developmental agencies, was another important manifestation of this structural contradiction. In fact, this contradiction, and its reciprocal operational responses, constitutes the core area of India's post-colonial developmental politics.

At the macro level this history underscores, on the one hand, India's assertion of national sovereignty in order to pursue its indigenous developmental priorities, based on self-reliance; and on the other hand, pressure from Western agencies-both direct and indirect-to globalize and pursue a policy of export-led growth, as imposed on other military allies across the world, including nearby Pakistan. In this historical contest of unequals within the world capitalist market, between nonaligned India and the advanced industrial democracies, the resilience of India's secular democratic instruments of governance has proven to be the major political dividing line.

All this took place during the cold war era of the "military-bureaucratic élite" as the main vehicle of "third world modernization" through military alliances and export-led growth, as envisaged by Western funding agencies. And this is what makes the Indian case so distinctive: from the inception of its republican era, India has generally conformed with the institutional imperatives of democratic governance, including universal adult franchise, but not to the Western strategy of "third world modernization".

The Western plea for "interdependence" has had small appeal in India's political culture of resurgent post-colonial nationalism which perceived them instead as imposing "dependence." In this confrontation, empirically, there has been a direct positive correlation between India's ability to resist Western pressures-and allurements-to globalize, and the relative strength of its democratic institutions of governance. Weak political leadership, and dented democratic institutions of governance, have generally been more vulnerable to such external pressures, and vice versa.

This trend can be seen clearly throughout the entire phase of India's planned developmental politics, from its beginnings in the early 1950s until the 1991 move toward economic liberalization and structural adjustment to promote globalization. The historical balance sheet shows India reinforcing the structural underpinnings of democratic governance. Paradoxically, this move also spawned space for the more strident phase of globalization of India's political economy in more recent times. The trajectory of this balance sheet is important for any future projection about the impact of globalization on democratic governance in India.

GOAL OF SELF-RELIANCE IN THE COLD WAR ERA

Historically, the second five-year Plan launched in 1956 spelled out the basic goals and priorities of India's post-colonial nation-building agenda. It envisaged a public sector dominating the "commanding heights of the economy," consisting of "heavy, key and basic industries;" carrying forward the infrastructural reforms of the colonial political economy in both agriculture and industry; a concerted Programme to create a reservoir of skilled technical personnel as human resource; and strict import control and foreign exchange restrictions geared toward industrial development and food self-sufficiency.

Difficult to enforce within the democratic structure, unlike in China, India aimed, like China, at promoting long-term "self-reliant growth" of the economy, in defense of national security and territorial integrity. But also unlike China, India's pursuit of development-led national security was at the cost of military build-up. Initially, the postwar Western alliance led by the United States opposed the goals and priorities of the Plan. The president of the World Bank called it" unrealistic and over-ambitious," and pleaded for a strategy of export-led growth, while the United States refused any aid to the public sector.

The Indian prime minister only had to "leak" the contents of the Bank president's letter for an outraged Indian public opinion to rally against such "Western interference" in post-colonial India's domestic policy and immediately endorse the Plan priorities. In 1957, a serious foreign exchange crisis sparked off another round of similar Bank initiatives and Indian response. The second general election in India in 1957 was also a referendum of the second Plan, and the overwhelming electoral verdict in favor of the Congress Party, its author, was a democratic endorsement of the party's goal of "self-reliant growth."

The triumph of democratic governance was highlighted with the first military coup in neighboring Pakistan in 1958, which aborted India's historic adversary's first visualized general elections. America's endorsement of the coup, and its diplomatic, military and economic support of Pakistan's" military-bureaucratic clique," coupled with general Western support for Pakistan's case in the Kashmir dispute, undermined the credibility in India of the Western alliance and its advocated strategy of development.

In 1958, the Western alliance constituted the "Aid India consortium", under World Bank sponsorship, to "coordinate" its aid strategy for India, largely along the lines previously visualized. However, from inception such strategies (and the institutions promoting them) were perceived in India as complementary to the pursuit of the "global military containment" of communism. In a context of resurgent post-colonial nationalism such efforts constituted an attempt by the West to introduce "imperialism through the backdoor."

The Sino-Indian border war of 1962 provided the first opportunity for the Western alliance to undermine the Nehruvian concept of "national security" with a substantial increase in India's defense budget at the cost of its economic development on planned lines. The Fund Bank and its Western alliance partners provided massive aid to ensure this shift in Indian policy on national security toward the "realist paradigm." This immediately helped improve the image of the West in India, but soon the Soviet Union, for its own cold war reasons, outdid the West in bolstering India's defense build-up.

This process fueled the arms race in South Asia between India and Pakistan, ultimately leading to their mutual nuclear deterrence capabilities in 1998. Nonetheless, throughout the 1960s, and despite considerable modifications in defense allocations, Nehru's death (1964) and another two rounds of the Indo-Pakistan war (1964 and 1965), India's macro-level Plan priorities remained unchanged. In fact, as a consequence, the goal of "self-reliance" was extended to the sphere of defense production.

The Fund Bank and the Western alliance continued to pressurize India along the same lines at all crisis points: for example, immediately after Nehru's death, and in the aftermath of the wars against Pakistan which resulted in a balance-of-payments problem. But the domestic political consensus, and Soviet support for Plan priorities, provided the political and economic underpinnings in defense of India's indigenous developmental goal of "self-reliant growth," and its vision of relative autonomy from the hazards of an inequitable global economic order dominated by the leaders of the world capitalist market, including the former colonial powers.

In 1966, and for the first time, Fund Bank pressure paid dividends when one of the periodic foreign exchange crises coincided with a major political battle for succession for the post of India's prime minister. The ruling Congress Party controlled by a "syndicate" of regional bosses was reluctant to endorse the candidature of the politically powerful Morarji; instead they supported a politically weak Indira Gandhi who announced the devaluation of the Indian currency to promote exports as her first policy step.

The consequent popular resentment against this "capitulation" to perceived Western pressures led the new prime minister to jettison her finance minister as scapegoat. She also quickly rid herself of the "syndicate," split the Congress Party, and established her authority over India's democratic politics, which, in the prevalent political culture, involved a dose of populist nationalism (the rhetoric of" anti-imperialism, and "threat" of "foreign hands"). She even defied the United States by intervening militarily in the disintegration of Pakistan, an American ally, and helping in the creation of Bangladesh after the war of 1971 The Western realist paradigm of national security had spawned its Frankenstein in the person of the new Indian prime minister; but this was a monster whose charismatic appeal contributed also to the stability of India's political democracy.

In the sphere of nuclear weapons, the Western model had to await its ultimate denouement until 1998, with successive explosions in India and Pakistan taking place against a backdrop of strident economic globalization. Ironically, by this point Western development strategy for the third world had dramatically transformed from its "national security"-based "realism" to the neo-realist neo-liberalism emphasizing human development, human rights, and human security alongside democracy.

By 1974, the emergence of dynastic "extra-constitutional authority" in the ruling Congress Party and the government had undermined the autonomy of most democratic institutions of governance. In 1975 the formal declaration of a "national emergency" put a moratorium on the functioning of political democracy. With the press censored, opposition leaders arrested, and freedom of speech denied, the economic policy of the Emergency regime shifted to boost exports, liberalize imports, and encourage foreign investments, without any formal change of earlier policy.

The Western powers and the Fund Bank turned a blind eye to India's Emergency regime, as did the Soviet Union, both for reasons of global power politics. Unsurprisingly therefore, successive Indian regimes have operationally conformed to the compulsions of the post-Emergency political economy by providing greater incentives to export, import liberalization, and foreign investment, all sharply at variance with earlier policy based on national consensus; none of the regimes have instituted a formal change of policy.

There have been some token gestures of defiance against the West. For example, the faction-ridden coalition government, after the elections of 1977, sought to reinforce its political legitimacy by periodic symbolic gestures against powerful American MNCs such as IBM and Coca-Cola. In 1980 Indira Gandhi was back in power after again splitting the ruling Congress Party. This time she openly continued her economic policies of the Emergency era, reinforcing them with a second devaluation of the Indian currency; in foreign economic policy she was more in tandem with Soviet diplomacy.

This operational version of "nonalignment" provided new external scaffolding for the domestic viability of Indian regimes. Her assassination in 1984, unrelated to her economic policies, brought about a wave of sympathy, and contributed to the massive electoral mandate in favor of her son Rajiv Gandhi in the general elections following. His political support base, and coterie consisted of high-profile corporate technocrats and computer whizz-kids, all committed to the Western version of "third world modernization."

This regime, committed to "economic reforms" and "modernization"-as political euphemisms for a total reversal of earlier economic policies-was also the most hyped in the Western media and its political elite. His assassination however paved the way for the beginning of the long era of weak coalition governments, lasting until the present day and threatening political stability. It was also the era of India's formal entry into the process of globalization, in conformity with long-standing Western strategy.

It was one such minority government led by a weak leader that confronted the newly elected Indian parliament with "Hobson's choice" of endorsing a new economic reform plan or facing a general election. The members of India's parliament elected in 1991, predictably, ensured against the risk of a general election. Most of the parties in the parliament also ensured that they were politically correct. For example, the erstwhile opponents of economic "reform," particularly the numerically significant parties of the "left," opted to abstain from voting in its favor, rather than voting against it.

This governmental strategy ensured parliamentary endorsement for its "reform" package for which, until then, there was no electoral mandate. In fact, no political party had even suggested these "reforms" in their election manifesto. The "reforms," suggested as "conditional ties" of the Fund Bank, consisted of measures which were a total reversal of earlier economic policies, and ensured conformity with Western "advice," in a situation comparable to the foreign exchange crises affecting balance of payments. Additional pressure was provided by the collapse of the Soviet Union and India's economic crutch.

This scenario provided the economic backdrop to the request for an IMF bailout by the Indian government, and the IMF's response outlining conditions for its aid. The package was negotiated by Mammohan Singh, an academic turned economic technocrat of the Indira Gandhi era, but with long formal association with the Fund Bank and its affiliate institutions. He was soon appointed finance minister and portrayed as a future prime minister. His political profile in 1991, when compared with his counterpart's fate during the devaluation of 1966, would be a reasonable indicator of the transformation of India's political economy in the intervening period and the social base of the new political elite viewing the world as its oyster, in sharp contrast to its counterpart in the aftermath of national liberation.

The political conjuncture of a weak leadership in a minority government was also typical of earlier regimes vulnerable to such Fund Bank "advice." This political scenario, rather than the periodic balance-of-payment difficulties, appears causally more related to the political decision to accept the "conditional ties" involving economic liberalization and structural adjustment to the process of globalization. The subterfuge of "reform" to this project involving a total reversal of existing policies was a conceptual mystification of policies without any democratic mandate and historically suspect. Not only the policy, but all its advocates were either political nondescripts or suffered from weak political legitimacy.

Admittedly, many of the domestic "vehicles" of India's reform package improved their political image later, when the general thrust of the reforms garnered an implicit ex-post-facto consensus among the mainstream political parties. At any rate, the cost of reversal of the reforms was increasing with time. But when the structural adjustment Programme of economic liberalization was initiated in 1991, neither the policy nor its advocates in India had any significant democratic legitimacy; and the Fund Bank, as the main architect of the "conditionalities," was historically suspect in India's political culture.

In this sense the political support base of India's dramatic decision to move toward globalization of its economy has remained inauspicious from its inception, for purpose of democratic governance of the country. Besides, India's economic liberalization began in an era of considerable deliberalization of its political democracy and atrophy of the post-colonial democratic institutions. In fact, historically, as already described, the very contest for political space within this externally inspired policy of globalization in India can be dialectically linked with the dent in India's liberal institutions of democratic governance.

Unrelated to the Indian scenario, this phase of global politics also coincided with the collapse of the socialist world, and the emergence within the global order of normative concerns like democracy, human rights, gender justice, environment and ecology. These events and concerns have also had their impact on democratic governance after economic globalization, influencing the latter's pace, scale, and impact in India.

IMPACT OF ECONOMIC LIBERALIZATION

It has been over a decade since the structural reforms for economic liberalization were initiated in India's political economy. It is important to assess empirically the economic balance sheet of this phase to enable us to make any political projections about its impact on the future of democratic governance in the country. It is also important to assess this balance sheet in comparative terms, between the earlier phase, when the external pressure for globalization was resisted in India, and the phase of political capitulation to such pressures in 1991. This would enable an assessment of the political viability of the new policy within the democratic process.

India's National Sample Survey (NSS) has recently published data which are quite revealing in this context. According to the survey, the reforms have produced unprecedented economic growth. Before the reforms in 1991, the rate of economic growth remained constant at around 3 per cent, which was popularly described as the" Hindu" rate of growth. But by the mid-1990s, GDP growth exceeded 7.5 per cent annually; agricultural growth also remained high; and social indicators like literacy and infant mortality and longevity also improved.

Paradoxically, this high rate of growth, distributed inequitably, has led to an increase in the number of poor people, and also to the widening of the regional disparity of the colonial era. The comparative figures of the period before and after the reforms are more revealing in this context. At the height of the era of controlled economy, rationing, price controls and nationalization of the 1970s and 1980s, poverty actually declined 2 per cent annually. By contrast, there was hardly any reduction in poverty between 1991 and 1997.

The survey conducted in 1997 show that every third person-34.4 per cent of the population-lived in conditions of absolute poverty, the same as in 1990. It also showed that the decline in poverty was marked in the period 1994/95-1997, despite the high GDP growth rate. NSS data on poverty between 1951 and 1997 is equally useful. This shows that between 1951 and 1955, more than half of all Indians (53 per cent) existed below the poverty line; the situation remained largely unchanged until 1971-1974.

But from 1973-1977 to 1986-1987, poverty declined steadily to 38 per cent; and, between 1989-1990 it declined still further to 34.07 per cent. In July 1991, when the reforms were launched, 36.34 per cent of Indians were poor, and at the end of 1997, 34.4 per cent were still poor, the same as in 1990, shortly before the reforms. These figures do not provide a particularly inspiring argument to sustain or widen the political will in favor of the reforms in a political democracy with universal adult suffrage.

Another "thin" survey with a smaller sample carried out by the NSS in 1998 reveals the contrast between the period before and after the reforms more sharply. In fact, it suggests that the number of people existing below the poverty line has actually increased to approximately 40 per cent. Along with "anecdotal evidence" of "immiseration" in some regions of the country, it underscores the plight among the relatively poorer sections of landless labourers in rural areas, who are also inequitably adversely affected by inflation and rising food prices.

An economic commentator highlights the wide-ranging variations in the impact of economic reforms in India. While the industrially more advanced states like Gujarat, Maharashtra and Tamil Nadu have prospered, the relatively poorer states like Bihar and Uttar Pradesh-with their very high electoral strength-have suffered declining economic growth and greater poverty since the reforms. The two poorer states account for a quarter of the country's total population and over one third of the country's poor.

The same survey also reveals that poverty trends in the five traditionally poorer states of Bihar, Uttar Pradesh, Orissa, Rajasthan and Madhya Pradesh worsened after 1990. More interestingly, Bihar and Uttar Pradesh had grown much faster in the 1980s, before the reforms, and actually experienced reduced poverty.

The per capita income growth in these five states (NSS, World Bank, TOI; *Times* 30 April 2000, quoting World Bank and NSS) in the period between 1981-1991 and 1992-1997 show similar trends. In Uttar Pradesh, it declined from 2.6 per cent to 0.7 per cent; in Rajasthan from 4.7 per cent to 2.9 per cent. Even in some of the relatively more prosperous states it declined: for example, in Punjab growth declined from 3.3 per cent to 2.8 per cent; in Haryana, from 3.9 per cent to 2.6 per cent. Meanwhile the prosperous states of Maharashtra, Gujarat and Tamil Nadu boomed, along with Karnataka, Andhra Pradesh, West Bengal and Orissa.

This uninspiring economic reality has to be viewed in the context of the pressures of the "conditionalities" of reform on fiscal policies, such as budget deficit, subsidies for the welfare of the vulnerable sections, poverty alleviation, the social sector, defense needs, etc. For example, the Union Budget for 2000 seeks to reduce subsidies for energy, transport, communication, education, the public distribution system and agricultural inputs, and also to accelerate the reduction of existing investments in the public sector.

At least in the short term, the incidence of hardship under such policies is inequitably harsh on the relatively poor and the deprived. While the politically organized working class, rich farmers and the urban middle class, with their larger operational leverage within the democratic institutions, are able to pressurize for" safety nets," the vast mass of unorganized rural and urban poor are at greater risk. This generally tends to undermine the cumulative political will in favor of reforms within a democratic system based on universal adult suffrage. There are winners and losers, with sharp cleavages between the two.

The patent regime of the WTO, one of the principal institutional agencies of the globalized international order, has also attracted adverse political attention in India by allowing traditional Indian food, spices, and medicines such as *Neem, Haldi* and *Basmati* rice to be patented by enterprising foreigners, thereby stoking the fading embers of India's post-colonial nationalism. This pro-nationalist movement has been reinforced by the inequitable global information order enabling an inundation of Western pop culture through films, satellite TV channels and other mass media, along with the brand-named jeans and fast foods.

The numbers of disaffected, drawn from India's traditional society in opposition to globalization, are significantly large within the political democracy to be managed by its party system and atrophying post-colonial democratic instruments of conflict resolution. There are reports of suicides by retrenched workers of disinvested public sector enterprises and municipal corporations denied welfare subsidies. There are also reports of the suicides of farmers unable to bear the failure of cotton crops in farms employing expensive genetically engineered seeds of American multinationals. Such events have not helped to make new converts to globalization in India's political democracy, which is faced with a quantum leap in the level of social and political violence, even before economic liberalization, which has merely stoked them further.

With the decline of the Congress Party, which spearheaded the national liberation, and the waning ideological appeal of communism, political parties are moving increasingly toward regionalism, based on one or another of India's myriad ascriptive social identities. Attempts by the BJP, the single largest party in the present parliament, to provide a national alternative to the Congress Party through a homogenized version of Hindu nationalist ideology have, predictably, floundered. India's democratic diversity-even within its macro-level Hindu majority-of language, caste, tribe ethnicity, and spatial location is simply too disparate for any single ascriptive identity to represent it. Even the ideological appeal of communism in India has been regionally specific.

Consequently, coalition governments consisting of political parties representing regional and sectional interests have become the rule, rather than the exception, and are likely to be so in the foreseeable future. The economic impact of the process of globalization, by widening the regional and sectional disparity is, on the one hand, reinforcing the structural imperative toward coalition governments and, on the other hand, making them difficult to manage. The fiscal incentives, and disincentives-"conditionalities" of globalization-inequitably affect the different constituents of India's system of universal adult franchise.

For example, withdrawal of subsidies for the public distribution system, or for fuel used by the poor, and for transport or agricultural inputs is affecting food prices; similarly, withdrawal of subsidies from education affect the middle-class youth. Tax incentives to boost exports and the stock market also affect existing regional and sectoral disparity, making the complexity difficult to manage through coalition governments within a democratic system with weak institutions of conflict resolution.

The Congress Party which, as the minority leader of the erstwhile coalition, initiated the process of globalization, is already under internal pressure to be less enthusiastic about some of the fiscal imperatives of the globalization process and its "conditionalities." The BJP, the present leader of the new coalition government implementing the reforms, is faced with similar contradictions. The present finance minister of the ruling coalition government has done his bit of tightrope-walking under such compulsions: first announcing strict fiscal constraints, then rolling some of them back as democratic concessions to public demands. But there are severe limits to such gamesmanship, particularly with regard to the ever-increasing allocation to the defense sector, a result of relations with Pakistan.

This part of the "conditionalities" of the reform process toward globalization is likely to remain unfulfilled within India's democratic structure, at least for the foreseeable future. Even on other problems, exacerbated by the existing impact of globalization and its fiscal pressures, four former prime ministers before the era of reforms have already joined hands, along with parties of the left, to provide a "third front," envisaging a slower and more cautious pace of globalization, allowing for allocations for poverty alleviation, social welfare for the weaker sections, safety nets for redundant workers and deceleration of public-sector disinvestment, subsidized public distribution systems for the urban poor, etc.

An all-India strike of Bank and other public-sector employees was held on March 11, 2000, many more such strikes have been threatened. The political culture of the era of the planned welfare state of the pre-globalized period is reasserting itself off the backlash of the immediate effects of the reform. There are also institutional constraints against a faster pace of globalization. The colonial legal system and its civil and criminal code are already overextended in dealing with the increasing level of social and political violence.

The proliferation of new instruments, and laws, for coercive resolution of such conflicts by the state is creating problems: economic costs are creating fiscal pressure on the budget; the state's actions are resented by domestic civil rights groups with global networks, thereby attracting attention from funding agencies that are under democratic pressure at home. In the upper-class urban areas, elderly relatives at home, deserted by the younger, skilled, professionals attracted by globalized employment opportunities, are increasingly becoming the victims of crimes by the vast army of the local urban unemployed.

In rural areas, remittance economies are creating new spheres of social tensions. Global human rights consciousness around bonded and child labour, gender equality, and environment are also creating new problems, paradoxically in the exporting industries, the principal beneficiaries of the globalization process, which are now faced with concerns of "business ethics" and "social audit." The institutions of democracy, including the machinery of law and order, are inadequately equipped to respond to the new challenge and are under pressure.

While funding agencies attribute the problems, causally, not to the reforms per se but to their inadequacy, thereby urging faster and more reforms, the domestic political will to accelerate its pace and scale remains weak, as yet at least. But even the present level of globalization, alongside its losers, has also created new winners, who are among the strong political pillars of the ongoing process of globalization. Those associated with computer software, telecommunications, food-processing industries and the burgeoning service sector, though still numerically marginal, remain the political vested interest for the ongoing process of globalization.

However slow, faltering, or reluctant, the process of reversal has already become quite expensive. In fact, all political parties, implicitly at least, acknowledge this. And this is the basis of the ex-post-facto political consensus around the general thrust of globalization. In the specific historical reality of the Indian experience as discussed here, any reckless increase in the pace of globalization has endemic risks for democratic governance, which is dialectically linked with the national security and territorial integrity of the country.

8

Problems at Home

It is easy to make a long list of staggering problems which India faces domestically-too high a birth rate, integration versus caste divisions, the difficulties of carrying out economic planning in a tradition-bound society, corruption in politics, the Communist threat, and the need for rapid agricultural and industrial improvement, among others. These problems are dealt with in this section. The first three articles in a sense provide the setting: an exploding population, still caste-ridden and with such great diversity that the communication on a national level of national purposes and goals is itself a critical problem.

Birth control efforts now under way are discussed first; then the status of untouchables in India is outlined; and facts are given about India's masses which indicate how difficult it is to develop a nation-wide sense of purpose for India's planning goals. In subsequent articles various authors deal with India's political scene, indicating that the dominant Congress party is experiencing great difficulties and may have more after Nehru's departure. The special problem of communism within India is also canvassed.

PROGRAMME FOR BIRTH CONTROL

After years of delays, bitter disputes, false starts, incredible snarls of official red tape and interminable meetings, India has at last embarked on one of the most fateful experiments in human history-a nation-wide attempt to control skyrocketing population as a matter of formal governmental policy. India is not the first overcrowded Oriental nation to turn to birth control. Since the end of World War II, Japan-once one of the world's highly prolific countries-has cut her birth rate in half.

This reduction is not the result of widespread teaching of contraceptive methods, but has been brought about mainly by a large-scale Programme of extremely cheap, government-approved abortions, performed legally at the rate of 1.5 million a year for mothers claiming that bearing additional children would damage their health or cause them economic hardship. "This is now war," says Lieutenant Colonel Bishen Lal Raina, the hard-driving army doctor who now runs India's family planning project."

We cannot wait for perfect methods, or perfect plans, or the blessing of all the rest of the world. We must fight with the weapons we have. Perhaps now we may save India in time." And time, he notes, is running out. India now has an estimated population of 400 million and a yearly increase of 6 million to 8 million. The world's leading authorities believe that this nation has scarcely one generation to put its house in order.

A study made by Princeton University's Office of Population Research, with the support of the International Bank for Reconstruction and Development, forecasts that if India's birth rate continues at its present high levels that country will have a population of almost 800 million by 1986. In that event, experts believe, India will have passed the point of no return. The country's resources could not conceivably support such a population growth; inevitably, they think, the ancient land would collapse into a terrifying shambles of famine, disease and anarchy, perhaps carrying most of Asia along with it.

Three people have played key parts in getting the vast control Programme under way-Colonel Raina himself ... ; R A.

Gopalaswami, an energetic and outspoken civil servant who has demonstrated his willingness to badger and battle everybody in or out of government to get action; and Lady Dhanvanthi Rama Rau, one of the best-known women of India, tall, gray-haired, charming, eloquent.... During the past years, these three and their dose associates have fought public and governmental apathy and inertia which would have driven weaker citizens to madness....

In 1947, when India won its freedom from Britain ... the government was pledged to "lay stress on self-control, as well as to spread the knowledge of cheap and safe methods of birth control." But for four years essentially nothing happened. "During the first years of our independence," the prime minister recalls, "we were terribly occupied with other matters-with the production of more food, with building more schools and more roads and more houses."

Under the direction of India's first minister of health, the distinguished Princess Amrit Kaur, daughter of the Raja of Kapurthala, about 145 birth-control clinics were opened, but were not operated actively. The health ministry was more occupied with malaria control, tuberculosis control and similar projects, all of which were important, but contributed to an even greater increase in population.

The 1951 census brought an abrupt shock. It revealed that even though the British had gone and India was managing her own affairs, the population was shooting up faster than ever. The help of the World Health Organization of the United Nations was sought, and the WHO promptly sent Dr. Abraham Stone, one of its top consultants who long had been prominent in the planned-parenthood movement.... But the American consultant soon found he would be strictly limited in his work in India.

Princess Amrit Kaur was a spinster, a respected member of the Church of England, and a firm believer in Mahatma Gandhi, whom she served as secretary for sixteen years. She made it dear the American would be expected to introduce only the rhythm or calendar method [of birth control].

Dr. Stone did his best. He set up teaching Programmes in two test areas and established a follow-up system. Finding that many village women were unable to count or had no access to a calendar, he adopted a "counting necklace," with the appropriate number of green beads to represent the" safe" days and red beads for the "unsafe" or "baby" days.

Whether or not the rhythm method had any real value in these trials is still a matter of debate. Some observers blame the lack of marked success on the general apathy of the villagers. A few doctors noted that the "counting necklace" was not being used according to plan....

The 1951 census report also led to bitter attacks against the government for its lethargy, and demands for immediate action. One of the most vigorous critics was Lady Rama Rau, a member of one of India's most influential families-her husband formerly was Indian Ambassador to the United States-and generally regarded as the leader of India's family-planning movement.

As president of the All-India Family Planning Association, she opened fire on the government. She denounced the rhythm method trial as a shocking waste of money and time. She called for establishment of thousands of birth-control clinics and for free contraceptives. She battled governmental red tape, internal jealousies, shortage of materials and general governmental inertia.

"You must realize," she says, "that the officials of my government surpass all others in the willingness to expend every effort to explain to you, with the utmost patience and tact, why anything which you might want-or anything which they might want-is totally impossible."

Owing in considerable part to her insistence, the government allocated about $1.3 billion for a national family-planning Programme under the first Five-Year Plan, from 1951 to 1956. Some of the funds were used to open about 150 family-planning clinics, a testing laboratory, the preparation of educational materials, and a variety of projects to investigate motivations and attitudes. Yet, by 1956, less than 75 per cent of the small first appropriation had been spent.

By 1957, however, it was generally agreed that the time for caution had passed. Princess Amrit Kaur retired as minister of health and was succeeded by the more aggressive D. P. Karmarkar. An enthusiastic army doctor, Lieutenant Colonel Bishen Lal Raina, was named Family Planning Officer, given an appropriation of about $10 million for the second Five-Year Plan, and promised more money if he needed it.

When he moved into his new job, Colonel Raina quickly laid out a plan for local family-planning centers, fitting them into existing health centers in each area wherever possible. "I want to make this a part of regular health care," he said. "It is to be entirely voluntary. Advice will be given only to those married couples who ask for it. The views of those who object to family planning will be scrupulously respected." He repeatedly emphasized that the goal was "not to prevent childbirth but to make it possible to bring up children in the best and healthiest social climate."

To get a family-by-family Programme moving quickly, he called for the training of 20,000 field workers and the establishment of 2500 family-planning centers by the summer of 1961. At present more than 2370 teachers have been trained and are at work, and more than 825 clinics have been established. "We will have all the people we need for this Programme ready and working within a year," he told me." By then we plan to reach at least 40 million families every twelve months....

A radically different approach has been pushed by R. A. Gopalaswami, a high-ranking member of the Indian civil service, a trained mathematician, and the man who directed the eye-opening 1951 census. "We are on the edge of disaster," he says. "We cannot waste time with uncertain Programmes. The only possible solution for us now is widespread surgical sterilization preferably sterilization of every parent with three or more children."

In his 1951 census analysis he calculated that India's population could never be limited unless each family produced no more than three children. "It makes no difference whether or not the mother's health or the father's wealth can let the family afford more than three children," he insists. "India cannot afford it." Three years ago Gopalaswami was assigned to a new position in Madras, in southern India.

He discovered there that individual physicians were already embarked on a modest Programme of sterilization operations-a simple, fifteen-minute operation for men, and a relatively simple operation for women which could be done after childbirth. He promptly sent assistants to interview patients who had undergone the operations and found that all were pleased with the results.

"That was enough for me," he said. "I went into action."... All government hospitals in the state of Madras were ordered to perform the operations without charge....

For the first year the Madras surgeons performed only a few dozen operations each month. Last year they were doing hundreds. By next year, Gopalaswami says, they will be doing thousands. In other parts of India doctors are following the lead of Madras and performing the sterilization operations in their clinics and hospitals. Still other surgeons have undertaken this work on their own. In the world-famed valley of Kashmir, for example, a group of surgeons-unaware of the Madras work - recently estimated that they have performed more than 10,000 sterilizations during the past five years.

As head of the family-planning project for India, Colonel Raina has approved sterilization as one effective method, but he has not gone overboard for it. "We will use whatever useful methods we can find," he says," and we will continue to look for new ones. Unquestionably, the most unusual new contraceptive under consideration is a pill, apparently effective when taken orally, which was developed by Dr. Sudhir Nath Sanyal, a physician working in a small, dark, overcrowded little private laboratory in Calcutta.

In New Delhi, Colonel Raina and his advisers feel the Sanyal pill still belongs in the experimental class, but they have approved further trials...."If the pills prove safe and effective under general village conditions, "Colonel Raina says," I will order them by the million and distribute them without charge."

Certain other Indian leaders are thinking along similar lines. Dr. H. J. Bhabha, India's world-famous atomic scientist, told a recent international conference that what India really needs is an "anti" "fertility chemical" which could be added to the staple food -perhaps to salt, flour or sugar-and eaten every day. It would have to be highly safe, he said, but it would not have to be highly effective.

"If it would only reduce the statistical probability of pregnancy by about 30 per cent," he said, "our population growth would halt and our problem would be immediately solved." Support for this proposal has come from such men as J. R. D. Tata, head of the huge Tata industrial empire and one of India's most vigorous industrial leaders." Development of such a chemical would require a massive, intensive research Programme," he says." This will be expensive, but we can well afford to buy such research."

Whether or not such an all-out research project will be undertaken, many American and European observers are beginning to believe that India may be on the way to solving its population problem. They note a growing sense of urgency throughout the whole government-a feeling that corners must be cut to get the job done before India's time runs out. Furthermore, many of them indicated that whatever happens in this country will have a tremendous effect throughout the rest of Asia, and in the overpopulated nations of Africa and Latin America.

THE UNTOUCHABLES OF INDIA

Segregation which in India is on a scale far vaster than in America, has been unconstitutional for ten years. But it is still flourishing. Attempts to abolish it still lead to violence....[In 1957] an outbreak against untouchables in Madras raged for almost two weeks and brought death to more than forty persons.... Large numbers of the 55 million untouchables-people who by tradition are looked down upon for reasons of their low birth-still find they must use separate water supplies, eat off different plates, live in separate communities. They have difficulty locating churches they can attend, have trouble sending their children to school, and often are discriminated against for jobs....

Those who try to treat untouchables as equals often find themselves in trouble.... What the untouchables keep encountering is resistance that stems from more than three thousand years of deep-seated tradition. During that time an elaborate caste system has been built up in India. It is given sanction by the Hindu religion. At the bottom of all of India's 2,000 or more castes are the 55 million untouchables-born so low in the social scale that they are not even considered members of any caste at all.

Most Hindus firmly believe that contact with an untouchable means personal pollution. Even the path of his shadow is defiling. Untouchables pollute water and food, it is believed. They are not given access to Hindu temples. Usually they are forced to live in segregated districts. Only about 3 per cent of them-as compared with 15 per cent for all Indians-have ever had an opportunity to learn to read and write.

In recent years a great many educated Indians came to feel that untouchability was morally wrong and should be eliminated. By the time India became independent, the feeling was so strong that untouchability was made unconstitutional. Laws have provided fines and imprisonment for discriminating against untouchables and reserve to them 20 per cent of the seats in parliament and 12.5 per cent of all government jobs.

In addition, big sums have been spent to provide schools and housing for untouchables. The government has carried on a steady campaign of propaganda-through films, pamphlets, lectures and so on-to discourage untouchability among caste Hindus in the villages. Prime Minister Nehru has called outbreaks of violence against the disdained millions" terrible ... primitive and foolish."

But all of this has barely made a dent. In most of India's 560,000 villages, untouchables are still segregated. They are restricted to the most menial jobs. Even in the cities, where they work in industrial plants, they often are forced to work in quarters separated from other Indians. At school their children are still required to sit on segregated benches.

There are many villages where untouchables are not allowed to enter residential neighborhoods occupied by caste Hindus, are not permitted to ride bicycles or wear certain kinds of clothing or use the public water supply. Often their only sources of water are the ponds where cattle are washed. They are forbidden to take the bodies of their dead through village streets.

The policy that 12.5 per cent of government jobs go to untouchables hasn't worked out in practice. For one thing, the educational level of most of them is so low they can't hold many jobs. For another, officials still tend to discriminate against them. In New Delhi, an untouchable who worked as an engineer in the public-works department-untouchables reaching this level of education is extremely rare-was passed over for promotion seven times.

Attempts to end school segregation haven't worked out, either. Some of the new schools opened up to untouchables now are attended only by untouchables. New hospitals for children are being run especially for untouchables. Reading rooms and even housing developments are being constructed for untouchables only. The penalties called for by law for discriminating against untouchables are seldom invoked. A government report ... [in 19561 said that throughout India only 297 cases were brought to court in a twelve-month period. The vast majority of un-touchables either accept things as they are, or are too backward to know about their legal rights.

In past years, many untouchables have sought to change their status by leaving the Hindu religion and becoming Christians. A great number found, however, that being a Christian made no difference. They were still looked upon as untouchable by the people in their villages. Some find that, having renounced Hinduism, they are worse off than before.

Many educated untouchables are able to "cross the line" by moving into the larger cities and hiding their origins. But, in attempting to do this, the color of their skins-which is usually darker than that of other Indians-acts as a handicap. In general, the darker an Indian's skin is, the lower his caste is likely to be. The members of the highest caste, the Brahmans, usually have comparatively fair skins. In choosing husbands and wives, Indians often place emphasis on color. Indians who advertise for wives in the columns of newspapers-an old Indian custom-frequently state their preference for fair-skinned brides.

Many Hindus will not permit their children to marry in a caste beneath theirs. Others will not eat at the same table with a lower-caste Hindu. It is this type of tradition that has helped make it impossible to eliminate untouchability just by passing laws against it. This fact is now being admitted in Indian government publications and official reports-one of which says: "Any number of enactments by themselves will not transform the situation unless there is a genuine change of heart on the part of every ... citizen." Complete integration in India, it is now being recognized, is still a long way off, and the road toward it is studded with trouble and violence.

INDIA'S MASSES

India is trying to build itself anew, and there are many visible signs of progress. But communications are still needed drastically. Only 18 per cent of the people in India can read and write. Two years ago a research team from Jamia Milia University in New Delhi surveyed 150 villages in selected areas of the four Hindi-speaking states of north-central India. They found that 6 out of 67 persons selected at random were entirely ignorant of the fact that the British no longer ruled India.

In response to another question, the researchers found that 54 out of 314 respondents did not know the name of their own country. Some, however, were aware of the word *Bharat* (India); they said they had heard people shouting *Bharat Mata Ki Fai* (Long Live Mother India). But when these same villagers were asked what *Bharat* signified, they said they did not know. It is difficult to try to communicate the complicated forms of modern democracy to a people who may not even visualize a nation. I accompanied Prime Minister Nehru shortly before a general election when he attempted just this.

The Prime Minister visited the lovely old ruins of Mandu in central India, where five centuries ago there lived in a king who, with eight thousand wives, put Solomon to shame. A special effort had been made to gather together thousands of Gond tribesmen, who form the penniless peasantry of the surrounding scrub-jungle-covered hills. Nehru, speaking through a translator, gave a simple lecture in civics. He said there were no more British; they had all gone away.

There were no more maharajas; they too were not ruling India. There were just the Indian people, who were ruling themselves. Everybody was an Indian, he said. He was an Indian and the Gonds were Indians. With no more British and no more maharajas, the Gonds like other Indians had the opportunity to choose who would be their rulers. He then went on to explain about the elections and what it meant to cast a vote.

Nehru was careful to speak slowly and to use simple terms that he repeated many times, as if speaking to children, but the entire idea must have been difficult for the Gonds to grasp. Nevertheless, Nehru delivers as many as a half dozen speeches a day during his tours because he knows that the only effective communication with the masses of India must be on a person-to-person basis.

The daily circulation of newspapers in India, with a population of 400 million, is only 3.1 million, and one third of these papers are in English. The dozen or so English-language papers are extremely important, since 99 per cent of the people are ruled by the one per cent who speaks English. But my own experience has proved it true.

An Indian who does not speak English cannot gain authority outside of his own limited circle. But the only persons who can afford the long education necessary to become proficient in English are those who were born with money or property. Thus the feudal system is perpetuated, and thus the English-language papers are so important; they help mold the opinion of the people who count.

But this should not be overemphasized. Newspapers have little impact even on many of those who are literate, either in English or the regional languages. Stanley and Ruth Freed are young American anthropologists who have spent more than a year working in a village only fourteen miles from Delhi. About two weeks after the revolt in Tibet began, when the Dalai Lama had just reached the Indian frontier, the Freeds asked several of the more educated people in the village what they thought of the matter. The newspapers were full of news about the Dalai Lama, yet only one of the persons the Freeds asked had even heard of him.

The sole exception was a young man studying for his master's degree. Among those unaware of the Dalai Lama's existence was their interpreter, a young English-speaking girl who had completed two years of college. There is no television in India, and there are only slightly more than 1.5 million radio sets in use, most of them in the four major cities: Delhi, Bombay, Calcutta, and Madras. The government has installed about 40,000 subsidized community radios in the villages, but this is just a beginning-there are 500,000 villages in India.

It is more than just a matter of poverty. There are no repair facilities in the rural areas, and so an entire system has to be set up to keep the community radios in working order. Besides, many villages do not have electricity and need battery-operated sets, which mean that the batteries must be brought into a district center at regular intervals to be recharged. Language is a further barrier to understanding. There are fourteen major languages in India, plus a few hundred dialects, and when Nehru speaks in his native Hindustani he is understood by less than half of the people.

Unfortunately, the intellectuals who run All India Radio, the government-owned radio network, scorn Hindustani as a polyglot tongue and insist on using a highly Sanskritized version of Hindustani called Hindi, which the government is trying to propagate as the national language. As a result, there are relatively few who understand the Hindi news broadcasts of AIR. The language pattern outside of north central India is even more complicated. AIR news broadcasts in Bombay and Hyderabad are delivered in five languages, while special Programmes for the hill tracts of northeastern India are spoken in fifteen separate dialects.

It is laid down in the Indian constitution that the government should try to switch over from English to Hindi by 1965. But there is so much opposition to Hindi that the government recently had to promise that it would not insist on this deadline. It is not that those who oppose Hindi love English more, but they fear that if Hindi becomes the national language their own languages will be neglected. They also fear that those who speak Hindi as their mother tongue would find it easier to get government jobs than those who would have to learn Hindi as a second language.

In most of the rest of the world language ties a nation together. In India language separates people and makes them enemies. India is such a complex country that it needs modern communications to bind it together, yet a great majority of Indians live in the age of the bullock cart. The Indian Airlines Corporation, the government-owned airline that provides all of the internal passenger service and almost all of the air freight traffic, has only 77 aircraft on regular service. More than two thirds of these are decrepit DC-3's used during World War II.

There are only 400,000 telephones, or one for every thousand persons. Most of the telephones, like most of the radios, are concentrated in the four major cities. There are only 110 pages in the telephone book for the entire state of Kerala, which has a population of 15 million, or almost double that of New York City. There is only one motor vehicle of any sort, including motorcycles, for every 850 persons. But there are 10 million bullock carts, or one for every 40 people.

Automobile drivers curse the bullock carts for slowing down traffic, and highway engineers hate them because their narrow, iron-rimmed wheels destroy the surface of the roads, especially in the summer, when the asphalt melts under the baking sun. Yet they are as much a part of Indian life today as they were at the dawn of Indian history. And, judging from ancient temple sculpture, the bullock cart has remained unchanged throughout the rise and fall of countless kingdoms. The cart has two wobbly wheels about five feet in diameter and is drawn by two humped bullocks with the yoke resting on the bullocks' necks in front of the hump and cutting into the flesh.

The Indian peasant is poor in money and technology; the bullock cart is the only vehicle he can afford or knows how to use. It is estimated that each bullock cart travels two thousand miles a year and that 70 per cent of the goods in India are carried by bullock cart. The 80 per cent of the Indians who live in villages are scattered as far as twenty miles from a motorable road. When the second Five Year Plan ends in 1961, there will still be but 138,000 miles of all-weather motorable roads, or one mile for every 9 square miles of territory. Only 1500 miles of this will be two-lane highways.

India depends primarily on its government-owned railroads for interregional movement. It has the fourth largest railroad system in the world, but it still does not meet India's needs. There are 35,000 miles of track, or 27 miles per 1000 square miles of territory, compared with 74 in the United States. There are only 9 miles of track per 100,000 people, compared with 138 in the United States. The Indian railroads were neglected during the depression in the 1930's. They were badly damaged and overworked in the war years and later when the subcontinent was partitioned between India and Pakistan.

Meanwhile, population has increased at the rate of 7 million a year, and there is the new and heavy burden of the industries and projects begun under the two Five Year Plans. Because of all this, the Indian railroads today are less able to meet the demands made on them than they were thirty years ago, even though about 20 per cent of the Five Year Plan allocations are spent for railway improvement. Traveling in an air-conditioned car on the Indian railways is about as comfortable as traveling Pullman in the United States, but third-class travel, which is what most Indians use, can be sheer horror.

About two hundred passengers are jammed along with mountains of luggage into a single dirty, hot carriage. The seats are narrow and made of wooden slats. The smell of humanity is reinforced by the odor from the inadequate and seldom cleaned toilet. There is no drinking water on the train, and the rush for seats is so great that even when the train stops, a person who has a seat does not dare leave it to get a drink of water at the station. Some improvements have been made, but not many. The failure is deliberate. India is trying to build its industries, and freight gets priority over people.

Thanks to this priority, most of the outdated freight cars have been replaced and the total number has increased by 40,000 in the past ten years, but freight capacity is still inadequate. Businessmen complain that they have to wait three months for a freight car to carry their goods and that, at times; when a car is made available they have to wait another month before it can be attached to a passing train. They also complain that the movement of freight cars is so chaotic that even after goods are dispatched it might take a month for the shipment to arrive at a destination only five hundred miles away. The shortage of freight cars is a major cause of governmental corruption. Businessmen say that the only way they can get a car is by bribing railway officials.

Governmental inefficiency is the keynote. All of the interstate communications are owned by the central government, and many of the individual states have nationalized interurban bus and truck lines as well as their municipal transport systems. Yet entering a government office is like stepping back fifty years or more. There are few filing cabinets and paper clips. Papers are attached by a string threaded through a hole in one corner and then wrapped in a folder tied together by another string. A code letter is pinned to the cover, and the name of the file is registered in a ledger. The file is then tossed on a shelf along with mounds of others.

The registers are tossed someplace else, and how any file is ever found again is a wonder. The rules for handling correspondence at the district level in Uttar Pradesh have changed little since they were drawn up in 1880. A letter has to pass through forty-one distinct steps and be entered in dozens of registers before it is answered. Throughout India, the government moves so slowly that it is not uncommon for an official to die before his pension is sanctioned and paid.

Fortunately, not all government organizations are so creaky. One of the most promising things in India is the Community Development Programme, which has shown itself receptive to new ideas and methods. It has sent thousands of village-level workers and others into the villages to teach everything from adult literacy to better ways of farming. It emphasizes the person-to-person approach and at times has shown great imagination. For instance, it has organized group tours of India by as many as five hundred villagers-tempting them with a chance to worship at the traditional shrines and, in the process, showing them the new factories and dam, which Nehru calls the modern places of pilgrimage.

In trying to communicate ideas, the village-level workers have a whole armory of new weapons. All branches of the central and state governments are turning out books, pamphlets, and leaflets; special movies have been prepared along with audio-visual aids. There are hundreds of mobile vans equipped with generators to penetrate into the darkest interior, and there are even a few publicity setups mounted on bullock carts.

But an urban Indian intellectual is often as much a stranger to an Indian peasant as an Englishman or an American. Even when they do speak the same language, they do not think the same thoughts. When an educational movie is prepared in a Bombay studio, using actors disguised as farmers, the real farmers will always flock to the mobile van to see it. But they laugh at the wrong places. It is often a parody of own lives and as such is entertainment, not education.

The problem is greater than just making more realistic films. Ideas not only have to be understood, they have to be accepted; and once accepted, they have to become permanent.

The Community Development Programme works intensively in blocks of one hundred villages for about four years, after which the area is given much less attention. There are many apparent changes in these blocks. But Community Development officials have now found much to their dismay, that the villagers quickly give up their new habits and ideas as soon as the external pressure is removed.

The reason for this is found in the word *dharma*, a religious term roughly meaning "the Hindu way of life." But since religion, especially in the villages, is intertwined with man's every act, it means more than the ceremonies of religion. *Dharma* includes all the ethics and mores of a man's family, caste, and community; it determines how a man dresses or plows his field or eats and even how he goes to the toilet. *Dharma* gives the sanction of heaven to the class and caste structure and lays down that superior authority must be obeyed. Thus a village-level worker, who represents authority, might easily get the peasant to change his habits.

But once the village-level worker goes away, other aspects of the *dharma*-mainly the spiritual pressure of tradition-reassert themselves. Foreign experts are often discouraged. I met a British nurse whom the World Health Organization had sent to Kerala, where she worked for three years establishing maternity and child-care centers. We had a long talk about all the things she had done, but as I got up to leave she remarked sadly that she would soon be going home and it would probably be forgotten.

He was sent to an area where another expert a year previously had taught the villagers how to install and use a large number of diesel pumps for their wells. When the second man arrived at the scene, he found that none of the pumps were in use. Some were mechanically defective; others had simply run out of fuel. Perhaps the best way of getting ideas permanently accepted would be to present them through religious channels. But Hinduism has no established church which can be used as a means of communication. There are only individuals like Vinoba Bhave, Gandhi's disciple, who is collecting thousands of acres of land as gifts for his Bhoodan movement.

Vinoba, with his asceticism and his long tours on foot, is operating within the *dharma* and is easily accepted. The landlords who give part of their holdings to Vinoba for distribution among the landless are the same men who strenuously resist all land reforms proposed by the government. But the Westernized administrators of India scorn Vinoba and his religion-oriented methods.

Nehru often says that he is not "religious-minded," and government spokesmen take pride in echoing that India is a secular state. After living in India for more than five years and realizing the force of the dharma, that there is a direct relation between the de-emphasis of religion since Gandhi's death and the fact that much of the enthusiasm that existed at the time of India's independence has now evaporated.

Many factories and huge new dams spring up, yet despite the best efforts of the government, per-acre yields remain among the lowest in the world, and thousands of ancient minor irrigation works are falling into disrepair. The level of literacy is what it was a decade ago, and the fine-sounding laws banning untouchability or child marriage are seldom enforced. That is, there is a failure of the things that require the active cooperation of the masses.

This cannot be accounted for solely by the lack of physical communications. Gandhi showed that despite the absence of roads and post offices it is possible to establish contact with the vast masses and mobilize them for action. But nowadays this spiritual rapport is missing; there is a vast gulf between the rulers and the ruled. This has serious implications. As long as there is no close contact between those at the top and those at the bottom, democracy in India has slender roots.

PROBLEMS FOR THE CONGRESS PARTY

India's Congress party is greatly in need of new and dynamic leadership both in New Delhi and in the various states. A few months ago Prime Minister Nehru said" provincialism, casteism, and communalism" (religious rivalry) had developed within the party" to a scandalous and shameful degree." More than two years ago he admitted that the average Indian believes most Congress men are corrupt. Congress leaders themselves are responsible for this impression.

The party's executive committee recently censured five top leaders of Rajasthan for "setting a bad example" by issuing a joint statement accusing their chief minister, M. L. Sukhadia (roughly equivalent to an American governor), of "favoritism, nepotism, and corruption." But others had set the example earlier.... In 1958 dissidents within the Congress in Punjab drew up a 3000-word "charge sheet" accusing their chief minister, Sardar Pratap Singh Kairon, of the same things.

There are dissident cliques in every state. Some represent economic groups like big landlords. Others represent caste groups, and others regional groups. Sometimes an entire group breaks off. In Andhra recently twenty-seven Congress members of the state legislature resigned and are now trying to form their own party. A similar group broke away in Madras state two years ago and fought the last elections as the Congress Reform party. But experience has shown that splinter groups are ineffective. The cliques generally remain within the party, since this is the source of power and profit.

The 1957 Communist victory in Kerala was due primarily to feuding and mudslinging which destroyed the people's faith in the Congress party.... Nehru used to spend a lot of time flying off to one or another of the state capitals to gather the feuding politicians behind closed doors and force them to patch up their troubles, at least temporarily. But it is growing obvious that Nehru's authority is waning. The party bosses in the states pay lip service to his calls for unity but openly continue their bickering, and the Prime Minister seldom even attempts to restore peace. Yet at the same time he holds most of the reins of power in his own hands, so that no one else is able to do what he is unwilling or unable to do.

Now even Nehru's personal reputation is being called into question. M. O. Mathai, the Prime Minister's special assistant, resigned following Communist charges that he had unexplained sources of income. The Communists want to know where Mathai got the money to buy a farm worth $25,000 and why leading industrialists contributed to a $225,000 trust fund in memory of Mathai's mother.

The Prime Minister has defended the integrity of his former special assistant and has flatly denied the implication that Mathai got money to influence his decisions." I do not think it proper for anyone to imagine that Mr. Mathai influenced me in anything or in any policy," Nehru said.

Proper or not, the Communists have reiterated their charges. They demand a full, public inquiry, but Nehru has agreed only to a secret investigation by a single government official. This has given the Communists the chance to pose as the defenders of democracy. They have repeated their demands for an open investigation and say they will not lay whatever information they have before the secret group. "Mathais may come and go," declared Bhupesh Gupta, the Communist leader in the upper house of parliament, "but our parliamentary system and our democratic standards shall remain and we have to protect them."

NEHRU'S POPULARITY

No one believes that Nehru himself is involved in corruption, but the Mathai case does disclose several chinks in his armor. He is a poor judge of men. He is also impatient of implied criticism and either tries to ignore it or loses his temper and says harsh things to those around him. As a result there are few independent men around him, and there are fewer every year as the old stalwarts of the independence struggle-the men who knew Nehru as a youth and who make allowances for his moods-die off. They are replaced by others, who are at best yes men and at worst sycophants....

Nehru is still the Congress party's greatest asset.... But the question is, what will the Congress party do for election material after he is gone? When Nehru's daughter, Indira Gandhi (no relation to the Mahatma) was elected Congress president, she spoke of bringing younger elements to the fore and of instilling a new sense of discipline. A. S. Raju, a Congress general secretary, said her election would check a" drift toward the rightist trend of thought."

Her moves so far have been disappointing. The Old Guard members of the executive committee handed in their formal resignations so that she could appoint whomever she wished. She promptly reappointed almost all of the old bosses, explaining, "I cannot deprive myself of the sound and wise counsels of our national leaders in my attempt to make room for young blood." Nehru was dropped as a regular member of the executive committee but added as a "permanent special invitee."

Nehru, contradictory person that he is, criticizes the Congress for its "provincialism, casteism, and communalism," but he also idealizes it. He once referred to the Congress as the "steel frame" of India, declaring that it was the only group which could hold the disparate elements of India together and at the same time provide democratic and socialist leadership....

However, there are doubts whether the Congress really represents socialism. The term is misleading. Congress socialism is generally devoid of any ideological content; it means brotherhood, humanity, and a better deal for the underdog. The trouble with the Congress party is that its representatives sometimes belie its socialist slogans....

THE POOR BECOME POORER

Out of a population of 400 million, 70 per cent are engaged in agriculture and allied pursuits. Of these, 30.4 per cent are without land or have so little land they are classified as agricultural labourers. They own one per cent of the land under cultivation and have a per capita income of $23 a year. Former Congress party president U. N. Dhebar admits that these agricultural labourers are "groaning under subhuman conditions."

Yet the Congress party, despite eleven years of majorities in most of the states of India, has not been able to bring about effective land reform. One has only to look at how some of these majorities were obtained to understand why. The Congress barely got a majority in Orissa in 1957 but promptly strengthened itself by absorbing three men who had been elected on the feudalist Ganatanra Parishad ticket and by forming an alliance with the five members elected on the equally feudalist Jharkand ticket. These new Congress members and Congress allies have effectively sabotaged land reform measures, and the old Congress party members, who are interested in power more than principles, refuse to get rid of them.

Western visitors to India are always impressed by the many new factories and development works, but Indians themselves are more conscious of the fact that one third of the entire work force is either unemployed or underemployed. Mr. Dhebar has admitted that "the circle of the rich becoming richer and the poor becoming poorer remains unbroken." This is the sort of atmosphere that can destroy a political party or can even breed a revolution.

Moreover, a new wind is stirring the countryside. Vinoba Bhave's Bhoodan (land gift) movement is gaining strength. It has collected more than four million acres, of which one million have been distributed and another million will be parceled out within a year. The rest is uncultivable. Bhave has also collected about 4500 villages as Gramdan-a plan whereby an entire village contributes all of its land to a common pool and farms it collectively. The Bhoodan movement aims at more than just land reform. Bhave wants a voluntary cooperative commonwealth built on a base of self-sufficient, self-administered villages.

To an American, Bhave's idea may seem too utopian to be practical. But India has its own traditions and ways of doing things, and Bhave is a product of these traditions. Thirty years ago much of what Gandhi said about how to oust the British also seemed wildly impractical. Bhave has been able to convince several highly respected Indian leaders, including former Praja Socialist Jaya Prakash Narayan, of the validity of his approach.

Narayan was once believed to be Nehru's logical successor, but he renounced politics five years ago to join the Bhoodan movement. He is convinced that parliamentary democracy does not meet the needs of India's conditions. He thinks bossism, corruption, and feuds are almost automatic under the present system because it is too easy for small, educated elite to take advantage of a vast, illiterate, and poverty-stricken peasantry.

Instead, he favors a series of indirect elections so that the peasants vote in small blocs for issues they can understand and for candidates they know personally. The persons elected from the bottom rung in turn vote for people to the next higher rung and so on up the line.

He also says the peasants must be given economic independence, and since there is not enough land for all, what there is should be worked cooperatively and the surplus labour used to produce most of a village's needs in clothing and small utensils and implements. Neither Bhave nor Narayan opposes large industries. They say that given the rapid population increase-now about 6 million a year-industries will never reduce the pressure on the land, so that capital-intensive heavy industries and labour-intensive cottage industries must develop side by side.

The Bhoodan ideas find ready acceptance among the Indian peasants. Bhave walks constantly, never stopping more than one night in any place. His march along narrow, dusty, backcountry roads has taken on the proportions of a triumphal procession. The villagers come from miles around to greet him as he passes and then gather at his halting place to listen attentively to what he has to say.

Basically, Bhave is helping to spread democracy. He tells the peasants to rearrange their lives and lands without waiting for the government to act. He insists that no coercion be used. Although he does not preach anticommunism, he is actually a strong antidote to communism. If the Indian peasants can learn to handle their own village and district affairs and not succumb to violence, they will automatically learn how to exercise better control of their political representatives at the state level, and eventually at the national level....

Ironically, although Bhave criticizes the Congress party for its obvious failings, there are usually a number of white Gandhi caps, signifying Congress workers, in his audience. Bhoodan is inspiring Congress district workers to become more active among the people. The old Gandhian idealism, which swept away the British, may again nourish the roots of the National Congress party.

COMMUNISM IN INDIA

India had its first experiment with peaceful coexistence of Communist and non-Communist governments during the period, April 5, 1957, to July 31, 1959, within its own borders. With the fall of the Communist government of Kerala state, this experiment has been interrupted, if not terminated. New state elections were to be held at the end of 1959. This, then, is an appropriate occasion for assessing Communist policy in India.

RECENT STRATEGY AND TACTICS

Current Soviet strategy in the underdeveloped countries may be compared to the "popular-front" policy in Europe during the years 1935-1939. Then it was "anti-Fascist," now it is "anti-imperialist" or, more specifically, anti-American. It is a strategy of mobilizing all" patriotic" forces within each country against the alleged threat of Western economic and military aggression. Applied to India, it is a strategy of collaboration with all groups of the population which support neutralism. Translated into tactics on the basis of India's circumstances, it means support of the " bourgeois" Nehru government so far as its actions are anti-Western in intent or in effect.

Within India the tactics of the Communist party (CPI) are to collaborate with all "democratic" parties and groups toward the goal of a" government of democratic unity," or a coalition government of Communist and non-Communist parties which have anti-imperialism and a diluted socialism in common. The CPI proclaims this goal both for each of the fourteen states composing the Republic of India and for the central government, but it concentrates on the state level of Indian politics.... The Indian Communists tend to collaborate with Nehru's Congress government in New Delhi while attacking the Congress governments in the state capitols. The main achievement of this policy, and its main test, is the Communist experience in Kerala state.

COMMUNISM IN KERALA

The state of Kerala is one of the most politically disturbed regions of the Indian subcontinent. The state has a great variety of communal problems. There are unusually large Moslem and Catholic minorities, severe caste animosities, and an exceptionally large and dissatisfied intellectual minority. The resulting social tensions have produced a multiplication of political parties. The Congress, dominant nearly everywhere else, has been reduced to a minority party alongside the Praja Socialist party, the Revolutionary Socialist party, the Moslem League and the Communist party. Before 1957, parliamentary government in the state meant minority or coalition government, and it was inherently unstable.

Until that year no government in Kerala (or, before the reorganization of states, in Travancore-Cochin) had held office for more than eighteen months. To cope with such instability, the central government, under the constitution, possesses emergency powers whereby in case of failure by a state government it can dissolve that government and administer the state by "presidential rule" until new elections. Between 1950 and 1957, presidential rule was declared on five occasions in India, and of these, two occurred in Kerala.

In the general elections of 1957 the Communists emerged as the largest bloc in Kerala's legislature. With the support of five independents whom they had helped to elect, they commanded an absolute majority and were thus able to form the government, under Chief Minister E. M. S. Namboodiripad. Confronted by the threat of New Delhi's intervention and by a precarious electoral base, the Communists' natural course of action was one of moderation....

Moderate as the Communists were by their standards, the effect of Communist rule was gradually to exacerbate communal and class differences. The Communists won an important by-election in 1958, regarded as a test of their record, but opposition increased. The potential strength of the opposition is indicated by the fact that it controlled an overwhelming majority of the newspapers and of the municipal and village councils in the state. All that was needed was an issue which would draw the lines for struggle.

The issue came with the government's Education Act, which stated, among other things, that teachers in all schools receiving state subsidies, public and private, must be appointed from a register maintained by the Public Service Commission. Charging political intervention in education, the Catholic Church announced its refusal to open parochial schools. This action catalyzed the opposition, and soon all parties rallied against the government.

OPPOSITION TO EDUCATION ACT

At this point a crucial decision was made: the opposition chose to resort to civil disobedience instead of awaiting electoral or judicial remedies. Under the aggressive leadership of Mannath Padmanabhan, spokesman of the Nair caste, opposition groups joined in a campaign to paralyze the Communist government and force either its resignation or its dissolution by the central government. Demonstrations and riots occurred, accompanied by police firings-not an uncommon event in India. The campaign was to culminate on August 9, "Save India Day," on which the opposition planned to undertake a full-scale general strike avowedly aimed at eliminating the Communist government from Kerala and the Communist party from India.

As "Save India Day" grew nearer, it became clear that no compromise was possible. The governor of Kerala and the Union President Rajendra Prasad recommended central action, and Nehru, at first reluctant, finally accepted it as necessary. On July 31 the Kerala government was dissolved. It retired quietly, and the local Communist protest was mild.... Published reactions after the event were characterized by relief, accompanied by regret over the methods used in bringing down the Communists and gloom over the prospects in Kerala.

LESSONS OF KERALA

Civil disobedience in Kerala was a bad precedent, not least because the Communists themselves are most likely to benefit from it. The CPI is best equipped, both by inclination and by organizational experience, to stage a similar civil disobedience campaign against a Congress state government. And shortly after New Delhi's takeover in Kerala it did precisely that in the traditionally turbulent state of West Bengal.

There are other potential benefits accruing to the CPI from the Kerala situation. Central intervention in state politics is generally unpopular, whatever the circumstances, and the prestige of the Congress may therefore be reduced both in Kerala and elsewhere in India. Moreover, given the circumstances of their fall, the Communists may evoke some sympathy by posing as martyrs....

The result {of the next election} will depend on the ability of the opposition to remain united. But it is reasonable to expect that, whatever the result, the elections will contribute to further polarization in Indian politics. Whether the Communists win (in which case they would probably face a second downfall) or lose, they may tend to conclude that they cannot gain and hold power anywhere in India by parliamentary methods.

Given their ideological bias, they may judge that a Communist government in India would have to fight for its life in a hostile environment, as Russia's infant Soviet government had to fight for its life in the "capitalist encirclement." They may conclude, in short, that peaceful coexistence of Communist and non-Communist governments is impossibility within India. In that case, the CPI may be disposed to swerve from its hitherto peaceful path and resort to more direct action.

AIMS OF WORLD COMMUNISM

The future direction of Communist policy in India will, however, depend more on the interests and attitudes of international communism than on those of the Indian Communists.

Like the earlier anti-Fascist line, the anti-imperialist strategy is subject to abrupt change. Indeed, the conditions under which change could take place can be anticipated. The strategy would naturally be terminated with the defeat of the "imperialist" bloc, and, short of that, it would be less urgent if that bloc were relatively weakened. The Soviet leaders boast of the ability of the Communist states to overtake and surpass the West in the economic factors of power. As they grow more confident, may they not feel less need to collaborate with bourgeois allies with whom they share nothing but anti-imperialism?

May they be less satisfied with the negative benefits of Indian neutralism, and more disposed to demand the positive benefits of Indian allegiance to the Communist bloc?...

More recently, and particularly since the fall of the Communist government in Kerala, the Chinese Communists have intensified their political and military pressures against border regions adjoining India and against India itself. However, this menacing situation may prove beneficial in terms of internal politics. Peiping's pressure on India has brought about a sharp split in India's Communist party, with some Communist leaders -among them Mr. Namboodiripad-declaring they are behind the Nehru government "for the defense of the integrity of the country and its freedom."

PLANNING IN INDIA

India's Five-Year Plans, their conception and magnitude, the resources and needs of the country, the difficulties in connection with foreign exchange, the desirability of foreign aid -all these and a number of related questions have received considerable attention in America. The extension of credit by the Export-Import Bank and the Development Loan Fund ... {in 1958} was evidence of the desire of the U.S. government to make an effective contribution to India's economic development.

The resolution introduced {in the U.S. Congress} by Senators John Kennedy and John Sherman Cooper (former U.S. Ambassador to India) for massive and coordinated support of India's plans and a strong plea by Senator Hubert Humphrey for large and sustained aid have served to make people increasingly aware of the importance of India's efforts for social and economic betterment. It is, therefore, essential to ask what is meant by India's planned development. Why is such a Programme necessary?

When India became an independent country eleven years ago, she faced enormous economic problems: a stagnant agricultural economy, an excessive population, woefully low standards of living, chronic unemployment and underemployment, lack of financial and technical resources. The lopsided nature of the economy was in no small measure due to retarded development under foreign rule. But the economic ills were also aggravated by postwar inflation and the after-effects of partition of the subcontinent.

On the other hand, the hopes for betterment of a people who had attained self-rule were understandably high. National freedom engendered "a revolution in expectations." Moreover, several projects for industrialization, power, and irrigation, and also Programmes for expansion of social services, had been formulated or were at various stages of implementation, and the necessity for some kind of coordinated effort for economic and social development was increasingly recognized.

After the adoption of the constitution in India in January, 1950, a planning commission was set up to survey the whole economy and devise ways of mobilizing and augmenting the economic, technical, and human resources of the country. The commission is an advisory and consultative body and formulates its proposals and recommendations in close cooperation with various ministries of the union (federal) government and the state governments. It consults continually with various groups of men: industrialists, business and labour leaders, consumers, economic and technical experts, and legislators. India's plan is thus essentially democratic in its conception and execution.

No facile solutions or ready-made rules exist for the improvement of a vast, impoverished nation. The methods by which Western Europe and the United States progressed over a century and a half can have only a limited application in a country with a large and growing population which has no unconquered frontiers, no colonial territories. Countries like India have to seek their own answers to problems of agricultural reform and industrialization, the role of the state in an underdeveloped economy, the encouragement of private enterprise, and the guarantee of social justice. We are trying to do in India what it has taken centuries to achieve in the West.

India's plan is to build up a "socialist pattern of society." We need not be frightened of words, whether "socialism" or "capitalism." All civilized governments today seek for their people some kind of welfare state or society in which concerted efforts are made to improve standards of living, to provide an increasing degree of economic security, and to enlarge the scope of essential social services. In wartime the state performs many functions to attain common objectives and mobilize national efforts; countries like India are waging a war against poverty, unemployment, disease, and illiteracy, and have to make a similar endeavor. In this sense, as Sir William Harcourt, a former British Chancellor of the Exchequer, observed," we are all socialists now."

The constitution of India itself has set forth the ideal of a welfare state based on social justice in which the ownership and the material resources of India are so distributed as to serve the common good and in which the economic system does not result in concentration of wealth and means of production to the common detriment. But a welfare state need not be a totalitarian state. The second Five-Year Plan has thus defined its objective:

The accent of the socialistic pattern is on the attainment of positive goals; the raising of living standards; the enlargement of opportunities for all; the promotion of enterprise among the disadvantaged class in the creation of a sense of partnership among all sections of India. These positive goals provide the criteria for basic decisions. The government and people of India are seeking to achieve these objectives through consent, not coercion. Our people are using the polling booths, not barricades; constitutional processes, not dictatorial ukases.

Moreover, India's constitution lays down that there shall be no acquisition by the state without compensation, and wherever such compensation has been paid, as in the nationalization of life insurance companies or a gold mining industry, it has been not only fair but generous. Measures are adopted for economic reform after full debate and through parliamentary procedures. In the Indian economy, agriculture, consisting of privately owned farms, is the predominant industry. No Programme is visualized for collectivization of the land; the emphasis is on development through cooperatives. While feudal estates are being broken up so as to make the tiller the owner of the soil, ceilings are provided for holdings of land in several states.

Private enterprise contributes nearly 98 per cent of the total industrial production, and it is actively encouraged by the state in its expansion. Thus, two private steel plants have been assisted in their schemes for doubling their capacity through governmental guarantee from World Bank loans, even though three government steel plants are being set up. In other words, the government is willing to help to achieve the maximum national product through private enterprise as well as through state owned and managed industries and services. The Indian people constantly remind themselves that the individual on the farm and in the factory is at the center of national development. We believe that a plan is for man, not man for plan.

During the period of the first Five-Year Plan (1951-1956) the spell of stagnation was broken. The national income increased by 18 per cent and the per capita income by 11 per cent, taking into account the growth of population. The output of food grains went up by nearly a fourth, or by 11 million tons, and agricultural production as a whole by 19 per cent. Through irrigation and land reclamation the area under crops increased by 26 million new acres.

Nearly 80 million people comprising one fourth of the rural population felt the impact of a dynamic community development Programme. This Programme is designed to revivify rural life by improving productivity and providing employment through rural industries. It also aims at improving the health, education, and communications in the village areas. A useful yardstick for measuring the success of such projects is the extent of voluntary contributions of the people; nearly half of the expenditure of this Programme has been made through voluntary contributions by villagers, in the form of free labour, materials, land, and even cash.

A silent revolution is spreading through the countryside. On its success depend the stability and progress of a land where 80 per cent of the people live in villages. Along with agricultural progress, industrial production increased by 30 per cent by the end of the first plan. Employment was provided for nearly 4 million more people; 6 million more children went to primary schools; the number of technical institutes and universities grew steadily; and health services were extended. But the success of the plan has to be judged not merely in terms of physical targets and percentages of increase in production and consumption, important as they are for an economically backward country.

What is more vital is the creation of a new spirit of enthusiasm, hope, and confidence. This the first plan, in a large measure, achieved. Unfortunately, it did not make an adequate impact on the economy. A start had undoubtedly been made, but it was recognized that future development had to be more basic as well as speedier. The second Five-Year Plan, therefore, is essentially an attempt to lay the foundations of sustained development. Briefly, its objective is to obtain a 25 per cent increase in national income-from $21 billion in 1955-1956 to $26 billion in 1961.

Production of consumers' goods is expected to rise by 21 per cent, with the balance plowed back into national development projects. In terms of per capita income the increase expected is 18 per cent, but in concrete terms this increase can hardly be regarded as ambitious. It would increase the per capita income from fifty-six dollars a year to sixty-six dollars. The ratio of investment to national income would go up from 7.3 per cent to 11 per cent, which is still low in comparison with that of many countries. Employment opportunities are to be provided for an additional 6.5 million people. Food production is to be increased by 25 per cent.

Manufacture of steel, which is basic to the Indian economy, would rise to 4.5 million tons a year, which is quite a modest target for a population of 380 million people. But with all the industrialization that is envisaged, India is and will remain a predominantly agricultural country.

To bring and conserve water for Indian farms, to supply fertilizer and manure to Indian farmers, to adopt more efficient practices in consonance with local conditions, organize the farmers for cooperative action, provide schools and health clinics, supply light and power to rural homes and industries, and develop better communications and transport-these are the primary tasks which the government is undertaking. We recognize that India cannot be prosperous unless her villages are improved; but the countryside will not be in a healthy state until the national economy is further diversified, the pressure of population on the land is reduced, avenues of employment extended, and industry built up.

This second plan has run into difficulties in regard to foreign exchange resources available for import of food grains, capital goods, and industrial raw materials. Therefore, the criticism is leveled that the plan has been" overambitious." It has undoubtedly set high targets for production of food and industrial goods and for increasing incomes and social services. But the country cannot attempt less under the intensive pressure of a rapidly increasing population and of insistent public expectations and demands. It should also be pointed out that difficulties in regard to foreign exchange have not been due to the importation of luxuries or misdirection of scarce resources;

by and large, the money has been expended on productive and remunerative projects.

In implementing plans of development, India has received a substantial amount of foreign aid from the United States, from the Colombo Plan, and from other countries, including Soviet Russia. The foreign aid received, however, constituted only about 10 per cent of the total developmental expenditure. The principal financial burden has been borne by the people of the country themselves. India is probably the highest taxed country in the world relative to capacity....

A national plan is not merely an inventory of schemes and projects; it must be bold in order to stimulate effort, inculcate initiative, and strengthen creative forces. And the people must feel that despite all difficulties and obstacles their government is making a maximum effort for their welfare and progress."

Against the danger of a big plan," Professor J. K. Galbraith observed after a visit to India and study of her plans," must be set even greater dangers of frustration of the democratic spirit which would follow from one that seemed reluctant, inadequate, or even insufficiently bold." In balancing the risks, we have to take into account the prevalence of chronic unemployment with its maladjustments, waste, and social discontent. These are facts which a realistic democratic government has to face....

NEEDED: MORE FOOD

India is facing a crisis in food production. More specifically, it is a crisis in food-grain production because food grains comprise two-thirds of the caloric intake of the average Indian. The crux of the problem is food enough for the rapidly increasing population.

Five million persons per year were added during the first Five-Year Plan, and seven million per year will have been added during the second plan period. Ten million per year probably will be added during the period of the third plan ending in 1966. Although there is considerable emphasis on family planning in India, no appreciable slowing down of population growth may be expected during the third plan period.

This means that food will have to be provided for 80 million more people by the end of the third plan. This explosive increase in population will raise the total from 360 million in 1951 to an estimated 480 million by 1966. Substantial expansion of food-grain production is necessary even to maintain existing consumption levels, which are among the lowest in the world. The present population places severe pressure on food supplies, and unfavorable crop conditions create an immediate crisis.

The successive Five-Year Plans have included food-grain production targets as major components ... The first plan set a target of 65.5 million tons by 1955-1956. This target was achieved quite easily as a result of greater emphasis on agricultural production, and with the help of favorable weather.

The second Five-Year Plan set a target of 80.5 million tons of food (including legumes) grains by 1960-1961. But the annual crop returns are less than the target rates.... Preliminary planning is now under way for the third plan. No specific targets have been announced, but discussions indicate that from 100 to 110 million tons of food grains will be required by 1965-1966. This assumes that population will continue to increase at projected rates, and that a small rise will continue to take place in per capita consumption of food grains.

A target of 100 million tons would permit a net daily consumption per person of 15 ounces of cereals and 3 ounces of pulses (legumes) for the prospective population. This compares with the consumption in 1956-1957 of 13.3 ounces of cereals and 2.4 ounces of pulses. A target at this level, therefore, would allow for some improvement in the diets of those who are now at bare subsistence levels, but it would not provide a safety margin for adverse weather nor for reserve stocks needed to stabilize prices and to meet other unforeseen emergencies. A target of 110 million tons is necessary to allow for these contingencies.

In addition to food-grain production, any balanced agricultural Programme should provide also for additional production of dairy and poultry products, fruits and vegetables to meet the demands of an expanding urban population and to permit gradual improvement in diets. But the conclusion is clear: the gap between needs for food grains, as indicated by the plan targets, and supply, as indicated by production trends, is growing wider.

The relatively favorable 1958-1959 season failed to reach the annual average of the food-grain target by 4.3 million tons, and the 1957-1958 crops was 9.3 million tons short. If food-grain production increases no faster than indicated by the present trend, the gap between supplies and needs in 1965-1966 will be about 28 million tons. In order to produce 110 million tons of food grains annually by the end of the third plan, the rate of production increase must average 8.2 per cent per year for the next 7 years. This rate of increase compares with an annual average of 2.3 per cent from 1949-1950 to 1958-1959, and an average of 3.2 per cent from 1952-1953 to 1958-1959.

The task is overwhelming. The urgency of an all-out effort is obvious. Adequate resources must be made available to accomplish the job. It is clear that the necessity for conserving foreign exchange requires holding imports of food grains to a minimum level, except as imports become available under special exchange Programmes. In any case, no conceivable Programme of imports or rationing could meet a crisis of this magnitude.

A third plan target of 110 million tons must be reached if the country is to go forward on its development Programme. In fact greatly accelerated expansion of food production is necessary to prevent hunger and possible civil disturbance. This target can be achieved if an all-out emergency food production

Programme is undertaken. The best in Indian agriculture is comparable to the best in other countries, but the average level is unduly low. The task before the country is to develop ways of raising the low average to the higher levels that many Indian cultivators have achieved.

THE SILENT REVOLUTION

In India-as in most of the less developed world-some four out of every five people live in rural villages or on farms. And in India, that means well over 300 million people-and some 200,000 villages. This suggests something of the vast scope of the current Programmes which India started from scratch in 1952 and which aim to establish community development projects or rural extension services throughout the land by the end of the second Five-Year Plan in 1961.

It also suggests why the Community Development Programme has been called "the silent revolution." On Mahatma Gandhi's birthday anniversary-October 2, 1952-India entered upon the first stage of community development with fifty-five selected pilot projects, each project covering an area of about 500 square miles and including some 300 villages.

Since then the Programme has expanded rapidly on two fronts: the National Extension Service and the Community Projects Programme. The first provides minimal basic services and a modicum of financial assistance to permit local groups to get started on small-scale Programmes of rural improvement. The second is a series of rounded Programmes designed to raise standards in agriculture, health and sanitation, education, housing, communication, women's welfare, and cottage and small-scale industry. As areas covered by the National Extension Service begin to make progress, they move into the more intensive Community Development Programme. The ultimate goal is to extend full-scale community development Programmes to all of rural India.

Underlying the entire Programme are the principles of selfhelp and mutual help. As projects are worked out in each area, the local communities qualify for assistance by meeting an agreed scale of voluntary contributions in money, in kind, or in labour. Publicly-provided financial assistance is shared by the central and state governments. For wealth-producing projects, such as irrigation works, funds are advanced by the central government to the state governments in the form of interest bearing loans.

And heavy emphasis is placed on the stimulation of local initiative and action through local institutions like the panchayats ... {village councils}.

By the end of the first Five-Year Plan in 1956 the interim goal of the Community Development Programme had been reached. One fourth of the entire rural population had been brought within the orbit of the Programme. Some 80 million people were involved in community improvement Programmes. Here are some of the results by mid-1957:

Some 150,000 community centers had been started. Nearly 4,000 primary health centers had been established. More than 1,200 maternity and child welfare centers had been created. Some 70,000 adult education centers were in operation and nearly 2 million adults had been made literate.

About 25,000 new schools had been built and 10,000 more converted. Nearly 3,500 production and training centers for arts and crafts had been established. Village housing projects were under way in 500 villages. And nearly 60,000 cooperative societies had been formed. Priority activities included the improvement of village wells, the extension of fruit and vegetable cultivation, the use of improved seeds and fertilizers, the upgrading of animal and poultry stocks, the construction of roads, and the drainage of land.

And for every dollar of contribution by the government, the rural people contributed the equivalent of sixty-one cents.

The United States-among other countries - has cooperated and provided a measure of assistance to India in the conduct of its "silent revolution." Over a period of about six years, some $15 million has been made available from Technical Cooperation funds. U.S. agricultural extension experts have helped develop study courses and demonstration projects. From the beginning the Ford Foundation has helped to train thousands of community development workers and has supported fifteen pilot projects in rural development.

Under the second Five-Year Plan, India has quadrupled the resources allocated to the Community Development Programme -and established the goal of reaching the entire rural population with either the National Extension Service or with full-blown Community Development Programmes. This will require the expansion of National Extension Service areas from 500 to 3,800 and the number of Community Development areas from 622 to 1,120.

Community development throughout the free world seeks to build economic and social progress on the traditional values and institutions of rural societies. India today is conducting the world's largest Programme of rural community development. And observers agree that its success or failure has significance for all of Asia and beyond-for throughout the less developed world the Indian Programme stands in stark contrast to the commune system of Communist China.

The Indian economy is now an unquestioned success story. But India's progress is not merely an example of how economic reforms have again worked to open up an economy to the benefits of free markets. It is also an example of how the commitment to democracy benefited economic progress as well. In a time when so many believe that democracy should be postponed until economic reforms are completed, India's success suggests that adhering to democratic values may indeed promote more durable economic growth. Despite the uncertainty created by recent elections, it is likely that the Indian economy will continue to thrive.

The idealism that drove Indian leaders to straggle for freedom, from the 1880s to the 1940s, was the pragmatic betterment of Indians. Indian leaders envisioned the economic life of the Raj, which they had come to appreciate through their British education in India or Britain. British education and its democratic political processes had left India's people with a drive to seek the same for their independent country and people. This strong attraction to and acceptance of the democratic process played a key role in the independence movement, which, by and large, was nonviolent and yet disobedient to its rulers.

With this solid grounding in democratic values, India set itself up as a parliamentary democracy with the same freedoms as in Britain, such as a vibrant free press. Its constitution incorporated parts of the American, British, and French constitutions. India is also a multiparty political system in which differing views are expressed and tolerated under constitutional guarantees of freedom of expression. India has lived its constitution in practice as well as on paper, avoiding totalitarian, authoritarian, and military regimes completely since its independence in 1947.

Democracy in India has survived wars with its neighbors, China and Pakistan; domination by a single political party, namely the Congress Party; three prime ministers from one party and one family, namely Jawaharlal Nehru, his daughter Indira Gandhi, and her son Rajiv Gandhi; left and right coalition governments; a socialist government; bribery and corruption scandals; low or no economic growth in some years; use of emergency powers of the central government by Prime Minister Indira Gandhi; abject economic poverty and a high degree of illiteracy; and much social strife. There have been ten governments and ten prime ministers, and all of them came to power through a peaceful electoral process. India demonstrates a deep-seated respect for and practice of democratic values.

Democracy is also a messy, noisy, and argumentative process as people with different views and values try to win public acceptance for them. Once a party wins power, democracy requires that the party serve the interests of the entire population. In this respect, the dominant view in India between the 1920s and 1990s was that of the Congress Party, which secured freedom for the people of India - a great achievement by itself. The general elections of 1996 produced a massive, confusing, but peaceful change of government.

Although a clear majority for any one political group did not emerge, new political alliances are forming. Since all parties agree that economic growth is the only way to make people's lives better, alliances are being formed based on economic policies and Programmes rather than ideology. Despite the fact that a coalition government can be reasonably stable, although not as stable as a one-party government, the next government, and possibly one or two following it, may not be able to complete the maximum tenure of five years.

The economic models practiced by India over the past fifty years have also had to take India's democratic political system into account. In response to the level of absolute poverty and the agrarian base of the economy on the one hand and the extremely unequal distribution of power and wealth and lack of industrial structure on the other, India adopted policies that would eliminate mass poverty and create an infrastructure for future industrial growth.

Logically, it required agriculture to produce a surplus for eventual industrialization. In the period following independence this meant postponing investment in luxury consumption goods such as automobiles in favor of setting up an educational system for the masses and infrastructure industries, such as steel, fertilizers, railroads, irrigation canals, and electric power generation in the public sector. This was done partly because of the large sums required, which few industrial families could finance. The public-sector companies were to provide an industrial base and would complement the private sector.

The government called this system democratic socialism. (In the West this is called a market, or mixed, economy; for example, in Europe railroads, aerospace, telephone, health care, and many other industries are owned and operated by the government and/or semi-government companies and autonomous organizations.) The Indian government was not against capitalism or capitalists. Scarce economic resources, however, had to be used to build the country rather than waste them on consumer luxuries for the few rich.

Although terribly inefficient from an operational economic viewpoint, its purpose was to create a base. Capitalists and entrepreneurs by the millions thrived as they engaged in full ownership, production, and economic activities and industries not exclusively controlled by the public sector. Gradually, the role of the public sector in investment, employment, and output decreased, and the role of the private sector increased. Since the early 1950s, the balance of the capitalism - socialism spectrum has shifted slowly but steadily toward capitalism.

Most of the output and employment in India today are in the private sector. Inefficiencies, bureaucratic waste, and licensing requirements most likely had a dampening effect on the overall growth rate of the economy. On the other hand, there were neither revolutions nor loss of freedom. Government investment policies were designed to exploit resource availability in deciding the location and priority of industries across the country.

Capital projects beyond government investment were set as national goals in the sense of French-type indicative planning. This resulted in more balanced development of various states. If some states had lower wages and less per capita income growth, then the central government provided subsidies to increase their per capita incomes. This relative stability of income levels in different parts of the country also avoided mass migrations chasing higher wages. Decisions regarding public investments followed a bottom-up approach, in which proposed projects in each state combined to form overall national goals in each industry.

The political process from local to national levels played an important role in the selection of projects at each stage of decision-making. Private-capital investments were expected to follow national industrial goals but there was no compulsion; decisions whether to invest were based on business's expectations of profits. India's record of economic performance is reasonably good given the limited available resources and the enormous problems of building an economy in a huge democratic society. Between 1966 and 1989, the economy achieved a real annual GDP growth rate of 4 per cent, yielding a per capita growth rate of about 2.2 per cent per year. For a shorter period (1975 to 1984), real GDP grew at 5 per cent per year.

The same is true for 1984 to 1993. Foreign exchange reserves grew from SDR (Special Drawing Right) 365 million in 1966 to almost SDR 4 billion in 1993 and over SDR 20 billion as of March 1995. Imports have grown from $3 billion to $26 billion over the same period. The current account balance was reduced from $1.5 billion in 1976 to a $7 billion deficit in 1989; recently, the deficit was about $1.2 billion. Clearly, India's economic achievement is no match for the Asian Tigers (Hong Kong, Korea, Singapore, and Taiwan). Could India have done better? Possibly, but given its unique circumstances, it is an achievement that India evolved into a major democracy as well as a capitalistic, mixed-market economy.

To achieve higher growth rates, India embarked on major economic and financial reforms and liberalization in 1991. By 1994 it had emerged as a market ready to be favored with worldwide attention based on its potential and attractiveness compared with other large emerging markets. What was the impetus for this transformation in world attitude toward India? What has been the process of change? What other reforms are needed to allow the economy to achieve its potential for a sustained period? Such questions are discussed in the following sections.

INDIA REFORMS ITS ECONOMY: 1991-95

India has matured as a country, as a political system, and as an economy that can stand on its own. Liberalization and opening the economy to the rest of the world was deemed essential not only to realize higher internal economic growth potential, but also to emulate the open economies of the Asian Tigers. Faster growth and access to more foreign exchange became essential to avert a major debt-service problem in 1991. The disintegration of the Soviet system, with which India had important but protective ties, also resulted in the loss of foreign markets for 10 per cent of its exports.

The new policies and Programmes implemented since 1991 included a significant reduction in import tariffs (from 135 per cent to 25 per cent and even lower for capital goods), the elimination of import quotas (except for consumer goods), as well as the elimination or reduction of restrictions on foreign ownership. There was a reduction and relaxation of anti-monopoly and restrictive trade practices to foster diversification and economies of scale and size in business. Banking and financial reforms allowed private-sector banks, recapitalization of public-sector banks, and reduction in their liquidity ratios.

Major Banks that were nationalized in 1969 began to be privatized along with public-sector companies. Licensing requirements, regulations, and red tape were reduced. Only six industries, compared with seventeen earlier, are now reserved for the public sector. Other changes included the reduction of the corporate tax from a 57.5 per cent to a 46 per cent flat rate, the reduction of the maximum income tax rate from 44.8 per cent to 40 per cent, and the reduction and rationalization of excise taxes to around 10 per cent.

Currency convertibility for current account transactions, the placement of a limit on central bank funding of the budget deficit, and the extensive use of a value-added tax in place of a unit tax have been introduced. The amount of mortgage interest that could be deducted from taxable income was doubled, and capital gains tax on domestic companies was reduced to 30 per cent and for individuals to 20 per cent, with the definition of long-term investment reduced to one year.

Finally, the government can now go to the market to finance the budget deficit beyond the limit set for debt monetization by the central bank. It is estimated that until now, only about 2 per cent of the populace paid income tax. The incidence of direct-tax burden is very low. India collects only 14 per cent of GDP in tax revenue compared with 40 to 50 per cent for most of the industrial countries. Reforms were adopted in March 1995 to increase tax compliance and to enhance incentives for growth in investment, including raising the exemption limit for income tax from 35,000 to 40,000 rupees - a five-year tax holiday for businesses that construct, maintain, and run the infrastructure.

The reforms were greeted with enthusiasm both inside and outside India. The changes were effectively implemented within the set time period. This boosted the credibility of the reform package in the private sector. The intended results of these reforms have materialized. Before the reforms, capital inflows were around $300 million a year. They increased to $1.2 billion in 1992, $3 billion in 1993, and $4.1 billion in 1994. Foreign exchange reserves have shot up to $15 billion in 1993 and reached over $20 billion in 1994-95. These levels of reserves can finance imports for an entire year, in contrast to ten days' worth of foreign exchange available in the beginning of 1991. Exports surged by more than 20 per cent in dollar terms in 1993 alone. Inflation and the budget deficit have come down.

The GDP is growing in the 5 per cent range. All this was accomplished in a short period of two and a half years, with many limitations still plaguing the economy. For example, regulations, although greatly diminished, have not really disappeared; quality and dependability of goods and services have a long way to go; transportation and communications networks have great limitations; and there is a chronic power shortage causing brownouts. To solve all these infrastructure limitations, however, contracts are being awarded to major foreign companies to build highways, power systems, telephone systems, and water and sanitation systems.

The government gave a major boost to the private sector and whacked away at the bureaucracy. These changes were hailed by the press as "an entrepreneurial treasure trove." Other statements in the press include:

- India's messy march to prosperity may look less exciting, it may also prove more consistent.
- India's steadiness is looking increasingly attractive to investors.
- India is solid, but has yet to unleash its entrepreneurial potential.
- One of the most diverse industrial economies in the world, India's reform Programme holds enormous potential commercial opportunities for American firms.
- U.S. companies will also need to reevaluate India's place in their global strategies if they are to take full advantage of its emerging market potential.

The reforms are bringing about better economic conditions in India. Economic growth of less than 1 per cent in 1991-92 has grown to 5.3 per cent in 1994-95. Inflation, which was almost 14 per cent in 1991, dropped to about 7 per cent in 1994. The fiscal deficit was under control at around 6 per cent in 1994-95 with a target of 5.5 per cent in 1995-96 - from a high of 8.3 per cent in 1990-91. Industrial growth has increased from just 0.5 per cent to over 8 per cent a year. Employment creation increased from about 3 million jobs per year to 6 million jobs per year.

REFORMS AND STABILITY IN THE FUTURE

The economy is growing because of increased investment, incoming foreign capital, and technologies along with increased competition and less state intervention. The middle class is estimated at between 100 million and 300 million and total consumers at over 900 million, approaching one billion. The safest way to achieve economic growth will probably involve an economic policy that seeks macroeconomic stability with control of inflation and the budget deficit, careful management of debt, and more use of equity markets to finance growth.

Economic and financial reforms already introduced and new ones yet to be approved (for example, further reforms of the financial sector in the areas of insurance and securities markets) will give a clear indication of future economic growth prospects as the reforms build domestic and international confidence in the system. At the base of the pyramid is the establishment of credibility. Credibility requires that monetary and fiscal policies be consistent with goals within an economic environment of market-based incentives and disincentives.

This environment includes deregulation where there is excessive regulation, privatization where there is excessive reliance on government enterprises, and creation of physical infrastructure for transportation, communication, water supply for drinking and irrigation, sanitation, health delivery, and education. An open trading and monetary system that links domestic and foreign markets through a convertible currency and tariff and commercial policies consistent with the World Trade Organization (WTO) are equally important for establishing credibility in the system. This open system will encourage competition.

To take control of these critical issues, India has initiated significant reforms to address all of the above since 1991. Many infrastructure reforms are being implemented on a continuing basis, reducing bottlenecks. India's policies and reforms are fully accepted and endorsed by the IMF. It is also generally believed that India's reforms will continue and that political competition among various political parties will not upset its trajectory for reforms and long-term growth prospects. India is very near full convertibility of the rupee, reflecting the maturity of the economy and its ability to withstand external competition.

Domestic price stability (now at about 11 per cent, down from 17 per cent in 1991) and the absence of capital flight (unlike the experience of Brazil, Mexico, Peru, Argentina, and Venezuela in the 1980s and the former Soviet Union more recently) have allowed India to adopt an outward-looking policy of convertibility of the rupee on the current account. India is maintaining macro-economic discipline, as shown by the 1994-95 budgets, which for the first time puts a limit on monetization of public debt as an automatic financing technique.

Beyond a certain amount of additional printing of the currency, the government will have to go to the market to buy funds in competition with other borrowers in the economy. This policy indicates India's commitment to prevent deficit financing and inflation from becoming problems. Once credibility is established, credit from external sources follows. Although India has not had a credit problem in world financial markets, its creditworthiness in private international banking and capital markets was lacking until the mid-1980s.

From 1950 to about 1985 India relied, due to its policy and lack of demand for its paper in private markets, mostly on official bilateral and multilateral capital to finance its foreign exchange needs for growth and development. It was cheap credit, but available only in limited amounts. Foreign banks began to find India attractive in the mid-1980s, as Latin America experienced severe debt-servicing problems and global banks were looking for new markets. Subsequent banking and financial reforms that began in 1989 made India even more attractive to global banking credits. India experienced a 75 per cent increase in its external debt between 1988-89 and 1994-95, most of which was in private debt.

This changed the character of India's relationship with foreign financial institutions. These reforms have reinforced India's credibility and access to credit in global banking markets, giving it the necessary liquidity for private and public projects. Capital inflows in the forms of portfolio and direct investment are now not only allowed but encouraged. Banking, credit, and equity markets are being integrated. Indian businesses are able to raise capital in international financial markets. Foreign financial institutions are expanding their presence and offering financial products and services in India in competition with local financial institutions.

Subsequent to the approval of the new General Agreement on Tariffs and Trade (GATT) and the creation of the WTO, India agreed, along with a group of mostly industrial countries, to a reciprocal home-country treatment of foreign financial institutions. The new agreement, therefore, is significant in terms of India's commitment to an open financial market environment and integration of its markets into the global financial system. Once credit is built up with foreign entities, capital flows into markets with credibility and credit. India has opened and reformed its capital markets to attract foreign capital.

Its economic credibility and creditworthiness have made it attractive to foreign portfolio and direct investment. Foreign and Indian financial intermediaries have formed mutual funds to invest in Indian companies, giving investors in the United States and Europe an opportunity to invest in India. Indian companies are able to issue their debt and equity in foreign capital markets. Foreign institutional participation in Indian equities traded on India's stock exchanges was flowing in at about $200 million a month in 1995. The linkage of India's capital markets and their integration into global capital markets has begun at a deliberate but steady pace.

The fact that the global investor is not euphoric about India is a good sign. It means that the investor is observing India's structural and financial reforms and taking a calculated risk-and-return approach, building a global portfolio with some Indian securities in it. The amount of foreign direct investment capital has been almost as much as portfolio investment. Foreign direct investment, which brings capital, technology, and management, is flowing into infrastructure as well as consumer goods sectors. Infrastructure projects include power plants, transportation systems (such as the automotive industry and road construction), and communication systems (such as telephones, cable, and satellite).

Consumer goods sectors attracting foreign direct investment include food processing, soft drinks, liquor, electronics and home appliances, household and industrial tools, and computers and computer software. Foreign direct investment is flowing in from North America, Europe, the Far East, and Australia. Familiar Western company logos can now be seen in India.

Foreign direct investment from such companies as Pepsico, Coca-Cola, McDonalds, IBM, Hewlett-Packard, Texas Instruments, Enron, GM, GE, Duracell, Black and Decker, AT&T, NYNEX, U.S. West, and similar companies from Great Britain, Japan, and Germany is flowing at a rate of approximately $200 million a month. All this is an indication that India has established its credibility, credit, and attractiveness to foreign capital. During the last two years, the democratic system established in the British tradition underwent a major test. In a case involving foreign direct investment by Enron, based in Houston, Texas, democracy and capitalism both passed the test.

To address India's severe power shortage and as part of a recent liberalization of the economy, the central government approved the construction of a power plant to be built jointly by Enron, General Electric, and other partners, including some

Indian companies. The project involved investment of more than $2.2 billion. The central government also negotiated a price for electricity. Enron was awarded the contract without following the normal competitive bidding and without gaining the approval of the Maharashtra state government, where the plant is to be constructed. Following state elections, the new Maharashtra government did not like the price of power and asked that the contract with Enron be renegotiated on the grounds that proper competitive bidding had not taken place.

It was a political fight between the central government and the state government, but it was also a legitimate questioning of the contract. Neither Enron nor the government of India liked it. Enron risked $300 million it had already spent in getting ready to construct the plant. Other companies interested in investing directly in India began to wonder if the country was open for business. Confidence in India suffered, resulting in less foreign direct investment.

After two years and high economic cost to all parties involved, Enron and the state government agreed to a new contract with a new pricing structure for the distribution of power to its consumers. The central government had no choice but to get the state government's approval under the autonomous rights and powers that the Indian constitution confers on the states. This case illustrates that India is a stickler for the democratic and bureaucratic procedures that it inherited from the Raj. It is unlikely that the mistakes of the Enron case will be repeated in India any time soon, and confidence in India has been restored.

Currently, there is another debate under way over the need for and role of foreign direct investment in India's growth. The debate is both academic and political. The former argues that domestic capital may be able to do everything that foreign capital will do, so why create dependence on foreign capital? The answer is that foreign capital brings with it technology endogenous to the equipment, process, techniques, marketing, and management of goods and services. Foreign capital usually is a net addition to capital stock. It may also create demand for new products and services. All these forces add to the output and availability of more choices, which spawn more economic activities.

The political debate centers on domestic and foreign control of economic activity and political influence. Some political groups in India prefer to allow foreign direct investment only in technologies not available within India, based on the assumption that the economy is a closed system. There are several problems with this method of selecting investment projects. First, foreign companies may not find it politically and economically attractive to enter such an environment. Second, no government or company can predict what technologies will be available in the market at any time.

Third, technologies and innovations that emerge in response to one another are not born in the absence of a systemic environment of openness, competition, and innovation. A closed system is always doomed to lag behind in creativity and growth, left with a continual choice of whether to import a technology or investment. There is another political transformation taking place that should ultimately strengthen the democratic process and the working of the competitive market economy. To make politicians and the political process more accountable, political corruption is being reformed.

There have been charges and counter-charges of corruption among politicians over the years. Usually nothing comes of it. In 1996, however, more than two dozen politicians in major political parties, including several cabinet ministers in the just-defeated Congress government, have been indicted on corruption charges. The indictments are a sign of the democratic maturity of the political system as well as the evolving independence of such investigative bodies as the Central Bureau of Investigation and the judiciary at the district, appellate, and Supreme Court levels. The court system will work to keep the cases and the issue before the public for some time to come.

One would expect corruption to be significantly reduced as a result of these trials and the punishment meted out to politicians of all political colors. The public's reaction was revealed in the recent parliamentary elections. This is a very healthy development in improving political ethics and the democratic process. One of the benefits of this would be an increase in foreign confidence and investment in India. In 1996, the Congress Party lost its majority in the parliament (it won only 25 per cent of the seats, whereas before the elections the party held 50 per cent of the seats). A key cause of this was corruption, actual and perceived, among politicians at the national level.

In the long run, the 1996 elections may signal a turning point in India's economic system. It is likely that India's dependence on politician-directed government will be replaced by a more democratic process. In addition, the Congress Party was unable to communicate its vision of the future to the masses. In terms of integrating India's economy with the rest of the world, the political parties on the left as well as on the right have consistently affirmed this goal. It is only at the margin that the left and the right exploited this issue for a quick advantage at the polls.

In practical terms, there may not be more than 25 out of 545 members of the newly elected parliament who may wish to limit global integration. Leaders of all parties have clearly stated that they are in favor of foreign capital and foreign direct investment for India's growth. The actual policy of the government is to allow foreign direct investment and majority control, if so chosen by members of a joint venture, in all industries except those deemed to be defense-sensitive and of such national interest that foreign entities cannot be trusted with

India's interests. Allowing repatriation of income and profit is also important to the foreign investor.

Mutual funds, investment banks, securities firms, and commercial banks are investing in Indian securities. Indian companies are raising funds in the world capital markets, merging with one another and with foreign companies. Stock market activity, participation, and capitalization are increasing. The fact that Merrill Lynch, Goldman Sachs, Citibank and many other securities firms, investment banks, and commercial banks have gone to India as part of their global financial services signals that India can attract additional financial intermediaries, including insurance and finance companies.

Promotion of competition in the economy continues to be pursued. Competition among domestic businesses, between domestic and foreign companies, among state enterprises, and between public and private capital should be promoted through economic policies, be those fiscal, monetary, exchange rate, or related to subsidies and indirect taxes. The recent opening of automobile, food processing, power generation, communications, oil drilling and distribution, and other industries to foreign investment and competition is likely to be expanded to other industries.

At the pinnacle of credibility, credit, and capital comes confidence. At this time, foreign business confidence in India's economy is high, based on the availability of capital, India's creditworthiness, and the credibility it has established in carrying out structural economic, monetary, and financial reforms in recent years. India should continue to introduce reforms (such as full convertibility of the rupee, fiscal balance, and monetary control), to deepen and broaden confidence in its stable economy and society, and to achieve full integration into the world trading system and word capital markets on a competitive basis.

This increased level of confidence has opened trade, enlarged financial flows (especially from private sources), created linkages to capital markets, and expanded India's overall competitive strength. India's economic and financial reforms are timely and appropriate for creating confidence among domestic as well as foreign investors. Foreign capital is important for its technological and economic multiplier effects. India has reached the apex of the pyramid of confidence, which it should maintain while implementing further reforms to broaden and deepen that confidence.

India has pursued policies that have produced a balanced achievement of personal freedom and economic betterment. The foundation laid in the past fifty years is poised to produce sustainable rates of 5 to 6 per cent growth in real GDP for the foreseeable future. India's future is promising. The chapter makes three arguments. First, a conflict between three different varieties of nationalism has marked Indian politics of late: a secular nationalism, a Hindu nationalism, and two separatist nationalisms in the states of Kashmir and Punjab.

Hindu nationalism is a reaction to the two other nationalisms. In imaginations about India's national identity, there was always a conceptual space for Hindu nationalism. Still, it remained a weak political force until recently, when the context of politics changed. The rise of Hindu nationalism can thus be attributed to an underlying and a proximate base. Competing strains in India's national identity constitute the underlying base. The proximate reasons are supplied by the political circumstances of the 1980s.

A mounting anxiety about the future of India has resulted from the separatist agitations of the 1980s and from a deepening institutional and ideological vacuum in Indian politics. India's key integrative political institution since 1947, the Congress party, has gone through a profound organizational decay, with no centrist parties taking its place. And secularism, the ideological mainstay of a multi religious India, looks pale and exhausted. Claiming Ashutosh Varshney is Associate Professor of Government at Harvard University to rebuild the nation, Hindu nationalists present themselves as an institutional and ideological alternative.

Second, India's secularism looks exhausted not because secularism is intrinsically unsuited to India and must, therefore, inevitably come to grief. That is the principal claim of the highly influential recent writings by T. N. Madan and Ashis Nandy. Insightful though their arguments are, Madan and Nandy do not sufficiently differentiate between different varieties of secularism. The secularism of Indira and Rajiv Gandhi was not a logical culmination of the secularism of Nehru. Politics over the last decade discredits the kind of secularism practiced by the various regimes in the 1980s. It does not discredit secularism per se.

Third, though a reaction to separatist and secular nationalisms, Hindu nationalism poses the most profound challenge to the governing principles and intellectual maps of an independent India. Hindu nationalism has two simultaneous impulses: a commitment to the territorial integrity of India as well as a political commitment to Hinduism. Given India's turbulent history of Hindu-Muslim relations, it is unlikely that Hindu nationalism can realize both its aims. What happens to India, therefore, depends on how powerful Hindu nationalism becomes, and the way in which this contradiction is resolved.

The national question is, of course, not the only contentious issue in India. Apart from the national order, two other orders-social and economic - have been challenged in recent times. The traditional caste hierarchy of the Hindu social order, slowly eroding due to the political equality of liberal democracy, has been explicitly confronted by politics emphasizing the mobilization of lower castes. The Fabian socialist core of the economic order is in its death throes, being attacked by an emerging market orientation and international openness in the count-y's economic policy.

Some of this change is welcome in India, but much of it has come suddenly and simultaneously. Because of the simultaneity of change at several levels, and especially because of threats to the nation's integrity-the most serious since independence-Indian politics in recent years have been experienced by a large number of Indians as an anxiety, as a fear of the unknown, and on occasions such as the demolition of the Ayodhya mosque, even as a loss of inner coherence. A yearning for re-equilibrating designs that can impose some order on anxieties is unmistakable. Politics remains central to this enterprise.

THREE CONTESTING NATIONALISMS IN INDIA

People everywhere have an idea of who they are and what they owe themselves. The liberation of spirit that has come to India could not come as a release alone. India was now a country of a million little mutinies. But there was in India now what didn't exist 200 years before: a central will, a central intellect, a national idea. The Indian Union was greater than the sum of its parts. - V.S. Naipaul

While one may disagree with Naipaul about whether a" national idea" existed in India in earlier times, he is rightly pointing to a paradox: both little mutinies and a" central" or" national idea" are surfacing at the same time. As disintegrative tendencies deepen, a sense of pan-Indian nationalism is also growing. The two tendencies-the mutinous disaggregation and a national resurgence-are fighting it out, with no clear victor at the moment. Recent accounts of India, especially the journalistic ones, have mostly concentrated on the disintegrative tendencies.

The merit of Naipaul's position lies in his recognition that the political tendencies are dualistic, not unitary. It is also the kind of duality for which direct evidence, privileged in the social sciences, cannot yet be provided. No large-scale surveys exist.

One has either to derive inferences from available political trends, or, like Naipaul, one has to travel, talk, hear, and see-that is, follow the method of a" writer." Separatist nationalisms in Kashmir today and in Punjab until recently have been the most powerful expressions of the disintegrative tendency. The other two varieties of nationalism-secular and Hindu-are committed to India's territorial integrity, though they seek to do it in different ways.

The three nationalisms do not have the same conception of the nation. Separatist nationalists claim that Sikhs and Kashmiris are not part of the Indian nation. They are nations by themselves. Their point is not simply that there is something distinctive about the Sikh and Kashmiri identities that separates them from India; rather, to use Ernest Gellner's words," the political and the national unit should be congruent." A nation is not merely a cultural configuration; it means investing a cultural community with sovereignty, and, at the very least, with political autonomy.

These movements, then, are not mere ethnic assertions. Ethnicity as a term designates a sense of collective belonging, which may be based on common descent, language, history, or even religion (or some combination of these). An ethnic group may function without a state of its own; a nation implies bringing ethnicity and statehood together. In principle, this congruence may be satisfied in a federal arrangement, in which case the concerned nationalism becomes sub nationalism or an ethnicity.

The larger federal entity, then, has the highest claims on that group's loyalty. Alternatively, one may opt for nothing short of sovereignty. That is what Sikh nationalists aimed at and Kashmiri nationalists are still fighting for. A Bengali can be both a Bengali and an Indian, so can a Gujarati. Bengalis and Gujaratis are ethnic groups: for separatists, Sikhs and Kashmiris are nations. However, for Indian nationalists-both secular and Hindu-the Sikhs and Kashmiris are ethnic groups, not nations.

The separatists, of course, may not succeed in their aims, in which case they may settle for the status of a state in the Indian federation. Sikh nationalism seems to have entered this phase already. It is important to remember, however, that the Sikh uprising was not simply a cultural battle for a separate identity; it was a political battle for nationhood. A nation, to repeat, is not just a cultural community; rather, it is a sovereign cultural community.

Unlike separatist nationalisms, secular nationalism, the official doctrine of India's national identity since independence, seeks to preserve the geographical integrity of India. In principle, it includes all ethnic and religious groups in its definition of the nation, and respects their beliefs and cultures. Giving security to the various ethnic and religious groups is considered part of nation-building. One can be a good Muslim or a good Bengali and a good Indian at the same time.

That, to Hindu nationalists, is the opposite of nation-building. A salad bowl does not produce cohesion; a melting pot does. Hinduism, to Hindu nationalists, is the source of India's identity. It alone can provide national cohesiveness. This claim inevitably begs the question: Who is a Hindu? Savarkar, the ideological father of Hindu nationalism, explains:" A Hindu means a person who regards this land ... from the Indus to the Seas as his fatherland as well as his Holy land."

The definition is territorial (land between the Indus and the Seas), genealogical (fatherland), and religious (holy land). Hindus, Sikhs, Jains, and Buddhists can be part of this definition, for they meet all three criteria. All these religions were born in India. Christians, Jews, Parsis, and Muslims, however, can meet only two criteria. India is not their" holy land." Can non-Hindu groups be part of India? Yes, but only by assimilation, say the

Hindu nationalists. Of the groups whose holy land is not India, Parsis and Jews are, according to Hindu nationalists, already assimilated, having become part of the nation's mainstream.

With the departure of the British, Christianity also lost its political edge, being no longer associated with foreign rulers. Ultimately, Muslims became the principal adversary of the Hindu nationalists, in part because of their numbers, but also because a Muslim homeland in the form of Pakistan caused India's partition in 1947. Twenty-five per cent of pre-1947 India was Muslim. Even after the formation of Pakistan, Muslims remained the largest minority, constituting about 12 per cent of the country's population today. This explains, in part, the enormous attention given to Islam by Hindu nationalists.

The Hindu nationalist claim is not that Muslims ought to be excluded from the Indian nation. While that may be the position of Hindu extremists, the generic Hindu nationalist argument is that to become part of the Indian nation, Muslims must agree to the following:

1. Accept the centrality of Hinduism to Indian civilization;
2. Acknowledge key Hindu figures such as Ram as civilizational heroes, and not regard them as mere religious figures of Hinduism;
3. Accept that Muslim rulers in various parts of India (between roughly 1000 to 1857) destroyed the pillars of Hindu civilization, especially Hindu Temples; and
4. Make no claims to special privileges such as the maintenance of religious personal laws, nor demand special state grants for their educational institutions.

They must assimilate, not maintain their distinctiveness. Through Ekya assimilation), they will prove their loyalty to the nation. It is interesting to note that the Muslim politicians who have accepted this argument-for example, Sikandar Bakht and Arif Beg-have been members of the Bhartiya Janata Party (BJP), the principal political party representing the ideology of Hindu nationalism in the electoral arena.

Hindu nationalism thus has two simultaneous impulses: building a united India as well as "Hinduizing" the polity and the nation. Muslims and other groups are not excluded from the definition of India, but inclusion is premised upon assimilation, on acceptance of the political and cultural centrality of Hinduism. If assimilation is not acceptable to the minorities, Hindu nationalism becomes exclusionary, both in principle and practice.

Created in 1925 in the state of Maharashtra, the Rashtriya Swayamsevak Sangh (RSS, National Voluntary Corp) is the institutional core of Hindu nationalism. The ideological trend, however, goes much further back. Viewed as a way to resurrect India's cultural pride, Hindu revivalism in the second half of the nineteenth century was a response to British rule. This revivalism preceded the national movement headed by the Congress party in the first half of the twentieth century, but it could not dominate the movement itself.

There were two principal modes in the national movement: Nehru's secularism and Mahatma Gandhi's Hinduism. Nehru's hostility to religion is well-known. Even a devoutly religious Gandhi could not be called a Hindu nationalist. He was a Hindu and a nationalist, not a Hindu nationalist. Gandhi's Hinduism was inclusive and tolerant. Being a good Hindu and having respect for other religions were not contradictory. Inclusion of non-Hindus in the Indian nation followed as a corollary of this position. Gandhi's love for Muslims even during the formation of Pakistan was, for Hindu nationalists, incomprehensible.

In 1948, when a Hindu fanatic assassinated Gandhi, Hindu nationalism was set back by decades. In popular perception, Hindu nationalists killed the Mahatma, the father of the nation. Many in the post-1948 generation were told by their parents to keep a safe distance from Hindu nationalists. A weak political force for a century, Hindu nationalism has acquired unprecedented political strength since the mid-1980s. At no point before 1989 did the Hindu nationalists receive even a tenth of the national vote. The average was 7 per cent. In 1989, this share increased to 11.4 per cent, and, in 1991, to over 20 per cent.

Electorally confined to northern and western India, Hindu nationalism has politically penetrated all parts of India, including the South and the East. In the southern state of Karnataka, it won nearly 29 per cent of the vote in 1991. In Gujarat, Mahatma Gandhi's home state in western India, its share of the vote in 1991 was a remarkable 51 per cent. The 1991 elections brought BJP governments to power in four states: Uttar Pradesh, Madhya Pradesh, Rajasthan, and Himachal Pradesh. Of these, Uttar Pradesh is the biggest state in India, and Madhya Pradesh among the biggest.

Equally important, by 1991 support for Hindu nationalism had gone beyond the urban trading community, its customary base, to include villagers and the modernized (and modernizing) middle classes. Hardly known for Hindu religiosity and Westernized in their daily life, nearly thirty retired generals, including a Jewish former general, joined the BJP in 1991. So did a host of former civil servants. For a party customarily associated with obscurantism, it was a moment of great symbolic significance. The BJP savored the moment and proudly displayed its modern recruits.

It is not clear whether the demolition of the Babri mosque in December of 1992 will ultimately hurt or strengthen the Hindu nationalists. That something as inconceivable as the mass demolition of a mosque could be undertaken and executed as a political project demonstrates, in and of itself, the new mobilizing capacity of this ideology. The assassination of Mahatma Gandhi in 1948 was the last politically critical act of Hindu nationalism, but that was neither a manifestation of its organized strength nor an expression of its capacity to mobilize the masses. It was an insane act of an angry individual who was motivated by the ideology of Hindu nationalism.

INDIA'S NATIONAL IDENTITY AND HINDU NATIONALISM

Who is an Indian? Deceptively simple, the question is hard to answer, as indeed it is with respect to several other nations in the world. Literature on comparative nationalism suggests that national identities have historically been based on several principles of collective belonging: ethnicity (Japan, Italy, Germany, and much of Europe), religion (Ireland, Pakistan, and parts of the Middle East), ideology (successfully in the United States, unsuccessfully in the former Soviet Union and Yugoslavia), and territory (Spain, Switzerland, and a number of Third World nations).

One should note that the territorial idea inevitably becomes part of all nation-states, but territory does not have to be the defining principle of national identity. Moreover, in some cases, there may be no clear principle of collective belonging. Rather, competing notions of identity may exist, one of which becomes dominant at one time, the other at another time. As Stanley Hoffmann argues, there are two competing views about the French identity. One is based on the French Revolution and the principles of freedom and equality, which bring French national identity quite close to the definition of the American nation.

A second one is based on quasi-ethnicity (conceptualized as history and heritage), which in French history leads to the Vichy regime and to Le Pen today. In the United States, as Samuel Huntington has argued, the key constituents of the" American creed"-liberty, equality, individualism, democracy, and the rule of law- have not always existed together, nor can they possibly, for they do not form a coherent logical set. What turns on the distinctive principles of national identity? Their political implications vary. Some of the most passionate political moments of America have been over the issues of freedom and equality, just as those of Germany have been over ethnicity.

Similarly, competing strains in national identity open up distinctive political logics. Excessive drift in one direction brings forth a reaction, and competing strains begin to acquire political momentum. A rising number of French people today are feeling threatened by the increasing ethnic diversity of France, which is conceptualized by some as a mono ethnic society, a conception opposed by others as too narrow and destructive of the principles of the Republic. In American history, as Huntington has argued, "Conflicts easily materialize when any one value is taken to an extreme: majority rule versus minority rights; higher law versus popular sovereignty; liberty versus equality; individualism versus democracy."

Since the rise of the Indian national movement, three competing themes about India-territorial, cultural, and religious-have fought for political dominance. The territorial notion is that India has a "sacred geography," enclosed between the Indus river, the Himalayas, and the Seas, and emphasized for twenty-five hundred years since the time of the Mahabharata. The cultural notion is that ideas of tolerance, pluralism, and syncretism define Indian society. India is not only the birthplace of several religions (Hinduism, Buddhism, Jainism, and Sikhism), but in its history it has also regularly received, accommodated, and absorbed "outsiders" (Parsis, Jews, and "Syrian" Christians-followers of St. Thomas, arriving as early as the second century, thus Christianity reached India before it reached Europe).

In the process, syncretistic forms of culture and even syncretistic forms of religious worship have emerged and become part of India. Apart from syncretism, which means a coming together and merging of cultures, pluralism and tolerance have also existed with different communities finding their niche in India and developing principles of interaction? Sarva Dharma Sambhava (equal respect for all religions) is the best cultural expression of such pluralism. Finally, the religious notion is that India is originally the land of the Hindus, and it is the only land which the Hindus can call their own.

India has the Hindu holy places (Benaras, Tirupati, Rameswaram, Puri, Haridwar, Badrinath, Kedarnath, and now Ayodhya) and the holy rivers (Cauveri, Ganga, Yamuna, and the confluence of the last two in Prayag). Most of India is, and has been, Hindu by religion-anywhere between 65 to 70 per cent in the early twentieth century and 82 per cent today. A great deal of ethnic diversity may exist within Hindu society: a faith in Hinduism brings the diversity together. India viewed in this fashion is a Hindu nation.

The three identity principles have their political equivalents. In political discourse, the territorial idea is called "national unity" or "territorial integrity"; the cultural idea is expressed as "political pluralism"; and the religious idea is known as Hindutva, or political Hinduism. The political notion of pluralism itself has two meanings, dealing with the linguistic and religious issues.

The principle of federalism was developed to respect the linguistic diversity of India: not only would the states be organized linguistically but the ruling party would also be federally organized, leaving enough autonomy for state-level party units. The political principle about religion has two levels. In general, religion would be left untouched so that religious pluralism in society could exist, but if the state did have to intervene in religious disputes, it would do so with strict neutrality.

The state would maintain a posture of equidistance, a principle that came to define India's secularism. These three strains have yielded two principal imaginations about India's national identity-the secular nationalist and the Hindu nationalist. The former combines territory and culture; the latter religion and territory. For the secular nationalist construction, the best source is Jawaharlal Nehru's *The Discovery of India.*

BIBLIOGRAPHY

Abbott, Jason P. "Democracy@Internet.Asia? The Challenges to the Emancipatory Potential of the Net: Lessons from China and Malaysia," *Third World Quarterly*, 2001. 22(1):99-114.

Ahmad, lmtiaz. *State and Foreign Policy: India's Role in South Asia*. New Delhi: Vikas, 1993.

Ali, S.H. "The Changing Faces of Politics and Repression in Malaysia," *Inter-Asia Cultural Studies*, 2001, 2 (1):115-126.

Aung San Suu Kyi, et al. *Freedom from Fear and Other Writings*. Penguin, 1995.

Austin, Granville. *The Indian Constitution: Cornerstone of a Nation*. Oxford: Clarendon Press, 1966.

Baker, Christopher J. *The Politics of South India, 1920-1937*. Cambridge: Cambridge University Press, 1976.

Basham, A.L. *The Wonder That Was India, 1: A Survey of the History and Culture of the Indian Sub-Continent Before the Coming of the Muslims*. 3d ed., rev. London: Sidgwick and Jackson, 1967.

Basham, A.L., ed. *A Cultural History of India*. Oxford: Clarendon Press, 1975.

Bayly. C.A. *The New Cambridge History of India, II.l: Indian Society and the Making of the British Empire*. Cambridge: Cambridge University Press, 1987.

Beaumont, Roger. *Sword of the Raj: The British Army in India, 1747-1947*. Indianapolis: Bobbs-Merrill, 1977.

Bedlington, Stanley S. *Malaysia and Singapore: The Building of New States*. Ithaca, NY: Cornell University Press, 1978.

Brass, Paul R. The New Cambridge History of India, IV. 1: The Politics of India since Independence. *2d ed. Cambridge: Cambridge University Press, 1994.*

Brown, Judith M. *Modern India: The Origins of an Asian Democracy.* New Delhi: Oxford University Press, 1985.

Case, W. "Malaysia's Resilient Pseudodemocracy," *Journal oj Democracy,* 2001, 12(l):43-57.

Chandra, Bipan. *Essays on Contemporary India.* New Delhi: Har-Anand, 1993.

Chandra, Bipan. *Modern India.* New Delhi: National Council of Educational Research and Training, 1971.

Chee Soon Juan. *To Be Free: Stories from Asia's Struggle Against Oppression.* Clayton, Australia: Monash Asia Institute, 1998.

Das, Arvind. *India Invented.* New Delhi: Manohar, 1992.

Davies, C. Collin. *An Historical Atlas of the Indian Peninsula.* London: Oxford University Press, 1959.

Ellinwood. DeWitt C., and S.P. Pradhan. *India and World War* I. New Delhi: Manohar, 1978.

Embree, Ainslie T. *1857 in India: Mutiny or War of Independence.* Lexington, Massachusetts: Heath, 1963.

Embree, Ainslie T., ed. *Encyclopedia of Asian History.* 4 vols. The Asia Society. New York: Scribner's, 1988.

Emmerson, D. "A Tale of Three Countries," *Journal of Democracy,* 1999, 10(4):35-53.

Fisher, Michael. A Clash of Cultures: Awadh, the British, and the Mughals. *New Delhi: Manohar, 1987.*

Ganesan, N. "Malaysia in 2003: Leadership Transition with a Tall Shadow," *Asian Survey.* 2004, 44(l):70-77.

Hardgrave, Robert L., Jr., and Stanley A. Kochanek. *India: Government and Politics in a Developing Nation.* 5th ed. Fort Worth. Texas: Harcourt Brace Jovanovich, 1993.

Harymurti, B. "Challenges of Change in Indonesia," *Journal of Democracy,* 1999, 10(4):69-83.*Bibliography* I 269

Inden, Ronald. *Imagining India.* Oxford: Oxford University Press, 1990.

Keay, John. Democracy and Discontent: India's Growing Crisis of Governability. *Cambridge: Cambridge University Press, 1992.*

Kulke, Hermann, and Dietmar Rothermund. *A History of India.* Rev., updated ed. London: Routledge, 1990.

Means, G.P. "Soft Authoritarianism in Malaysia and Singapore," *Journal of Democracy,* 1996, 7(4): 103-117.

Metcalf, Thomas R. *Modern India: An Interpretive Anthology.* London: Macmillan, 1971.

Pandey, B.N. *The Break Up of British India.* London: Macmillan, 1969.

Sarkar, Sumit. *Modern India, 1885-1947.* Delhi: Macmillan. 1983.

Singh, Surinder Niḥal. Rocky Road of Indian Democracy: Nehru to Narasimha Rao. *New Delhi: Sterling, 1993.*

Spear, Thomas George Percival, ed. *The Oxford History of Modern India, 1740-1975.* 2d ed. New Delhi: Oxford University Press, 1978.

Tully, Mark. *India: Forty Years of Independence.* New York: Braziller, 1988.

Vorys, Karl von. Democracy without Consensus: Communalism and Political Stability in Malaysia. *Kuala Lumpur, 1976.*

Wah, Francis Loh Kok, and Khoo Boo Teik. *Democracy in Malaysia: Discourses and Practices.* Surrey, UK: Curzon Press, 2002.

Welsh, B. "Attitudes Toward Democracy in Malaysia: Challenges to the Regime?'" *Asian Survey,* 1996, 36(9):82-104.

Wolpert, Stanley. *A New History of India.* 4th ed. New York: Oxford University Press, 1992.

Wolpert. Stanley. *India.* Berkeley: University of California Press, 1991.

Woodward, M. "Indonesia, Islam, and the Prospect for Democracy," *SAIS Review,* 2001, 21(2):29-37.

INDEX

M

N

O

P

R

S

T

U

W

Y